£30.00

D1616883

EQUALITY POLITICS AND GENDER

Equality Politics and Gender

edited by
Elizabeth Meehan
and
Selma Sevenhuijsen

SAGE Publications
London · Newbury Park · New Delhi

Chapter   1, editoral matter and arrangement © Elizabeth
    Meehan and Selma Sevenhuijsen 1991
Chapter   2 © Ian Forbes 1991
Chapter   3 © Tuija Parvikko 1991
Chapter   4 © Jet Bussemaker 1991
Chapter   5 © Carol Bacchi 1991
Chapter   6 © Selma Sevenhuijsen 1991
Chapter   7 © Joyce Outshoorn 1991
Chapter   8 © Amy Mazur 1991
Chapter   9 © Jennifer Jarman 1991
Chapter 10 © Evelyn Mahon 1991
Chapter 11 © Birte Siim 1991

First published 1991

SAGE Publications Ltd
6 Bonhill Street
London EC2A 4PU

SAGE Publications Inc
2455 Teller Road
Newbury Park, California 91320

SAGE Publications India Pvt Ltd
32, M-Block Market
Greater Kailash – I
New Delhi 110 048

British Library Cataloguing in Publication data

Equality politics and gender. – (Sage modern
politics series)
    I. Meehan, Elizabeth   II. Sevenhuijsen, Selma
    III. Series
    320.082

    ISBN 0–8039–8482–0
    ISBN 0–8039–8483–9 pbk

Library of Congress catalog card number 91–052966

Typeset by The Word Shop, Bury, Lancashire

Printed in Great Britain by Biddles Ltd, Guildford, Surrey

Contents

List of Figures and Tables

1

Problems in Principles and Policies

Elizabeth Meehan and Selma Sevenhuijsen

This collection of essays comes from the 1989 European Consortium of Political Research (ECPR) Workshop on Equality Principles and Gender Politics: Theories, Programmes and Practices. The purpose of the workshop was to bring together papers that discussed principles of equality from different perspectives and empirical areas. Equality has been a central normative concept for the modern women's movement all over Europe and in many other parts of the world. Experience in devising policies, evaluating them and using litigation to secure their implementation has led to extensive debates about the meaning of equality and related concepts like equal rights and equal opportunities. For example, renewed attention has been paid to the question of whether equality implies the same treatment for men and women or whether different treatment is needed to ensure equal freedom for both sexes. This goes beyond the technicalities of the by now well-known matters of direct and indirect discrimination to more fundamental problems. In the course of the debates, the viability and desirability of equality as a goal has been questioned and the connection between equality and related concepts like difference, sameness, autonomy, justice, interests and citizenship is debated as well.

It was the significance and the excitement of debates on these topics at the 1987 Amsterdam meeting of the European Consortium of Political Research that inspired the 1989 undertaking. At the 1989 workshop, sixteen papers were presented. The editors have selected ten of them which appear to fit together particularly well in the issues that they cover from their different perspectives. The way in which these interrelate stems from their discussion of competing conceptions of equality. The chapters in this book show that similar concerns emerge from philosophical analyses of politics and the state and from policy analyses of the decision-making processes.

Whether primarily conceptual or empirical, the chapters deal with the problems of analysing equality which participants were specifically invited to treat under the general question of whether the goal of equality between men and women requires the same or different treatment. Questions about equality include whether it should be procedural or substantive. That is to say, what promise does equal treatment hold for people in unequal situations? Is it 'just' to single out categories of people for 'special' treatment? And what conceptions of justice could be employed when discussing this question? Should the ideal for feminists be the model of participation in public life as set by men, an ideal that seems to be inherent in contractarian concepts of citizenship and rights? Are these concepts themselves really gender-neutral, as a superficial reading of contract theories does suggest, or do they implicitly assume a model of the rational citizen that is male? Do feminists who argue that gender differences concerning moral reasoning and citizenship should be recognized run the risk of justifying the case of those who are against women's liberation? On the other hand, if feminists do not call for a recognition of differences, how can equality policies, which assume the possibility of gender-neutrality in politics and at work, ever improve the lives of women who, by and large, are not in the same situation as men with respect to family obligations, the labour market and sexual expression?

In dealing with these kinds of question, many of the chapters reveal common concerns that are outlined in the next section. In addition to discussing the meaning of equality itself, the chapters show the need to consider equality in relation to other concepts and philosophical schools of thought that provide alternatives to the idea of equal rights in contractarian frameworks. They also reflect the significance of different historical experiences in different countries of equal opportunity policies, which may influence the conclusions drawn by the writers in this collection. Some chapters are quite pessimistic about finding answers to the kinds of question posed above in ways that genuinely advance the concerns of women's movements. Several refer to the ways that dominant intellectual traditions and political structures exclude from the start or subsequently dilute questions about gender politics, definitions of issues and solutions to problems. But several chapters also show that there are conceptual openings in established intellectual traditions which can inspire feminist theorizing or policy 'windows' in modern institutions which can be used by those who are aware when a configuration of socioeconomic and political factors exists that is conducive to advancing women's interests.

The Main Themes of the Book

The chapters discuss the meaning of equality, other related concepts such as fairness, justice, autonomy and dependence/independence, the connections between class and feminism and the family and feminism, and the nature of political traditions and institutions through which feminist demands may or may not be met. They also address the question of the respects in which political concepts can be seen as 'gendered' and whether, therefore, it is possible to frame feminist goals in the received languages of politics.

Feminism and Equality

What is obvious in virtually all of the chapters is that the concept of equality is problematic. As Forbes points out, it 'may denote a moral belief, a rationalist precept, an *a priori* principle, a right, a means to an end, or an end in itself'. To add to this, another difficulty should be noted. The 'logical' opposite of equality is not difference, but inequality. Concepts of 'difference' can also be used in a confusing way; contrasted with similarity and involved in other pairs such as identity–diversity and distinction–non-distinction (Komter, 1990). And the use of these concepts is not only a semantic question but refers to diverging philosophical and political traditions (Phillips, 1987).

An essentially contested concept (as well as a political slogan which, for some, implies an unacceptable limitation to liberty and intrusion into family life), conservative theorists sometimes wish to banish 'equality' from political discourse. Yet, as Forbes and Parvikko also point out, without constant demands made in its name, little progress would have been made in extending rights and freedoms to previously excluded groups. This is no less true in the particular case of women. Mitchell (in Phillips, 1987), for example, argues that the idea of equality for eighteenth-century women was revolutionary. Its transformatory potential is acknowledged by Bacchi in connection with the American feminist movement of the early 1960s and by Parvikko and Siim in relation to Finland and Denmark. In referring, however, to the United States and Scandinavia, we are confronted with the two most frequently encountered problems for feminists in the use of equality both as an analytical concept and a political demand. One of these is procedural, involving the requirement that likes be treated alike and the idea that women are *not* fundamentally different from men. The other is whether what is wanted is not procedural equality but material equality which may be realizable only by recognizing, when it is appropriate to do so, that there *are* differences between men and women. Both possibilities point to the underlying question of who should become equal to whom, in which spheres and in what respects. In other words, the employment of equality as a concept and as a goal supposes a standard or a norm, which, in practice, tends to be defined as what is characteristic of the most powerful groups in society.

A frequent theme in this book is the dominance of the idea of equality that is present in social contract theory. Liberal social contract theory, as formulated by its founding fathers, Thomas Hobbes and John Locke, was expressed in opposition to patriarchical political theory which, seeing all power relations as homologous, argued in favour of the absolute power of the sovereign king by comparing it with the natural patriarchal power of the father. Against this idea, contract theory sees society as a contract of equal individuals who agree to transfer their sovereignty to a central government, in order to protect their own interests and to construct a general will. Numerous political theorists have pointed out that equality in social contract theory is a hypothetical construction: individuals are taken *as if* they are equal, equality being conceptualized as equality before the law. Equal rights discourse discounts differences unless they are being seen as natural, trivial or 'just'.

This way of thinking is embedded in liberal legal systems and in the prevalent discourses on justice. The dilemmas to which this gives rise are the primary focus of Carol Bacchi's essay. The best-known maxim on justice states that similarly situated individuals should be treated in the same way. A heavy burden of proof lies on those who would differentiate. This can lead to protracted, mostly speculative, contests over whether women are *by nature* different from or the same as men; such disputes are, in a way, an inevitable consequence of contractarian modes of thinking. As Bacchi points out, the liberal version of equal rights is especially prevalent in the United States and has resulted in the judicial 'strict standard of scrutiny' in cases of racial discrimination. This means that racial classifications can be upheld only if they are for an overriding public purpose, such as the security of the state, and if there is no other means of meeting that purpose. The standard is less strict for women because judges have been less inclined to reject the idea that sex differences are irrelevant to other lesser public objectives. Consequently, it seemed necessary to American feminists of the 1960s to emphasize the fundamental similarity between men and women in order to defeat sex classifications that were used as a barrier to women's entry to the sphere of paid labour and political decision-making. Such classifications limited women's rights as citizens to the equal protection of the civil and criminal law and their rights to equal pay and job opportunities. But the removal of arbitrary barriers does not, as Forbes and Mahon point out, lead to equal material outcomes; indeed, equalizing the starting points can legitimize a system that deliberately differentiates, even if on grounds of fairness, desert or merit instead of ascriptive status.

The Scandinavian model of equality, unlike the American, has a much greater material element. But, even though there is a much stronger tradition that collective responsibility for welfare is fundamental, the dominance of contractarianism in Finland restricted the idea that women might legitimately make specific demands upon the state (Parvikko). Siim argues that, in Denmark, there was – and, to some extent, still is – a dual concept of citizenship; the 'citizen-worker' and the 'citizen-mother'. But, as in Finland, it is the notion of class solidarity rather than feminism that informs the goal of material equality, even though this has brought about policies which could facilitate the capacities of women to act as citizens. Despite the presence in Scandinavia of a notion of citizenship with a material dimension that is absent in America, here, too, it has been thought necessary for women to emphasize their similarity to men in order to be the beneficiaries of public policy. Both Parvikko and Siim point to the existence of a social norm in Scandinavian countries that both men and women should do paid work and be equally interested in family affairs – even in the politics of abortion. The fact that the same stratagem has been necessary in two types of polity that differ widely in their ideologies about positive state intervention corroborates the point made by Forbes that general ideologies of liberalism, radicalism, conservatism do not give rise to unequivocally parallel conceptions of equality and policy prescriptions. Both Forbes and Bacchi draw attention to the capacity of some liberal thinkers to move to what might be thought to be a denial of liberalism's own first precepts. In the original sense of liberalism, the first priority is the removal of barriers to equality, particularly direct impediments; once that is done, there is no further proper duty upon the state to provide 'special' treatment. But some modern liberals incorporate an element of the material notion of equality in so far as they accept that present material circumstances arise from a history of past discrimination. This means that they acknowledge that, despite the removal of barriers, women or racial minorities are still not at an equal starting point and that some 'affirmative action' is necessary, albeit as a temporary measure.

Other lessons that a superficial association of particular conceptions of equality with general political ideologies is inadequate are provided by Bussemaker and Parvikko. Bussemaker draws attention to the fact that, in the Netherlands, a material dimension has been added to liberalism of the equal rights type. Here, policymakers state that equal treatment and equal access to opportunities in welfare policies will lead in the long run to standards of living undifferentiated by sex. However, they seem to accept uncritically the fact that well-intentioned measures can have an adverse effect on the position of women in the short term. Parvikko makes the interesting observation that, in the early days of Finnish feminism, it was the radicals, because of their quasi-Marxist emphasis on the liberating potential of paid employment, who most strongly stressed the natural similarity of men and women and conservatives who stressed differences; whereas, now, radicals take up the different needs of men and women, conservatives tending towards equal treatment.

Feminism, Autonomy and Justice
It has been noted already that the concept of equality, defined in the procedural terms of equal treatment and linked to concepts of fairness and just deserts, can lead to degrees of inequality – which may or may not be regarded as acceptable. The legitimacy of such arrangements rests upon what is often regarded as a fiction of universalism in liberal theory. This, in turn, stems from a notion of the individual which is apparently gender-neutral but which, in many respects, can be argued to conform to a male standard or male perspective. This would imply that women cannot be that easily included in a contractual mode of reasoning.

Pateman (1988, 1989) exemplifies this position in the most radical way, arguing that the overthrow of patriarchal theory, which had legitimized a system of power based on the supremacy of fathers and a hierarchy of families culminating in the royal family, was only half a revolution. It brought about equality among bourgeois men but women were incorporated into civil society, not as individuals, but as the subordinates of husbands or fathers. Pateman interprets the term 'fraternity' not, as most political theorists do, as something like solidarity or communality, but as a literal description of a system governed by men as brothers. The social contract supposes, according to her reading of contract theory, an underlying, hardly visible sexual contract by which men appropriate women's bodies.

Although several elements of Pateman's methods and interpretation can be questioned, her work convincingly makes clear that many of the concepts and frameworks of the contractarian tradition should be deconstructed with respect to their 'gender-loadedness'. The association of women with naturalness and the private sphere not only leads to a practical exclusion of women from political life but also constructs conceptions of politics, rationality and justice in such a way that faculties associated with femininity are excluded, by definition, from these realms. In other words, the meanings of sexual difference are inscribed in the way rationality and autonomy tend to be constructed. Dichotomies between body and mind, love and justice, emotions and reason, nature and culture, female and male, or motherhood and fatherhood, are embedded in the contractarian tradition and, indeed, in other strands of political philosophy as well (Pateman, 1989; Coole, 1988; Lloyd, 1984).

This may imply a rejection of concepts like autonomy, rationality, rights and justice as irretrievably 'male'. But it is also held that they can be uncoupled from their adverse association with sexual difference in order to be more usefully employed in feminist thinking and feminist politics. More radical thinkers in the liberal tradition like Mary Wollstoncraft and John Stuart Mill have contributed in many respects to this project. As an advocate of individualism as well as democracy, John Stuart Mill was also an active campaigner for women's rights. In so far as he argued, as Bussemaker points out, that if women were not rational enough to be full citizens it may be because of artificial constrictions imposed upon them by society, his ideas about female emancipation might be said to be similar to those of some liberal feminists in America and radical feminists in Finland: that women are, if social arrangements allow them to be, similar to men. Moreover, so long as the comparison is put in this way – instead of the possibility of men being similar to women (Parvikko, Bussemaker) – women are forced to adopt the strategy of convincing people that they require the same treatment. However, Bussemaker revisits Mill's conception of autonomy, essential to his ideas about individualism and diversity, to argue that it can be used by feminists to criticize strict concepts of equality and to provide a starting point for alternative approaches. Individuals are never completely autonomous, freedom and the desire to act upon it always existing within a social framework. But, as a goal, autonomy can circumvent the question often put – exasperatedly, as Bacchi points out – about whether women want to be treated the same or differently; comparable capacities to behave autonomously sometimes require one, sometimes the other. Bussemaker's argument coincides with the point made by Bacchi that what genuine advocates of universalism and equal treatment are really worried about is not the differentiation in itself but the purposes to which it is put; that is, they are worried about the detriment that can follow, and often does, from classificatory schemes.

Sevenhuijsen also questions the social contract assumptions of demands for equal rights because, through their connections with property, they embody concepts of the individual and rationality that appear neutral but, in practice assume male norms. She reads equal rights discourse and theories of distributive justice in the

Rawlsian tradition as normative frameworks, as discourses that have not only enabling but also restraining effects on feminist ways of thinking; in this case, over issues connected to parental rights and child custody. Reasoning in terms of equal rights and contractarian justice has recently been criticized by feminist writers as corresponding to a male model of moral reasoning and moral maturity. Carol Gilligan's work (1982) has been highly influential in this respect. Sevenhuijsen argues, together with authors like Joan Tronto (1987) and Anette Baier (1987), that Gilligan's ideas about differences in moral reasoning should be seen as fitting into an alternative tradition in moral philosophy that can be traced back to the morality of virtues in the work of David Hume.

In the contractarian model, conflicting interests and disputes are regulated by laws based on the idea of a universal rationality, whereas David Hume argued that moral reasoning was context-bound and that conflicts about what was just or right should be resolved by 'rearranging situations so that interests are no longer opposed'. The one requires impersonal, equal treatment, the other recognizes different interests and the need for the development of virtue through community participation and discussion. As Sevenhuijsen argues, by reasoning in terms of a morality of care, feminist thinking about child custody can construct new ways of framing the issue, in which children are no longer seen as objects of legal contestation. A 'caring' attitude supposes respect for the autonomy of women who care for children and respect for the rationality of their considerations in doing so.

Feminism and the Family
Sevenhuijsen develops her arguments in the context of recent reforms of family law which, in the name of equal rights, are re-establishing the idea of father-right. She shows that the dominance of equal rights discourse tends to marginalize considerations of care. It is no accident that the family is a key factor in all these chapters. But the way in which it is so in the world at large is by no means predictable. Forbes, for example, argues that the New Right embodies contradictory views on the family. Modern liberals in the classical tradition balk at the pursuit of equality because it would involve intrusion into family life in which are to be found the sources of future life-chances; for them, this is an area of privacy and liberty that must be beyond the reach of the state. Yet neo-conservatives, for whom equal opportunities lie in the ability to be independent, see the need for close interest in the family as the source of cultural attitudes and the need for the state to ensure that the right values are being instilled. They share with radicals and

welfarists, though in different ways, a belief that the family is a proper object of public policy. Moreover, in many strands of feminism, gendered family structures and uneven power relations in the family are the sources of women's oppression, either in primary terms or because of a secondary impact upon women's capacities to act in other spheres; for them, too, public policy needs to take account of this or family roles need to be reconstructed.

Bacchi's chapter shows that there is a profound conflict in the American feminist movement about the best way of enabling pregnant women workers to maintain employment rights. The equal rights strand, worried by the detrimental consequences of the tradition of classifying women as different, want pregnancy to be treated as a temporary disability, like illness, for the purpose of insurance, leave and pay. This group is opposed by those who argue that, since it is only women who become pregnant, 'special' treatment is necessary to take account of the fact that women workers are not in a similar situation to men; in any case, pregnancy is not a disability but a normal event of life which public policy should take into account. Bacchi's major point is the need for feminists to challenge the way in which 'equality' and 'difference' are set against each other in much contemporary political discourse. She also argues that the disagreements in the United States provide lessons for controversies elsewhere that involve the 'same' or 'different' treatment.

Jarman's chapter is about just such an issue in British political history. Her topic is the abolition of protective legislation, a condition made by the Confederation of British Industry in return for support for equal pay. Whereas the Trades Union Congress wanted the 'same' treatment through the extension of protection to men, the 'same' treatment has been achieved by the abolition of restrictions on the working hours of women. Jarman takes the Equal Opportunities Commission to task for justifying this on the ground that women said they wanted the opportunity to work at night (upon which better pay and prospects are often contingent), their husbands, on daytime shifts, being able to look after the children. As she points out, the survey of their opinions gave them no opportunity to say that they would really prefer better child-care facilities during daytime hours so that they could combine work with normal family life.

The provision of child-care facilities, support for other dependent family members and other assistance to combine work and family roles are strikingly better in the Scandinavian countries than anywhere else. Although a model for feminists elsewhere, Scandinavian feminists, Siim argues, have been alarmed by the

possibility that welfare policies may not increase women's independence but transfer their dependency from the private sphere of
men to the public sphere of the state (Siim, 1988; Hernes, 1988).
Siim, however, explains in this book that she has come to revise her
earlier doubts, arguing here that the provision of social protection
does give women space to act in the public sphere and the
opportunity to contribute to the definition of problems and
solutions.

Feminism and Class
The power to define one's own needs, or the absence of it, is a key
part of both Parvikko's and Siim's chapters. In both cases, the
argument is that, however advanced Scandinavian and Finnish
social welfare systems are from a comparative point of view, the
existence of support owes little to recognition of women's rights of
citizenship. As noted earlier, the central issue in both countries has
been one of class solidarity and a strong sense of the idea of the state
being 'a tool to be used' by the people in the collective pursuit of the
common good, not to be feared as a source of coercive authority
and regulation. While Parvikko, in particular, worries about the
inhibition of this class-based version of equality on the growth of an
autonomous women's movement and the acknowledgement of
women's interests, it is clear from Jarman's chapter that the absence
of a commitment to class solidarity through welfare policies in
Britain means that the way in which problems and solutions are
defined will reflect the interests of employers more than those of
working-class women. Mahon's chapter, too, on equality policies in
the Irish Civil Service shows that when a 'sameness' version of
equality is combined with formalism instead of material outcomes,
middle-class women are more likely than working-class women to
benefit, albeit with some difficulty, from new rules about employment.

Feminism, Power and Public Policy
Several policy areas have been referred to already: welfare,
pregnancy, child custody, protective legislation and employment.
Two other chapters, by Outshoorn and Mazur, go more specifically
into issues of employment; these are accounts of how positive action
and the abolition of discrimination came to be on the political
agenda in the Netherlands and France.

It is a common theme that women's autonomy, their capacity to
act as full citizens and the achievement of satisfactory policies
depend critically upon the existing distribution of power. Bussemaker and Outshoorn point to the dilemma of what stratagems can

be chosen by those who lack power; the question is whether to try to define women's needs in completely new terms or to define needs in terms that are compatible with prevailing frameworks and ideologies, thus containing some hope of success. The former may not even be possible, as Parvikko suggests when she proposes that the absence of feminism in Finland can be explained by a common consciousness, embracing women too, of class solidarity, as Mahon suggests when she points to the dominance of patriarchal thinking in Ireland, and as Jarman suggests when she points out that women were excluded from political life when protective legislation was first articulated and inadequately consulted when it was reformed. The second approach was adopted in the Netherlands, where, in the views of Bussemaker and Outshoorn, it was relatively easy in the early 1970s to make demands for equal rights in the terms of the prevailing discourse of liberalism and welfarism. But, as Outshoorn points out, this stratagem had led, in the wider context of partisan changes, to such a dilution of the demands of the Dutch women's movement, that actual policy – a weak version of positive action – is no more than symbolic. Dilution is also characteristic of French equal treatment policies in which positive action has also come to be voluntary and in which enforcement mechanisms are virtually ineffective. The chapters by both Outshoorn and Mazur corroborate arguments of authors like Edelman (1969) and Skocpol (1988), who state in other contexts that, if policies are, indeed, to have a redistributive effect upon the supposed beneficiaries, the existence of committed members of bureaucracies and political institutions are necessary.

On the other hand, just as collective social protection has been said possibly to encourage public patriarchy, so too, the creation of 'women's bureaux' and the appointment of women to public bodies have been characterized as a form of 'state feminism' which, according to some, may give the appearance but not the reality of progress towards the elimination of subordination. As both Mazur and Siim point out, however, the crucial matter is the power potential of women in such positions and whether they use it to promote women's interests. Siim is relatively optimistic about what has happened so far as the Danish women's movement has permeated trade unions, political parties and state-sponsored corporate institutions but she worries about the gaps between women of different classes that are likely to open up as developments in the economy reactivate the expression of class interests at the expense of the articulation of shared, feminist interests.

Plan of the Book

Although the above-mentioned questions, problems and possibilities run through all of the chapters, the book is divided into two parts. The first is primarily on theory and discourse. The second part takes political processes and public policies as its main subject. But the two parts are not divorced. The conceptual section touches upon policy matters because the deconstruction of the language of law and politics helps in the construction of a picture of what it is that societies, or different elements in society, think about the issues raised in this book. This, as well as the work of philosophers, helps to elucidate the promises and pitfalls of feminist strategies. Equally, the stories of policies are not simply chronologies of 'facts' but bring out the underlying assumptions and values of policy-makers and help to corroborate or refine conceptual developments.

In chapter 2, Ian Forbes discusses radical, liberal and conservative understandings of 'equality of opportunity'. In doing so, he demonstrates, at a general level, what is also argued by other contributors with respect to specific feminist issues: the impossibility of relying upon the concept of equality as the driving force of women's liberation. A key element of this chapter is the connection between each of the three understandings of equality and the status of the family as the source of moral development and an object of public policy. Of particular significance is the chapter's observation that, while liberals draw a strict line between the pursuit of equality and the privacy of the family, the family is a battlefield for radicals and conservatives. The argument is that radicals have chosen a set of welfare options for dealing with the family that have given rise to a powerful new right critique which seeks to re-emphasize the family as the source of moral independence instead of allowing a culture of dependency on the state to flourish.

The next chapter, by Tuija Parvikko, also deals with the kinds of welfare issue taken up by Forbes' radicals. But, while the shortcomings of the notion of equality, even in its welfare form, have been discussed by feminists in many countries, this chapter deals with the startling absence of political dissatisfaction about the Finnish notion of equality. On the face of it, this is surprising because Finland legislated much earlier than other European countries on equal political rights and Finnish women have a much longer history than others of substantial participation in the labour market. This pioneering position has not been perfected but, as Parvikko points out, continuing inequalities are inadequately explained because social thought, originally influenced by Sweden, is dominated by contract theories and the ideals of class equality and welfare democracy. An endeavour, referred to in chapter 2, of finding what degree and types of differentiation would be acceptable to egalitarians has some tradition in Finnish social theory but its main concern has been with which class-based, more than sex-based, differences are tolerable.

Like Parvikko, Jet Bussemaker, in chapter 4, deals with the difficulty for feminists of the embodiment of gender-neutrality in the notion of equality in contractarian theories, while, at the same time, it may seem politically sensible to employ a discourse that fits in with existing frameworks of political theory. While appeals for equal treatment may be accepted relatively easily by the holders of political power in liberal, welfare society, Bussemaker shows that a new problem of unequal consequences of formal equal treatment is arising in the Netherlands through the insistence that all social security claims must rest upon a demonstration of willingness to work. As she points out, for many women paid employment is less rewarding than it is for men since they are more likely than men to be in the secondary labour market. The new policy does make an exception for mothers of young children but, by doing so, confirms the idea that the family is a matter for private decision-making. As already mentioned, Bussemaker's proposal is to re-examine the idea of autonomy. Autonomy is a concept that is liberal in its reference to the idea of the self-fulfilling individual but which, if the social context is part of the conceptualization, can also accommodate the different situations of men and women.

Both the empirical subject matter and the major arguments of chapter 5 by Carol Bacchi have been outlined earlier. Like Bussemaker, she discusses the conflict between 'sameness' and 'difference' principles but with reference to the way the issue of women's reproductive capacities is laid down in American legal discourse and to the divisive impact this has had on the feminist movement. In addition to emphasizing the need for feminists to challenge the use of 'difference' as an opposite to 'equality' and to the importance of distinguishing between concerns about a differentiation and its purposes (see above), she commends Ashworth's preference for 'specific' instead of 'special' treatment, the former being a term without the self-serving connotations of the latter.

In chapter 6 Selma Sevenhuijsen also points out, in connection with child custody, how difficult it is for liberal feminists to argue against the human right to family life employed by father-right advocates without, at the same time, appearing to want to keep old gender differences intact or reifying an ideology of motherhood. In her case, she adopts Waltzer's (1983) view that different spheres must be governed by different principles of justice and styles of moral reasoning, which enables her to synthesize the work of Gilligan and others on ethics of care with the Humean tradition as described on p. 98. In her view, this enables debate to focus not on the possessive right of one parent or the other but on the interests of children and quality of their care.

Part 2 of the book is more explicitly about political process and public policies. In chapter 7 Outshoorn tells the story of 'issue perversion' in the Netherlands. Early feminist ideals included consciousness-raising, role change, equality in education and child care, adequate public child care, jobs, the availability of contraception and the legalization of abortion; later on, demands were developed in relation to sexual violence and incomes policies. Preferential hiring was proposed in the 1970s as one means of achieving labour market equality. The last was compatible with Dutch welfare philosophy that something 'extra' must be done for the less privileged. But, however readily accepted in political and administrative circles, it came to be defined by elites as *the* woman question to the exclusion of all the other issues and, even so, watered down so much as to become ineffective.

At least in the Netherlands, as Outshoorn's 'agenda-setting' approach shows, the women's movement had some initial influence in defining the issue; in France, initiatives were almost entirely elite-inspired. This is the subject of chapter 8 by Amy Mazur, who uses a similar model for explaining the advent of equality legislation. She points out that there was no chance for French grass-roots organizations to have a major impact upon problem identification or definition, and argues that employment policies of the 1960s were limited by gender bias at powerful levels of French society. The events of 1968 provided a 'window' for some activists outside and within government and led to two reforms in the 1970s. The election of President Mitterrand, whose party had adopted the idea of women's equality, led to a further law in 1983. Even so, the story of the French reforms is really one of non-decision-making, the issues barely discussed in the Assembly, enforcement being left to individual litigants and judges disposed to favour the rights of employers to manage.

The subject of chapter 9 by Jennifer Jarman has already been referred to. In contrast to France, a comparatively strong British Equal Opportunities Commission exists to enforce anti-discrimination legislation but, even so, Jarman's account of its role in the reform of protective legislation reveals that consultation with women workers had no more impact in securing legislative recognition of their interests than is the case in France, the upshot being similar to that in the Netherlands – a law which reflects, or does not seriously challenge, the interests of employers.

In chapter 10 Evelyn Mahon deals with public sector employment in a country that she describes as more patriarchal than other liberal democracies in ideology and in practice. Because of the strength of traditional attitudes, changes in the Civil Service, initiated in 1983 and intended to improve women's opportunities, have had some impact but at personal cost. Profiles of senior women reveal that they have had to become 'superwomen', to adopt male work patterns and to behave at work as though their families did not exist. To do so, they are critically dependent on good child-care arrangements – usually achieved by employing other women.

In chapter 11 Birte Siim shows that in the Scandinavian countries there is a remarkably high degree of political participation by women compared to Anglo-Saxon and Catholic countries. It has been noted already that, in Scandinavia, ideas of welfare have been based on universalism and social solidarity. In the late 1960s, the state began to be used to change the borders of the public–private division, a shift that women have been able to use to expand their roles as citizens in economic and political life.

Though Scandinavian practice is criticized as a possible source of a new form of patriarchy and is vulnerable to downturns in the economy, Siim's chapter, like that of Parvikko on Finland, shows how far public philosophy about the specific needs of women, if they are to be as fully citizens as men, has travelled in those countries in comparison to Ireland.

The editors would like to thank the ECPR for enabling this workshop to take place, the contributors for their efficiency and goodwill in revising their chapters and all the other participants in the workshop whose papers do not appear here but who contributed so much in discussion to the refinement of those chapters that are in this volume. The editors are also grateful to the Nuffield Foundation for enabling Birte Siim to travel to London to present a version of her chapter at a conference on Women and Citizenship. This was held under the auspices of the Women and Politics Group of the Political Studies Group and the Sexual Divisions Study Group of the British Sociological Association.

References

Baier, Anette (1987) 'Hume, the women's moral theorist?', pp. 37–55 in E . Feder Kittay and D.T. Meyers (eds), *Women and Moral Theory*. Ottowa: Rowman & Littlefield.

Coole, Diana (1988) *Women in Political Theory. From Ancient Mysogyny to Contemporary Feminism*. Brighton: Wheatsheaf Books.

Edelman, Murray (1969) *The Symbolic Uses of Politics*. Illinois: University of Illinois Press.

Gilligan, Carol (1982) *In a Different Voice. Psychological Theory and Women's Development*. Cambridge, MA: Harvard University Press.

Hernes, Helga (1988) 'The welfare state citizenship of Scandinavian women', pp. 187–213 in Kathleen B. Jones and Anna G. Jónasdóttir (eds) *The Political Interests of Gender*. London, Newbury Park and New Delhi: Sage/ECPR.

Komter, Aafke (1990) *Macht van de Dubbele Moraal. Verschil en Gelijkheid in de Verhouding Tussen de Seksen*. Amsterdam: Van Gannep.

Lloyd, Genevieve (1984) *The Man of Reason. 'Male' and 'Female' in Western Philosophy*. London: Methuen.

Mitchell, Juliet (1987) 'Women and equality', pp. 24–43 in Anne Phillips (ed.), *Feminism and Equality*. Oxford: Basil Blackwell.

Pateman, Carol (1988) *The Sexual Contract*. Cambridge and Oxford: Polity Press in association with Basil Blackwell.

Pateman, Carol (1989) *The Disorder of Women*. Cambridge and Oxford: Polity Press in association with Basil Blackwell.

Phillips, Anne (ed.) (1987) *Feminism and Equality*. Oxford: Basil Blackwell.

Siim, Birte (1988) 'Towards a feminist rethinking of the welfare state', pp. 160–79 in Kathleen B. Jones and Anna G. Jónasdóttir (eds) *The Political Interests of Gender*. London, Newbury Park and New Delhi: Sage/ECPR.

Skocpol, Theda (1989) 'Comparing national systems of social provision: a polity centred approach'. Paper presented at meeting of the American Political Science Association, 1–4 September, Washington, DC.

Tronto, Joan (1987) 'Beyond gender difference to a theory of care', *Signs: Journal of Women in Culture and Society*, 4: 644–62.

Walzer, Michael (1983) *Spheres of Justice. A Defence of Pluralism and Equality*. New York: Basic Books.

PART I

POLITICAL THEORY AND LEGAL DISCOURSE

2

Equal Opportunity: Radical, Liberal and Conservative Critiques

Ian Forbes

Equality principles are among the most powerful in political thought and practice, despite the variety of available conceptions. Equality may denote a moral belief, a rationalist precept, an *a priori* principle, a right, a means to an end, or an end in itself. Such a wide range of possibilities means that coalescence of interest and commitment around the concept is maximized, notwithstanding quite sharp analytical differences between the protagonists for equality of a particular kind. As a consequence, the language of equality principles has a complex set of philosophical references whereby demarcation lines between contrasting positions are subtly etched. In the process, the range and applicability of equality discourse has been extended as new dimensions of understanding emerge and as fresh attempts are made to improve the situation of disadvantaged groups and individuals. Inevitably, therefore, the content and role of ideas about equality are subject to constant revision. Nevertheless, equality principles, as an identifiable category in thought and as a basis for political action, have remained an essential element in continuing attempts to organize, institute and achieve change in society.

One of the most striking examples of the association of equality principles with practical political action to bring about change concerns equality of opportunity. Equality of opportunity has long and strong connections with gender politics in particular, stemming from seventeenth- and eighteenth-century demands for practical improvements in the legal and social standing of women in European society. The assumption that women are rational human agents lay at the heart of these campaigns for equality.

Since then, equality of opportunity has developed a status of its own in political thought. Certainly, equal opportunity is something of a portmanteau concept, consisting of and conveying a variety of political principles. Some of these are associated with antagonistic theoretical perspectives. The women's movement, ethnic minority groups, other disadvantaged groups and some on the Left have for an assortment of reasons developed a maximalist application of the concept. This is sometimes referred to as 'genuine equality of opportunity', and refers to the means to egalitarian ends, or as an essential element in emancipation, in freedom from discrimination and oppression. Liberals and the neo-liberal Right have resisted such developments. For them, liberty resides in choice and the absence of constraint. Equality in practice threatens liberty, so only minimalist interpretations are consistent with individual freedoms, the prevention of harm and proper limits on state intervention. More straightforwardly, some theorists of inequality wish to abandon any commitment to 'genuine' equal opportunity altogether, while others insist instead that strict procedural equal opportunity alone is desirable because it will nurture a healthy hierarchy.

As a political principle relating to equality, equal opportunity can have an array of justifications, which may conflict with one another. As a procedural argument in respect of opportunity, chance or access, equal opportunity seems most congenial to theories of justice which have a preference for starting-gate equality. This leads to arguments about the basis for justice – fairness, desert, needs – about where the starting gate is perceived to be and about how we should deal with those who start the race with differing and/or unequal abilities. Partly because of this, equal opportunity is now rarely enacted without reference to end-state arguments, and is implemented most notably by means of monitoring and positive action programmes. Arguments abound over the distinctiveness of affirmative action and the validity of reverse or positive discrimination. Positive discrimination is usually rejected,[1] but the same writers usually go on to confirm arguments in favour of equal opportunity policies (Edwards, 1987; Sumner, 1987; Radcliffe Richards, 1982; Cohen *et al.*, 1987).

Ideological as well as analytical considerations are also at issue. In general, radical proponents of equality wish to weave into their accounts some notion of social and historical circumstance, whether in terms of class, gender, 'race', needs or socioeconomic rights, whereas liberal thought gives precedence to an individualist human agency as the basis for formal political and legal rights. Neo-liberal and conservative thought similarly validates individual agency as a way of minimizing state action, but complements this with an account of civic responsibility. Thus equal opportunity is a fertile ground for analysis; the concept characteristically plays host to ideological conflict, stimulates theoretical refinements and leads to public policies which act as a testing ground for the adequacy, implementation and assessment of the concept. Equal opportunity is, variously, a principle, a cause and a practice. But the competing approaches of equal opportunity, it will be argued here, are becoming less distinguishable in one important respect. The family – whether it be seen as a socialization agency, a social institution or a private realm – is increasingly the critical focus for the development and application of equality of opportunity.

Radical Equality of Opportunity

Equality, when adopted as a foundational value and prerequisite for social justice, generates antagonism to a limited or procedural version of equal opportunity. John Schaar (1971: 135–6) argues that the doctrine of equal opportunity, while 'attractively simple', is inherently 'very conservative'. His critique highlights the way that simple versions of equal opportunity can presume, reproduce and magnify inequality in society. Equal opportunity, when restricted to making unlike individuals submit to a single pattern of achievement, unequally hampers the ability of some to benefit. There cannot be equal opportunity to engage in an unequal competition, and there is neither equality nor opportunity for the person who knows that to enter the competition is to reproduce the hierarchy. In Schaar's opinion, the crucial factor is the kind of social values which are recognized and incorporated into the concept:

> The doctrine of equality of opportunity is the product of a competitive and fragmented society, a divided society, a society in which individualism . . . is the reigning ethical principle . . . In other words, much of the demand for equality, and virtually all of the demand for the equality expressed in the equality of opportunity principle, is really a demand for an equal right and opportunity to become unequal. (Schaar, 1971: 142–3)

Effectively, equal opportunity confirms existing inequalities and is capable of transforming original equality into inequality. How, then, could the concept have been so readily accepted and incorporated into post-war public policy? Some point to the nature of the political systems within which this transformation has taken place. Derek Phillips cites the example of the United States, where

> Because of the tradition of individualism and egalitarianism, there emerged a need to in some way combine the justification of inequalities

with certain elements in the American creed . . . This combination . . .
is manifested in the idea of equality of opportunity . . . The major
reason, of course, is to bring about a greater equality in people's 'life
chances' and to increase the general level of equality in society. (Phillips,
1979: 42)

There are actually two major reasons here – changing the situation
for individuals and changing society –\and the latter is the more
controversial because it infers an agreed social commitment beyond
an individualized notion of justice[In any event, equal opportunity
is about legitimation as well as policy outcomes, about appropriate
political progress as much as a conception of the good society.\If so,
the experience of the post-war women's movement provides a
further indictment.\Women have fought for emancipation and
liberation. They have aimed to remedy inequality and injustice, to
challenge patriarchy and the entire social hierarchy, to change it
politically, socially and ideologically.\One of feminism's successes is
in the area of equal opportunities, or so it seems. Yet, as Hester
Eisenstein observes:

As incorporated into the capitalist democracies, feminism came to mean
a narrowly defined form of social change, most notably, the recruitment
of women into some areas of power and privilege from which they had
been previously excluded . . . in the United States, the 1970s saw . . .
the passage of legislation to ensure equal opportunity in matters of
education, credit and employment . . . The structures oppressing
women, especially the nuclear family, were not dismantled. Rather, the
changes that took place appeared to accommodate and co-opt feminist
demands, in the familiar pattern of American liberalism, without
making any basic changes in the structures of political, economic, or
social life. (Eisenstein, 1984: 136–7)

The British experience is even less encouraging. The various Acts
individualize equal opportunities, such that there must be endless
one-woman struggles for even the limited kind of change described
above to occur. As Susan Atkins remarks:

the problems faced by women cannot be solved merely by increasing the
number of Davids sent out to throw stones at Goliath. For the basis of
that fight was a gentlemen's agreement. If David won, the Philistines
would hand over power to Israel (1 Samuel, 17). The Sex Discrimination
Act is no gentlemen's agreement, but a diversionary tactic. While the
female Davids are busy fighting Goliaths, the Philistines continue to
wage war on the rest of womankind. (Atkins, 1986: 62)

While individual successes are possible, neither equality nor
emancipation for women as a practice or a principle is established or
advanced. Such criticisms presuppose a more developed account of
equal opportunity – radical equality of opportunity. This position is

methodologically collectivist. It sees individuals as social beings, the understanding of which derives from their group origin and characteristics. Liberty is conceived as a particular combination of freedom and ability. Freedom is limited if ability is absent, and upon this belief hinges the demand that equality refers to end states. For Richard Norman (1982: 97), that end state should be an 'equally worthwhile and satisfying life' for everyone, and 'equality of liberty'. Without definite and demonstrable openness of outcomes or results, the egalitarian can justifiably claim that the present pattern of inequalities represents a hard and entrenched hierarchy.

Equal opportunity, on this view, may be a necessary but it is certainly not a sufficient condition for equality in society. Nor is it sufficient to secure equal liberty. Sufficiency is supplied by the attachments to the understanding and practice of equal opportunity generated by the account of the impediments to equality (rather than the nature of liberty). These arise out of the commitment to treat like persons in a like manner, and to provide the opportunity for a worthwhile and satisfying life.

The egalitarian is faced with a number of difficulties here. S/he has to show how difference may and may not amount to inequality, and must demonstrate: that the good pursued is general, non-trivial and attainable; that opportunity exists to get it; that scarcity requires distributive justice; that redistributive action is justified; that some individuals will have a less equal chance to gain the good; and that this diminution of chance stems from impediments of an historical, social or political nature outside of that person's control.

Additionally, William Darity Jr (1987: 176) argues that 'the fundamental issue is the acceptability or non-acceptability of hierarchy and, if there is to be a hierarchy, what criteria are used to distribute inequality across members of a society'. Thus the egalitarian has to establish the distinction between the existence of inequality or difference in society, and the hierarchical organization of society. For the methodological collectivist, equality is a notion of the *general* good. Inevitably, it concerns a prior interpretation of social existence as unequal. It also entails a view of the social whole, within which individuals are to be understood and defined in relation to others with respect to their endowments, status and economic situation (seen by critics as a 'sociological alibi' and hence a claim against the state and others). Egalitarianism interprets the good in such a way as to incorporate: a view of human nature; a policy-making principle; a commitment to a procedure and means of implementation; and a particular kind of general social outcome. Equality between social beings in respect of the benefits and burdens of that society is sought.

What is *not* offered is numerical equality, nor any kind of strict equalization of outcomes between individuals *per se*. Yet, as Felix Oppenheim (1981: 122) points out, numerical equality of the Aristotelian kind is the only treatment which is truly egalitarian, given a direct correlation between aim and outcome. Any trimming of outcomes, or stretching of the relationship, or lack of success in implementing the good introduces *degrees* of equality and inequality.

Thus the egalitarian must admit that unequal outcomes are acceptable; s/he must present equality of outcome as a specified set of parameters which must arise out of a strict but unrealizable notion of equal treatment. The objection to this use of the notion of equality is that it is actually a doctrine of acceptable *inequality*. The discussion is no longer about equality at all, but about the range and kind of inequality we might accept.

Even accepting that outcomes cannot be numerically equalized, radical proponents of equal opportunity will still insist that efforts must be made. Inequality and hierarchy are rejected, but not the conceptually distinct notions of (Millian) diversity, (Derridean) *différance* and (feminist) difference (Fuss, 1989; Grosz, 1989; Moi, 1985; Marks and de Courtivron, 1981). Equal opportunity, described as the best procedure for selection to scarce social positions, or as equal access to opportunity or to a worthwhile and satisfying life, or even in terms of positive action can introduce the benefits of diversity to the previously biased or unrepresentative workforce or institution. This has strong Millian overtones, but is an argument which can be forwarded by the staunch communitarian.

Equal opportunity is a change agent. It is not necessary to claim that 'better' people from an enlarged skills base will accede to positions in the meritocracy. 'Meritocracy' can be as fluid in its meaning as the right or the good. Benefits accrue from opportunity and access being available to a wider population. Less elitism, uniformity and rigidity means more flexibility and awareness of difference and alternatives in the institutions of society. Englightenment notions of progression, development and perfectibility need not be included in what is a predictive claim. Diversity can be preferred without expecting it to produce improvement.

The consequences for liberty follow similar lines, in so far as the use of collectivist rather than individualist precepts means that liberty is judged by altogether different criteria. Liberty concerns social and political outcomes in respect of (individuals as representatives of) groups and humanity. Liberty is not capable of atomistic or exclusive enjoyment but is dependent upon it being a general condition of existence. Therefore, equal opportunity may be used as a means of bringing about equal liberty, since collectivists cast an early eye on the historical and material circumstances which may inhibit particular enjoyment of liberty. The definition of and conditions for liberty, therefore, present no major obstacle to the radical proponent of equal opportunity, but the same cannot be said for the liberal.

Liberal and Neo-Liberal Equality of Opportunity

For the liberal, equal opportunity is a matter of justice, or the right balance between equal treatment and individual liberty. There are several versions of note. The first is what Amy Gutmann (1980: 218) calls the 'old egalitarianism', which 'took as its primary aim equality of opportunity'. It is this rather simple version which is so strongly attacked by radical thought. The second is John Rawls' (1972: 301–3) notion of fair equal opportunity, turning on arguments that are more to do with justice than equality. The third is a pluralist model of equal opportunity best expressed by James Fishkin (1983, 1987), who sees limitations to an absolute commitment to the principle of equal treatment by virtue of the need to protect liberty. For a truly liberal political theory, the family must have primacy, since a major realm of liberty resides in the autonomy of the family:

> Consensual relations within a given family governing the development of its children should not be coercively interfered with except to ensure for the children the essential prerequisites for adult participation in the society. (Fishkin, 1987: 39)

Fishkin admits that the bulk of inequality in society is related to the nature and existence of the family, but he wants its political and social sanctity preserved intact. This rules out even modest proposals relating to equal opportunity. As S.J.D. Green points out: 'Any social order which does not disrupt the integrity of the family unit allows for the possibility of particularistic provision in the educational opportunities of each generation' (1988: 23). This is the reality which prompts radical egalitarian proposals. Fishkin is typical of liberals who wish to prevent the consequence of an egalitarian commitment to equal opportunity, which in R.S. Peters' (quoted in Phillips, 1979: 44) view cannot exist unless one is 'prepared to control early upbringing, size of families and breeding'.

Such overtly illiberal proposals are deemed to clinch the argument against radical equality of opportunity. However, these kinds of objection are a distraction from the naturalistic and functionalist accounts of the family that underlie these conclusions. Nor can the liberty argument, of an individualistic kind, be easily deployed here. First, as the arguments of feminist thinkers have demonstrated so forcefully, the family has always been constructed to serve as a partriarchal institution of unfreedom. For women, consent is dubious, if not absent, individualness is subsumed under the authority of the husband, and freedom is effectively negated. Non-liberal feminist thought has 'complicated and subverted traditional definitions of male politics', and is dismissive of the priority of a liberty systematically denied to women (Eisenstein, 1984: 139). Secondly, children are not completely counted as individuals either. Considerable harm can legally be caused to them, short of some forms of physical and sexual abuse. Routinely, they are 'positively controlled' and their freedom of choice 'is under arbitrary control' (Harris, 1982: 35). Female children, of course, bear the double burden of unequal treatment on the basis of their sex.

Far from establishing indications for the right balance between commitments to the competing demands of equality and liberty, the liberal position asserts that political action must not involve the family, even though it is an openly acknowledged source of unequal opportunity and an institution which in virtue of its constitution violates individual freedom. Fishkin (1987: 47) at least sees the problems faced by liberalism: 'Either we must learn to expect less, or liberalism undermines itself as a coherent moral ideology; it undermines itself by robbing itself of moral legitimacy, of claims to moral validity.' He therefore opts for 'a limited liberalism': 'As a matter of public ideology this requires a revision of expectations, a revision of moral culture. As for equal opportunity, we do not need a *systematic* theory and the demand for one is part of the problem' (Fishkin, 1987: 48).

This conclusion is interesting in two ways. First, labelling as a problem the demand for a systematic theory is to blame the victim. The second and more important observation concerns the choice of an alternative change agency to the state. Why is it unacceptable to impose a political vision, but reasonable to revise moral culture? Who has the authority to determine and prescribe an (implicitly) exclusive culture? Why is this not an equally great, perhaps greater threat to liberty? That such questions can be asked of a liberal thinker is an indication of the difficulties equality principles can pose for a libertarian approach.

Clearly, the institution of the family carries a heavy burden of responsibility for inequality in society. The refusal to subject that institution to a substantive or critical revision produces somewhat incoherent and illiberal conclusions. The New Right exploration of this ground reveals some remarkably similar analytical manoeuvres but quite different conclusions concerning action.

Equal Opportunity and the New Right

Building upon the classical liberal approach to liberty and equality, neo-liberal attitudes to equal opportunity have two dimensions. One is a critique of egalitarianism, wherein equal opportunity is the Trojan Horse of social policy, ready to disgorge the multiple evils of affirmative action, positive discrimination and equality of outcome – what Thomas Sowell (1984: 175) calls 'statistical parity of retrospective results', and Michael Novak (1990: 13) sees as 'a new soft despotism'. The spectre is raised of the imposition and enforcement, ultimately by a coercive state, of a preconceived conception of social justice which *guarantees* equal outcomes. The objections to this are several. Philosophically, neo-liberals are suspicious of compulsory views of the good society, since liberty is threatened (Joseph and Sumption, 1979). Empirically, it is denied that the desired ends can actually be achieved; rather, there will only be a levelling down (Barry, 1981: 144). Politically, harm will be done by the growth of an intrusive state which will seek in vain to produce the good intended. Normatively, individual responsibility will wither, thus militating against the realization of the good as each individual sees it. Equality of opportunity is, on this account, bad social theory leading to bad social engineering.

A second dimension shares some of these concerns but is far less antagonistic to equal opportunity policy. The difference arises from positive claims concerning inequality in society. Unequal outcomes between unequals in society are approved, as are equal outcomes between equals; unequal outcomes between equal individuals are not, nor are equal outcomes between unequals, if some restriction of the freedom of the individual is entailed (Novak, 1990). The focus on merit, often employed in utilitarian fashion to bolster the radical case, is turned against that position. As J.R. Lucas has pointed out:

> If we are to attach any weight to merit – and it is difficult to claim that fairness is preserved where merit is disregarded – we are committed to possible inequalities of some sort, because although it cannot be shown *a priori* that people do have different deserts, it does follow from the nature of the concept that they could . . . We can secure Equality in certain respects between members of certain classes for certain purposes and under certain conditions; but never, and necessarily never, Equality in all respects between all men for all purposes and under all conditions. The egalitarian is doomed to a life not only of grumbling and everlasting envy, but of endless and inevitable disappointment. (Lucas, 1971: 150)

Theorists of inequality, who openly admit that there must be unequal outcomes, claim to have a more forthright or realistic approach. However, not too much weight should be attached to these apparently clinching arguments. The 'certain respects' in which equality can be 'secured' cover no more than the least controversial cases. Secondly, the egalitarian seems doomed to being misunderstood, due to the persistent but erroneous assumption that a commitment to equality as a foundational principle means a determination to seek an equalized and uniform end state, regardless of the cost in liberty and variety.

Notwithstanding the theoretical niceties, the practical consequence of this position is a strong commitment to procedural equality, to ensure that meritocratic principles adjudicate admission to valued positions in society. The unequal society is thus improved and strengthened, and the considerable rewards it offers go to those who most deserve it, namely those who can most successfully differentiate themselves as 'better', according to the criteria set by those persons, agencies, institutions and practices which control and administer selection, recruitment and promotion agenda to the elite positions in society. In this case, equal opportunity is the mirror image of the egalitarian position, since it is a necessary but not sufficient condition, not for equality, but for justice between individuals, the defence of liberty and a dynamic and productive society. As Darity observes, Sowell's preferred society is based on an equal opportunity vision compatible with:

> a set of values and ideals that idealizes a society that competitively weeds out winners and losers . . . Equal opportunity is procedural equality, dictating uniformity in procedures across all persons, and guaranteeing nothing about the outcomes across individual or ascriptively differentiated groups . . . Sowell purports to desire a world where human achievement can be accomplished in a color-blind environment : . . . . (Darity, 1987: 178)

Here, equal opportunity is not rejected, just redefined, and this vision of a perfectly competitive society is supported by 'New Consensus' thought (Novak, 1987). However, there are important differences in conservative thought concerning equal opportunity. Unlike Sowell (who is a black conservative thinker), others are prepared to acknowledge the existence of groups (for example ethnic minorities, the poor, the disabled and the aged) and see the need to treat them differentially. The intention is to end poverty. Among the principles for understanding poverty are the ideas that:

> Every able-bodied person ought to have the opportunity to exit from poverty. If the poverty of some is persistent, or if it persists among particular groups over long periods, something seems seriously wrong.
> Those of the poor unable to exit from poverty, through no fault of their own but because of disability, illness or old age, should find

adequate assistance from others, including government as a last resort . . . Given an open society and personal effort, talent should often emerge (and be rewarded) among persons born poor; and their invention, creativity and personal liberty should flourish. Thus, the free circulation of individuals in both upward and downward mobility should respond primarily to individual talent, effort and opportunity. (Novak, 1987: 7)

The recognition of genuine impediments to opportunity is matched by the admission that the state is ultimately responsible. The New Consensus approach makes further concessions to the social welfare function for government, just when so many are busy rejecting such functions in keeping with what must by now be the 'old consensus' of the New Right. The persistence of poverty under a variety of economic, social and political conditions in post-war United States experience, the lack of effect of 'the heroic achievements of the Civil Rights movement' (Novak, 1987: 73), has forced New Consensus thinkers to concede that, 'under current conditions: (1) economic growth is not enough; (2) opportunity is not enough; and (3) welfare as now constituted is not enough' (Novak, 1987: 74).

Lest this be taken as an outbreak of agreement with left of centre critiques of the capitalist welfare state, the predicates of this three-part finding need clarification. For example, it is argued that 'the problem of behavioural dependency' is at 'the heart of the poverty problem in 1987' (Novak, 1987: 72). As the work of Glenn Loury is quoted approvingly: 'For a significant proportion of (welfare) recipients, their dependency . . . is a long-term condition arising from behaviours for which they might appropriately be held accountable' (Novak, 1987: 37).

This is the other side of the conservative view of freedom. A narrow or negative view of liberty must be accompanied by a means of accounting for the failure of so many to raise themselves up, to avail themselves of the benefits of economic growth, take advantage of the wealth of opportunities and to be nurtured by existing welfare provision. Instead of a fear of freedom, there is now the *failure* to be free, culpable since freedom is already available; it does not have to be created, daringly, in concert with others. Since the liberal state cannot be held responsible for the failure to be free, the individual must be. But current society, in their view, also has responsibility for the way that it endorses and protects welfare aspects of public policy and expenditure. In New Consensus terms, such attitudes and practices promote behaviour which keeps individuals 'in a dependency on the public purse – and, worse still, in an inward dependency' (Novak, 1987: 98). Furthermore, the magnitude of 'the problems of dependency and dysfunction . . . corrodes a free society' (Novak, 1987: 100).

For these thinkers there is no puzzle here, no dilemma of freedom that so many are unfree. After all, it is the nature of liberty to set a challenge to humans in society: 'The free society sets unusually high expectations for its able citizens. It demands the self-reliance of each, so that each may contribute directly to the well-being of all' (Novak, 1987: 121).

Remarkably, New Consensus thought adopts a *prescriptive* theory of the good. It is not an *indirect* contribution that is valued on the assumption that general well-being will emerge. For internal consistency, the principle that all should be free to determine their own interpretation of the good should not be violated. If politics is about the search for that notion of the good which does not rule out this logical prerequisite, this may at first blush sound like a commitment to open and expressive democratic participation, whereby the people could deliberate, choose the good for their society and accept the implicit Rousseauian obligation to honour the decisions thus made. Or it could approximate a woman-centred perspective – 'an ethic of sharing, cooperation and collective involvement' – and indicate a feminist vision of the future, 'tending in the direction of greater equality, shared decision-making, and justice' (Eisenstein, 1984: 144–5).

However, the freedom of all to determine the good refers to all private *individuals*, distinct, autonomous, and associated with other individuals only to the extent that each wishes to exercise the capacity to decide upon and pursue the good of their particular choosing. The New Consensus critique ushers in a definite set of ideas to bring about their prescriptive vision of society; 'a community of self-reliance, in which independence is made possible by mutual cooperation and in which community is aimed at self-development' (Novak, 1987: 121). Things must change; governments, policy-makers and all the institutions of society must accept responsibility for past mistakes. The main task, reducing dependency, 'will require working together as a national community to increase the numbers of self-reliant citizens' (Novak, 1987: 101). It can be argued that this represents both a notion of unity which must ultimately be coerced and a commitment to greater end-state equality by another route.

Even more surprising is the identification of the institution most problematic to the implementation of change in society – the family. Conservative thought since Burke has esteemed the family as the prime transmitter of culture and creator of individual selves. Now, however, the family is part of the problem because it fulfils that function to such devastating effect. Fishkin's liberal unease over the implications of a thoroughgoing application of the principle of equal opportunity deserves further review:

> it raises stark conflicts with the one area of liberty which touches our lives most directly. Once we take account of the family, equal opportunity is an extraordinarily radical principle, and achieving it would require sacrifices in liberty which most of us would regard as grossly illiberal. (Fishkin, 1987: 40)

Crude and all-too-familiar spectres of the ungodly communist and the rabid feminist wreaking havoc with our most private and precious of institutions and therefore the fabric of liberal society lie not far behind Fishkin's sentiments. But compare his nervous, hands-off liberal approach with the brisk New Consensus opinion of the family:

> With accumulating power, the blurred, sometimes disordered set of expectations for behaviour portrayed by our major institutions reaches directly into family homes; *one must insist upon* personal responsibility and social obligation. Since personal values do not arise in a vacuum, *one must attend to* the health of the national ethos. . . . In short, the family is the arena in which the battle to reduce poverty – both in its material and in its moral components – should be most hotly contested. (Novak, 1987: 18, emphasis added)

This inversion of priorities is not for the faint-hearted. In the recent past, there was much concern if little agreement over the public/private divide. Feminism extended political analysis to include the family, despite accusations of extending the notion of politics to breaking point (Miller, 1987: 391). No such boundaries of the private and political seem to be agreed by the New Consensus. The ideology has moved from validating a divide based on private wealth versus the public political realm in favour of the quite different concern for personal responsibility for the common weal. The family is, suddenly, the acknowledged battleground of both equality and morality. The state has a vital role in bringing about this change, with government assigned the 'fundamental tasks that . . . are indispensable to the common good', so that it can 'show leadership' and inspire 'all citizens and all institutions of society to focus their talents and resources upon desperate needs' (Novak, 1987: 100).

This kind of 'leadership' to overcome the dependency problem entails a significant transitionary period. It effectively means a *dictatorship of the libertarians* until the appropriate moral prescriptions have taken hold and have created newly 'self-reliant citizens' and the uncorroded free society. Given the New Consensus view of one moral community, the need to bind together in a quasi-corporatist manner all the institutions of society in pursuit of a common purpose, the violability of every aspect of a person's life from cradle to grave and the absence of alternative ideological frameworks, their vision may fairly be described as a totalitarian one.

Principle Differences and Policy Convergence

This examination of radical, liberal and conservative accounts of equal opportunity shows marked variations in interpretation on the one hand and a good deal of convergence on the other, both within and between ideological perspectives. The limitations that are placed on the implementation of equal opportunity in general concerns the insufficiency of the ends produced. Those ends are undesired for a variety of reasons; for some, the ends attained fall short of expectation, while for others the ends are unsought and negatively valued. It is slightly surprising to find that there is no automatic correlation between ideology and preference for equal opportunity.

Convergence emerges, perhaps unexpectedly, in three areas. First, radical, liberal and (some) conservative proponents of equal opportunity all see the need for a wider programme to tackle social problems. Radicals want 'genuine' change, a verifiable progress towards equality and are willing to endorse a conception of equal opportunity only if it will secure that progress. The other positions see the inadequacy of current provision of opportunity by itself and wish to augment it with a sweeping moral regeneration.

The second convergence concerns the family. All are now agreed that the family is an obstacle to the implementation of equal opportunity. Only some radical thinkers have been prepared openly to acknowledge this and accept the theoretical and policy implications; feminist thought is in the forefront of the search for alternatives to the family given its crucial role in the socialization of gendered subjects. Other radicals join with liberal thinkers in general and some conservative thinkers in particular; they remain prepared to subjugate equality to liberty, thereby protecting and privileging the family in the face of the need for social change. Other conservative thinkers are now ready to discard this central tenet of liberal thought and build the case for 'family engineering'. Thirdly, each position appeals to a conception of the good, and has a commitment to impose it (liberal thought by imposing agreement on the 'ungood' to be avoided). All views entail some justification of acceptable diversity and even difference.

Technically, therefore, the concept of equal opportunity, as a specific combination of assumptions and arguments, is essentially contestable on the usual seven counts (Gallie, 1955–6). It is appraisive, internally complex, open to a variety of initial descriptions and modifiable under different circumstances. Moreover, it is in constant and disputed use in political argument, and has an authoritative exemplar which argument has developed and augmented.

Politically, is it significant that all are agreed on the necessity of opportunity if not equality. Derek Phillips (1979: 45) doubts that substantive as distinct from (the much weaker concept of) formal equality of opportunity can ever be reached, yet concludes that without 'a continued *demand* for formal equality of opportunity, even modest advances will not be forthcoming'. Fishkin (1987: 41), in a more complex way, indicates that liberty is insolubly in conflict with equality, so equal opportunity must be a part of an unsystematized liberal programme to approach 'asymptotically' its aspirations without full prejudice to either. Whatever the difficulties of his attempt to grapple with the theoretical and practical issues, Fishkin's contribution is in marked contrast to Barry Gross' consideration of 'real' equality of opportunity, which deserves a brief mention if only for the breathtakingly blithe way he concludes:

> When we awake from the dreams of perfect equality where all enjoy the same means and all prospects are equally sweet, when the warm light of day has brought us back to reality, then we will say that meaningful, possible, real equal opportunity exists and can only exist in a liberal society, a reasonably open society, a society like ours. (Gross, 1987: 142)

Egalitarians like Schaar would dispense with equal opportunity altogether in favour of its antithesis, the radical democratic conception of equality, one 'stripped of the antagonistic and privatistic overtones of the equal opportunity principle': 'This is the equality that obtains in the relations among the members of any genuine community. It is the feeling held by each member that all other members, regardless of their many differences of function and rank, belong to the community . . .' (Schaar, 1971: 149).

Radical proponents of equal opportunity have responded by developing affirmative action practices to offset the practical limitations of mere procedural equal opportunity and the empirical buttressing of the existing hierarchy. This signals an antagonism to inequality, a commitment to a non-individualistic set of social values and a determination to bring about change in the face of an adverse social and political context. As Goldman (1987: 102) sees it: 'A genuine concern for equal opportunity therefore must be part of a broader egalitarian program, and, as such, it is certainly a concern that genuine egalitarians can endorse.'

This kind of discussion worries conservatives like Sowell (1984). They trust liberal society, but not liberal policies, since they see in them a tendency to compromise on liberty to secure social 'improvement'. Inequality is the value to be defended here and a robust and meritocratic hierarchy to be developed. The only way to achieve this is an equally genuine concern for strict procedural equality of opportunity. New Consensus thought goes still further, saying that more needs to be done in the way of social and political engineering.

Concerns over liberty or freedom stem from the visions of society that underpin these views. The dominant model is that of the 'free society', and the effect of equal opportunity on it has been the issue. What has not been considered is any alternative to the fairly narrow, market-oriented conception of the free society that has been encountered. Gutmann (1980) offers a vision in some sympathy with the radical egalitarian determination to move away from the competitive model of human nature and society. For her, 'liberal egalitarianism looks forward to a further development of the cooperative nature already revealed in the development of the liberal welfare state' (Gutmann, 1980: 229). Unlike Fishkin, she sees no need for 'a complete remaking of moral consciousness' (Gutmann, 1980: 229).

Conservative thought adds references to culture, nation and community, as if these were truly collective notions describing a single entity and a universal set of values. These conservatives wish to impose a single culture and social norm on the whole society, in direct contradiction to the minimal state commitment and the argument that governments are simply unable to impose outcomes on society. Without departing from the 'free society' model, an alternative is possible by reinstating the concept of a pluralist society at the level of culture (Nickel, 1987). This would mean acknowledging the validity of different practices of community, of family and of right, not just ideas and beliefs, and requires the admission that their programme of moral regeneration and re-education is neither politically nor ethically sustainable.

By far the most interesting finding of an analysis of the three critiques is that the family is the major focus of analysis and action, in terms of ideology and policy. In the process, the liberal account of equal opportunity falters alarmingly, and liberalism itself demonstrates its incapacity to maintain any internal coherence in the face of the need to introduce change in society. In this last respect, it is intriguing to note that radical and New Right critiques converge. They both conclude that the family is a legitimate target for public policy in the service of social ends, but it is the New Right critique which is far more developed in terms of contemporary justifications and ideas for implementation. The radical critique, by contrast, reveals its historical and materialist origins by tending to focus on change at the workplace and within the formal public institutions. Where it has dealt with the family, it has chosen a range of welfare policy options which have given rise to such powerful critiques of the welfare state in general. Unless radical critiques of equal opportunity develop more sophisticated accounts of change and the family, then it is likely that, once again, some on the Left will be forced into a defence of an institution they originally rejected.

Notes

* The author is grateful for the encouragement and advice of Diana Coole, Elizabeth Meehan, Selma Sevenhuijsen and the members of the ECPR Panel on Gender Politics.

1. The effects of past discrimination call for a specific policy response. It is possible to compensate for past injustice by creating a new set of losers in the short run from among the more privileged groups (male, white, undisabled individuals). This 'positive' or 'reverse' discrimination, often through the use of imposed quotas, is legal in a few places even though it does override justice considerations. Even the suspicion of its practice tends to cause conflict and dissatisfaction among beneficiaries and losers alike. More sophisticated responses assess the discrepancies brought about by past discriminatory action in terms of expected and actual percentages of groups selected or preferred. Targets with a specific time-frame are set. Targets are intended to improve recruitment and assessment practices (not to affect *individual* decisions) and produce a manifestly fairer result in the future. This form of approach is known as 'positive action', and will often include special training arrangements, efforts to attract candidates from under-represented groups, and a reassessment of the assumptions underlying decisions concerning suitability, qualifications and experience. Positive action does not transgress justice considerations, and can be a vital inducement in the change process.

References

Atkins, Susan (1986) 'The Sex Discrimination Act 1975: the end of a decade', *Feminist Review*, 24 (October): 57–70.

Barry, Norman P. (1981) *An Introduction to Modern Political Theory*. Basingstoke: Macmillan.

Barry, Norman P. (1987) *On Classical Liberalism and Libertarianism*. New York: St Martin's Press.

Cohen, M., Nagel, T. and Scanlan, T. (eds) (1987) *Equality and Preferential Treatment*. Princeton: Princeton University Press.

Darity Jr, William (1987) 'Equal opportunity, equal results and social heirarchy', *Praxis International*, 7(2): 175–6.

Edwards, John (1987) *Positive Discrimination, Social Justice and Social Policy*. London: Tavistock.

Eisenstein, Hester (1984) *Contemporary Feminist Thought*. London: Unwin.

Fishkin, James S. (1983) *Justice, Equal Opportunity and the Family*. London: Yale University Press.

Fishkin, James S. (1987) 'Liberty versus equal opportunity', pp. 32–48 in E.F. Paul, F.D. Miller Jr, J. Paul and J. Ahrens (eds), *Equal Opportunity*. Oxford: Basil Blackwell.

Fuss, Diana (1989) *Essentially Speaking*. London: Routledge.

Gallie, W.B. (1955–6) 'Essentially contested concepts', *Proceedings of the Aristotelian Society*.

Goldman, Alan H. (1987) 'The justification of equal opportunity', pp. 88–103 in E.F. Paul, F.D. Miller Jr, J. Paul and J. Ahrens (eds), *Equal Opportunity*. Oxford: Basil Blackwell.

Green, S.J.D. (1988) 'Is equality of opportunity a false ideal for society?', *British Journal of Sociology*, 39(1): 1–27.

Gross, Barry R. (1987) 'Real equality of opportunity', pp. 120–42 in E.F. Paul, F.D. Miller Jr, J. Paul and J. Ahrens (eds), *Equal Opportunity*, Oxford: Basil Blackwell.

Grosz, Elizabeth (1989) *Sexual Subversions*. Sydney: Allen & Unwin.

Gutmann, Amy (1980) *Liberal Equality*. Cambridge: Cambridge University Press.

Harris, John (1982) 'The political status of children', in K. Graham (ed.), *Contemporary Political Philosophy*. Cambridge: Cambridge University Press.

Joseph, Keith and Sumption, J. (1979) *Against Equality*. London: John Murray.

Lucas, J.R. (1971) 'Against equality', in H. Bedau (ed.), *Justice and Equality*, New York: Prentice-Hall.

Marks, Elaine and de Courtivron, Isabelle (eds) (1981) *New French Feminisms*. Brighton: Harvester.

Miller, David (1987) 'Politics' in D. Miller (ed.), *The Blackwell Encyclopaedia of Political Thought*, Oxford: Basil Blackwell.

Moi, Toril (ed.) (1985) *French Feminist Thought*. Oxford: Basil Blackwell.

Nickel, James W. (1987) 'Equal opportunity in a pluralistic society', pp. 104–19 in E.F. Paul, F.D. Miller Jr, J. Paul and J. Ahrens (eds), *Equal Opportunity*. Oxford: Basil Blackwell.

Norman, Richard (1982) 'Does equality destroy liberty?' in K. Graham (ed.), *Contemporary Political Philosophy*. Cambridge: Cambridge University Press.

Novak, Michael (1987) *The New Consensus on Family and Welfare*. Washington: American Enterprise Institute for Public Policy Research.

Novak, Michael (1990) *Christianity, Capitalism and Democracy*. London: Institute of Economic Affairs.

Oppenheim, Felix (1981) *Political Concepts: A Reconstruction*. Oxford: Basil Blackwell.

Phillips, Derek L. (1979) *Equality, Justice and Rectification*. London: Academic Press.

Radcliffe Richards, J. (1982) *The Sceptical Feminist*. Harmondsworth: Penguin.

Rawls, John (1972) *A Theory of Justice*. Oxford: Clarendon Press.

Schaar, John H. (1971) 'Equality of opportunity, and beyond', pp. 135–6 and 142–3 in A. de Crespigny and A. Wertheimer (eds), *Contemporary Political Theory*. London: Nelson.

Sowell, Thomas (1984) *Civil Rights: Rhetoric or Reality?*. New York: William Morrow.

Sumner, L.W. (1987) 'Positive sexism', in E.F.Paul, F.D. Miller Jr, J. Paul and J. Ahrens (eds), *Equal Opportunity*. Oxford: Blackwell.

Weedon, Chris (1987) *Feminist Practice and Poststructuralist Theory*. Oxford: Basil Blackwell.

3

Conceptions of Gender Equality: Similarity and Difference

Tuija Parvikko

In contemporary discussions about equality there are few people who claim that Finnish women and men are equal in all respects. Just as rare are those who would insist that perfectly achieved equality would resolve all problems in gender relations. What is predominant, however, is the fact that equality is still considered to be a basic parameter in the Finnish discussion of gender relations. It is assumed that the achievement of equality is essential; without equality more profound changes cannot take place in the way people think and act.

This chapter focuses on the question of how the notion of equality still prevails as an ideal in the Finnish discussion of gender relations. Do we still mean by equality the same thing as twenty years ago? Has the concept of equality remained unchanged during the past three decades, and if not, how has it changed?

How to Define Equality?

According to Adriana Cavarero (1988: 60), who among others has written about the genesis of modern political theory, it is through theories of social contract that the invisible commitments of the contemporary equality concept must be deconstructed and analysed. It is characteristic of the concept of equality that all differences are obscured with the result that all human beings are considered to be basically alike. Western political theory outlines a picture of a neutral individual – a so-called subject – for whom categorization by gender/sex is secondary. Human beings are primarily seen as human and only secondarily as men and women. Cavarero notes that this gender/sexless, neutral individual is a theoretical abstraction not to be found in reality.

More importantly, Cavarero (1988: 70) points out how theories of social contract do not maintain their 'logic of neutrality', but the individuals who are sexless at the moment of contract are later seen as exclusively male. In Western political thought the self-evident and privileged parameter of human action is man. At the same time the sexual difference of woman is made insignificant. If a woman aims at becoming a political subject, she is obliged to compare herself with a man, and the parameter of her political action is male (Cavarero, 1988: 71). Gender is thus both evident and inherent in political thought – but only as male sexuality. A woman finds herself with the destiny of Sisyphus. She can try to become similar to men but the result of this effort can never be perfect.

On the basis of Cavarero's analysis it can be argued that from women's point of view the notion of equality is a double-edged sword. It is through the ideal of equality that women have gained the same political rights as men have and the equal legislation prevents (at least partly) the arbitrary treatment of women. However, the principle of similarity is inherent in the concept of equality. The system works in such a way that those different from each other are compared with the same parameter, which is assumed to be valid for everyone. In other words, the demand for equality is based on the presumption that women and men are commensurate, that is essentially similar, individuals.

Equality and difference have been understood to be alternative concepts in the liberal political tradition from the times of the social contract theories until today. Difference has become the reverse side of equality. One of these terms has gained a positive value whereas the other one has obtained a negative connotation. In the liberal political tradition it has been the concept of equality that has been considered positive. In addition, it has been assumed that the ideal of equality could be realized by means of (equal) legislation. Another version of equality as a positive value speaks about equal resources. This means that the possession of the same or equally appreciated social resources must be combined with the abolition of formal hindrances to enable the realization of substantial equality. In this chapter I regard equality as a concept which obscures differences. At the end of the chapter I ask if there are other possible ways of delineating the relation between equality and difference.

Finnish Gender Ideology in Transition

In this chapter I shall examine the different definitions of equality which have been in use in Finland from the 1960s onwards. Basing my considerations on the notion of sexual difference and on the idea of the 'hidden masculinity' of Western political theory, I shall examine how the concept of equality and gender ideology have changed in Finland. First of all I outline the definitions of equality on the axes of equality–difference and progress–reaction. I ask if the question of equality has been understood as a question of 'hindrances' or a question of 'resources', or something else. I also discuss how the rise of women's studies influenced the terminology and the concepts in use. How is the concept of gender defined by women's studies in the 1980s? Does the reconsideration of the concept of gender entail the reformulation of the concept of equality? Finally, I make some suggestions about how to advance both theory and practice in women's studies in the social sciences. This entails discussing the possibility of surpassing the equality–difference dichotomy by critically reconsidering the relationship between gender and sex.

As a way to investigate these questions I have examined studies and pamphlets published in the field of social sciences from the 1960s onwards, which can be seen as reflections of gender ideologies of the period. Through the analysis of these texts it is possible to distinguish some essential features in the Finnish way of understanding gender relations. I have chosen texts that discuss explicitly the concept of equality and give an explicit definition of it. By comparing different definitions from different years I have outlined the conceptual changes, as well as conceptual continuities.

The Debate on Sex Roles

The debate on sex roles started in Finland in the middle of the 1960s. In the 1950s there was a Scandinavian discussion of and research on sex roles based on the role sociology of that decade, which turned into a predominant form of thinking in the 1960s. Each sex was linked with more or less distinct social 'roles'; women and men were seen as carriers of these roles. The sex role debate of the 1960s meant a step away from the previous gender ideology, according to which the most important mission of women is motherhood.

According to a Swedish sociologist, Edmund Dahlström (1963: 20–1), there were two main sex role ideologies: moderate and radical. Along with social progress, the main aims of the so-called general 'old liberal' ideology had been realized in the Nordic countries. Thus, legal and formal equality between the sexes had been achieved, although in practice it was often found deficient. According to Dahlström (1963: 22–7), attitudes towards housework formed a clear boundary between moderate and radical sex role ideologies. While moderates claimed that the value of housework must be recognized, the radicals claimed that women should have an equal opportunity to work outside the home. From the radical viewpoint role differences, as well as any other differences, served to discriminate against women, and because of that radicals called for equal opportunities and treatment for everyone.

The moderate concept of the differentiation of roles is derived from the belief in the essential difference between men and women, while the radical concept of equality is based on the idea of the essential similarity of men and women. We can now see that in the Scandinavian debate on gender relations the borderline between radical and moderate thought was drawn in such way that any acknowledgement of differences was seen to be reactionary. Employment was seen as a necessary precondition for the emancipation of women. Housework was regarded as an unavoidable burden, something to be minimized. It must be emphasized that the sex role debate of the 1960s was never limited only to relations between men and women but extended to include humankind as a whole, involving class equality, as well as man's new role (see Fredriksson (ed.), 1966).

The goal that lurks behind these demands was not the 'feminization of men' but the notion of sexual neutrality as an ideal. Sex role differentiation and inequality were understood as problems which could be resolved in a relatively short period by extending democracy and increasing equality. In the ideal future society one's sex would no longer have any social significance.

Adverse Laws of Male Society
The main principle of the Finnish sex role debate in the 1960s was the endeavour to de-emphasize distinctions in sex roles by mixing them. Gender relations were called into question at about the same time as in many other Western countries. In Finland, there was no question about men's participation in the debate; their involvement was considered important. The 'narrow' debate on woman's condition was widened to include general discussion on equality. The question of emancipation was linked to a wider social vision of a better future. Separate women's organizations were declared outdated, because they emphasized the 'woman question' as a specific matter and underscored the specificity of women. Essential in this Finnish way of identifying and understanding women's condition is the belief that the exploitation of women could be abolished in conjunction with wider social and political reforms: there was no need for a separate women's struggle.

What made Finnish women believe that the problem of women's subordination could be resolved through wider social reforms without the need for a separate feminist movement? A partial answer may be found in the view of a contemporary. Katarina Eskola (1968: 12–14) searched for an answer to the question why the sex role debate in Finland began in the 1960s. She specifies five crucial factors. First, women attended school and went to work outside the home in higher numbers than before, but society did not support this change in any way, for example by arranging child care. Secondly, there were expanded opportunities for family planning. Thirdly, there was the influence of an international sex role debate. Fourthly, social sciences had broken through and become 'fashionable'. Finally, the sex role debate penetrated to the state apparatus.

The 1960s are usually considered to be a decade of great social upheaval. The factors enumerated above may be seen as indicators of this upheaval. In the 1960s Finnish women were in many respects in a new situation, a turning point of old and new, which presented new pressures for them. Was the edge of women's protest broken off by the legislative reforms aimed at reducing these social contradictions (as the fifth factor suggests)? It does not seem so, because many reforms introduced in the 1960s were not realized until the 1970s. At the end of the 1960s women still came across many practical difficulties in everyday life, among others the shortage of child-care facilities and the problem of the 'double burden'. Besides, although family planning was possible, attitudes towards contraception were still quite secretive and the abortion law was extremely limited.

Evidence shows that women in Finland were also left outside the major decision-making processes. Clearly, many factors in everyday life in Finland in the 1960s would seem to have awakened questions about women's inferior position. Women active in the sex role debate responded to this by directing their demands to the political and state apparatus. This belief in state-centred solutions was not only characteristic of women; above all, it was characteristic of the Finnish Left to believe that permament solutions should and could be made through legislation. Underlying this belief was the ideal of democratic socialist society, in which every person is able to participate in the decision-making process. While bourgeois society was declared rotten and corrupt it was also held that profound changes in the social system could be achieved only by using the apparatus of the very same system.

It has often been argued that Finnish women have long been more independent of men than women in many other countries. This argument is usually based on the fact that Finnish women have 'always' worked a lot also outside the home and they have had to shoulder responsibility for household duties when men have not been able to do so. Thus it could be imagined that, because of this higher rate of independence Finnish women would also have been more ready to keep their distance from male-centred political society. Yet as we have already seen, this was not the case, at least in the 1960s. Another usual argument is that class conflict has been severe in Finnish society, which may have made sexual difference seem secondary. Woman's status in society has depended strongly on her class, too.

The Finnish women's trust in general social reforms reflects the fact that sexual difference as such has not been considered a decisive factor determining the existence of an individual. Other factors, such as class, education, age and so on have been considered much more important. This still leaves the decisive question open: why has sexual difference been so 'hidden' in Finland?

Finnish Woman and Man
So the social atmosphere in Finland in the 1960s was not very favourable for women's separate political action, nor were women willing to withdraw themselves from male or mixed political organizations. However, in the 1960s there was a certain demand for studies concerning women. The literature on sex roles available in Finnish expanded. One of the influential books of the 1960s is Elina Haavio-Mannila's pioneering study on women, *Finnish Woman and Man*, published in 1968. Here I am interested in placing the book in the context of the then contemporary debate on equality.

Haavio-Mannila (1968: 1–3) makes a distinction between liberty and equality. For her liberty is clearly a judicial concept, almost synonymous with the concept of justice. Women are officially free, that is they are not legally in a lower position than men. They have the same legal rights. Equality, instead, is for Haavio-Mannila a concept which describes the actual situation between women and men: it refers to 'real circumstances'. For Haavio-Mannila the problem is practical and not a question of principle. Official equality under the law had not yet led to equal treatment in practice.

Haavio-Mannila (1968: 2–3) pointed out that women did not have the same individual opportunities as men to realize their liberties and rights in practice. There were some hindrances, primarily based on deeply rooted values and attitudes, attitudes which were justified by referring to the biological differences between women and men. She suggested that legal rights were indispensable but not sufficient preconditions for equality between the sexes. The sufficient preconditions would come into play only when all other possible ways of social participation were realized. What are these other possible ways? Haavio-Mannila pointed out that men and women have different means available to attain a socially valued status. Equality is not a synonym for similarity.

I believe this sentence is decisive for understanding Haavio-Mannila's viewpoint. She sets the 'common good' as a goal of social action, but emphasizes that women and men have different means of contributing to the common good (Haavio-Mannila, 1968: 2–3). By saying this, Haavio-Mannila clearly tried to avoid the trap of similarity and commensurability, which always lurks behind the idea of absolute equality. She conceded that the action of women and men can be different without being unequal.

Haavio-Mannila's formulation differs from other concepts of equality in the 1960s, because it does not automatically consider the possibility of women's different action reactionary. On the contrary, she demanded more room for women 'as women' in social action for the common good. She also pointed out that women, as a new group breaking into society, are in a sense 'marginal persons'. The process of becoming independent, liberating themselves from the exclusive family role, breaking into the labour market and other social activities has led for the time being to a situation where women are tottering between the family and full social participation (Haavio-Mannila, 1968: 15–21).

I think the idea of women as marginal persons illustrates women's situation in the 1960s quite well. On the other hand, its limitation is the fact that it directs attention towards male society without questioning the existing values and modes of action of this society. On the contrary, a male model of women's full participation becomes an ideal. In the final analysis it does not question society itself.

Equality Seen as Same Social Resources

The sex role debate of the 1960s did not disappear without leaving any trace. In 1972 the Council for Equality between Men and Women was founded. During the 1970s some international 'classics' of feminism were published in Finnish. In addition, research on women's position in the labour market and political decision-making was published. Thanks to these studies there is now a lot of 'hard data' on women's position in society. Compared with the public sex role debate of the 1960s, however, the following decade is relatively silent about the 'woman question'. As far as I can see, this is mainly due to two factors. For one thing studies made by women on women did not arouse much public attention. Here we come across the well-known invisibility of women's activities. Secondly, the new feminist movement was born in Finland some years later than in many other Western countries.

At the beginning of the 1970s the discussion of women's position in society was often linked to the discussion of social and family policy. The abortion question was one of the most illuminating examples of the Finnish way of posing the question.

The feminist movements of the 1970s called for women's right of self-determination, including control of their own body and sexuality. The availability of abortion was understood to be a part of the reacquisition of one's own body, and a new abortion law was passed in Finland in 1970. This happened without the kind of struggle that was needed in many other Western countries, yet there was lively discussion. But the new abortion law was seen as part of reformist social policy; abortion was not considered solely a woman's concern – the interruption of pregnancy was a decision belonging equally to men and women, a matter to be decided together. The positive side was that this interpretation stressed men's responsibility in pregnancy but, on the other hand, it also emphasized men's right to influence women's decision whether to give birth or not. Also the argument of what was best for the child was invoked; it was claimed that every child should have the right to be born as a desired child.

The Finnish attitude towards abortion shows how women's position was continuously treated according to the principle of equality and how this way of thinking often turned against women in practice. The abortion case illustrates both shared responsibility and the denial of the right to autonomous and different individuality, based on the fact that it is women who actually give birth (Räsänen, 1984: 149–50).

It has been pointed out that Finnish legislation mainly embodies the similarity version of the concept of equality. The laws written in the 1970s and affecting women continue to have at their heart the idea of sexual neutrality and that everybody should be treated in the same way (Koskinen, 1983). Despite Finland's reputation as an exemplary country of formal equality, which might have provided an impetus for more substantive change, the very laws which feminist movements in other countries chose as their objects for struggle did not take a very radical form in Finland. The abortion law mentioned above is quite moderate generally and from a feminist point of view it clearly disregards women's right to self-determination. (The interruption of pregnancy may be made on medical or social grounds. The decision is made by one or two doctors and the State Medical Board.) Laws concerning other women's issues were passed quite late in comparison with other Western countries. It was only in the 1980s that a new surname law was passed as well as a new equality law (which mainly concerns equality in employment). A law against sexual violence has not yet even been discussed in Finland.

In the 1970s, Riitta Auvinen (1977) continued Haavio-Mannila's tradition with her doctoral thesis, 'Woman in Man's Society'. For Haavio-Mannila it took only one sentence to mention that equality does not mean similarity, whereas Auvinen tries to define it more precisely. She notes that the Western concept of justice requires equal treatment of people. Yet differences between individuals create some problems. According to Auvinen (1977: 123) the traditional definition of justice runs as follows: 'For everyone that which pertains to him.' This definition contains two parts. The first part states that all humans are equal. The basis of this lies in similarity. The second part, however, has difference as its basis; justice does not mean simply equal treatment of like people. Auvinen interprets this to mean that equality between women and men cannot mean similarity between like persons but, instead, must mean relative equality; women and men should be equal in relation to a certain criterion.

Reasoning thus, Auvinen (1977: 123–4) ends up by suggesting that the availability of resources is decisive for the equality of women. Without resources it is impossible to gain access to the group which defines the criteria of equality. The advantage of this formulation is in its political nature; equality is a question of definition, its contents can be influenced, it can be changed. On the other hand, Auvinen does not question the ideal of equality as the main parameter of human relations as such. On the contrary, she suggests that in modern society the spheres in which men and women act are becoming more and more alike; in the society of the future it will no longer be possible to speak about men's sphere and women's sphere. (Auvinen, 1979: 120). In this way Auvinen sets the gender-neutral way of looking at things as an ideal.

From Studies on Equality to Women's Studies

From the 1960s until the end of the 1970s, studies on women were mainly studies on equality. From the vantage point of equality, it was first of all preferable to examine women's work. It can still be asked, though, where this emphasis came from. As far as I can see, the answer lies in the already mentioned fact that Finnish women were very active in the wage labour force. As long as women's difference was not realized (or perhaps admitted) women were studied in the same terms as men – in terms of work and equality. It is important to note that the Finnish gender system is such that it is not possible to make a simple division between 'a public world of men' and 'a private world of women'. To a large extent, Finnish women were integrated into society (although not very often to the top positions) quite early. The differences between women and men may come to light by asking how they relate to private and public spheres. On the other hand, it can be argued that, just because women have been so integrated into society, the apparent similarity between the sexes has been emphasized.

In 1980 the Academy of Finland arranged, along with the Council for Equality, a seminar on women's studies. The report ('Suomen Akatemian ja tasa-arvoasiain neuvottelukunnan naistutkimussemi-naari') of this seminar provides a picture of the watershed that arose in the Finnish way of thinking about gender relations. For the first time a great number of scientists tried to distance themselves from studies on equality and attempted to define a concept of women's studies.

At the beginning of the 1980s, Finnish women's studies were no longer studies only on equality but attempted to go further. Studies on equality were not totally ignored or abandoned: they were recognized as having their own significance in terms of producing hard data, but they were only one component. Just using the term women's studies already served to distinguish current work from the previous equality-directed point of view, which was considered insufficient and even partly erroneous or misleading (Hakulinen, 1980: 7–10).

According to Haavio-Mannila (1980: 28), who among others participated in the 1980 seminar, the studies on equality could be criticized for being value neutral and too cautious in bringing up criticisms of society, being too distant from the everyday life of women, and finally for defining equality as similarity of the sexes. Avoidance of the use of the concept of subordination meant that the research point of view became narrower. Women's position was explained by using the concepts, theories and methods of men's studies.

The breakthrough of women's studies in Finland signalled at least two things. First of all, feminist researchers and activists tried to keep a critical distance from earlier interpretations of equality and locate a new, more women-centred point of view. Secondly, public discussion of women's position in society took on a new life as did the academic activities. However, the women-centred viewpoint did not always prevail. Especially in books directed towards a 'wider reading public' a clear effort was made to surpass the 'narrow sex-oriented' point of view and take 'humanity' into account.

In 1984 the Ministry of Education published a collection of articles called 'Man – Woman – Human' (Mies – nainen –ihminen), which is a good example of this tendency. The title alone emphasizes the entirety of humankind and the uniformity of men and women. The subtitle, 'Viewpoints of science on the differences between the sexes and equality', refers to something the articles confirm; it is argued that, at the present time, there are no scientific reasons to consider women essentially inferior to men. The subordination of women is seen as a socially produced condition which can be changed if so desired. In this book, Osmo Lampinen (1984: 211–13) divides definitions of equality into traditional and radical. He defines the traditional as one calling for women's equal opportunities to participate as individuals in social action. He connects the radical interpretation with the new women's movement, which has identified women as a group or category with common values and endeavours. Women have common characteristics and inclinations, which separate them from men. According to Lampinen, the new women's movement emphasizes a demand for deep and substantial equality.

In the discussion on gender relations, equality is still defined as an ideal of these relations in the 1980s but, at the same time, the definition of equality has changed. The new women's movement suggests that pure equality is not enough, but its significance as a sort of minimum aim is not denied (Pietilä, 1983). It has been stated (Koskinen, 1983) that the road of formal equality may have come to its end; the case of Finnish sexually neutral legislation demonstrates that difficulties in gender relations cannot be intermittently repaired by means of legislation. In addition, gender-neutral treatment does not necessarily do justice to individuals, who in any event are never abstract human beings, but always men and women.

The new discussion of the insufficiency of equality may be understood as an endeavour to surpass the previous narrow viewpoint of the similarity of the sexes. At the same time, the continuing adherence to the importance of equality may stem from a profound conviction that the sexual origin of an individual should not constitute a destiny, which restricts his/her possibilities in life. In my reading, it is against this background that women's studies in the field of social sciences in the 1980s have tried to redefine the concept of gender.

Gender as a Socially Produced Category
According to Saarinen *et al*. (1987: 5), gender is a socially produced category and a system of relations which is closely and in many ways entwined with the institutions of the political system and their operation at every level. On the other hand, Rantalaiho (1988: 38–9) points out that Nordic women's studies in general are marked by a concentration on the relation between the sexes in the labour market and on the parental relations but that sexuality and corporeality have been forgotten. She calls for more courageous

and many-sided studies in order to make theoretical progress.

These views are from books published quite recently in the field of women's studies. I think they provide a good example of the stance from which social scientists have examined the notion of gender during recent years. To say that gender is a socially produced category is in principle a definition elastic enough to leave room for many interpretations. In practice, however, gender is sometimes reduced to mean a category produced in the sexual division of labour in society. It can be asked, why the concept of gender is defined by means of the concept of labour. Obviously this is partly due to the labour-centred vantage point of the research. From the standpoint of sexual difference, this labour-focused definition of gender is not necessarily erroneous but it is quite narrow and, even more importantly, it is also in a way bound to the 'male perspective' of the public sphere, whose main components are often considered to be work and politics. Gender, however, is not only a question of the division of labour but is something which also exists in other ways. In other words, the structure of human culture cannot be reduced to the division of labour.

Towards a Conclusion

Lampinen's classification scheme of traditional and radical interpretations of equality reveals an interesting conceptual transition from the 1960s to the 1980s. In the 1960s Edmund Dahlström spoke about moderate and radical sex role ideologies. He defined moderate sex role ideology as something that emphasized differences between the sexes, while radical sex role ideology was based on the idea of essential similarity of the sexes. In the 1980s, in contrast, Osmo Lampinen regards the traditional interpretation of equality as something that is based on the similarity of the sexes, whereas the radical interpretation of equality, which aspires to substantial equality, is based on the differences between the sexes. Thus what was radical in the 1960s has become traditional in the 1980s and vice versa. It is also important to note that, along with this conceptual transition, ideas about progress and reaction have also changed places. In the 1960s radical sex role ideology based on the similarity of sexes was considered progressive, whereas in the 1980s the traditional concept of equality based on the similarity of the sexes is classified as reactionary. Correspondingly, in the 1960s reaction was associated with the moderate sex role ideology based on differences, while in the 1980s it is linked to the traditional concept of equality based on similarity.

At the beginning of this chapter I asked if the notion of equality still prevails as an ideal in the Finnish discussion of gender relations. On the basis of my analysis it can be concluded that the ideal of equality has maintained its position as the basic parameter in the discussion on gender relations. Yet at the same time, the definition of equality has changed. It can be asked, to what extent the equality discourse of the 1980s is equivalent with that of the 1960s. In the 1980s the concept of equality is clearly understood to be a twofold concept. For one thing it refers to *formal equality*, which can be achieved by means of legislation. On the other hand, it refers to *substantial equality*, which aspires to being able to deal with relations between individuals in different original positions. Contemporary criticism of equality for the most part concerns the capacity of formal equality to guarantee equal treatment of different individuals.

Though an advance on formal equality, substantial equality is also problematic, because it coexists with the traditional concept. It has to be asked to what extent it is reasonable to try to prescribe the relations of different individuals in terms of the concept of equality. There are at least two kinds of problem. First of all, the acknowledgement of differences leads to practical difficulties in formulating legislation: should the aim of legislation be equal or different treatment? Secondly, remaining in the framework of equality means the same as keeping in the 'male paradigm' in two ways. First, the questioning of the principles and basis of society and its political, ideological and cultural structures is not needed. Secondly, although the concept of equality has been broadened in the 1980s, it has not fully lost its apparently sex-neutral nature, behind which the masculine gender as a parameter is hidden. This is because it directs attention to the sphere of labour, while the other spheres of human action remain intact.

I have shown how in social scientific studies on women in Finland there has been a shift from the more or less sex-neutral concept of equality of the 1960s to the concept of gender as a socially produced category of the 1980s. In order to progress both theoretically and in practice, I suggest that the notion of gender should not be taken as a self-evident category to be used in women's studies. On the contrary, we should reconsider the dichotomy gender/sex. To escape the danger of biological reduction, this dichotomy is very useful. In social sciences it is a widely accepted principle that analyses should avoid biological reductionism. Yet we are often reminded of the fact that women have 'always' been defined as inferior beings by means of sexual/natural/biological difference; arguments based on sex/nature/biology can be and are used against women all the time. However, the example of the Finnish sex-neutral legislation shows that this problem cannot be resolved by simply forgetting sexual difference. More importantly, I would say that if the dichotomy gender/sex is accepted without any doubt, the real basis of women's subordination may disappear from sight.

To define gender as a socially produced category tells only part of the story of the terms of women's subordination. As Carole Pateman (1988) shows, women are subordinated as a sex. The social contract, made by brothers, is constructed in such a way that women can become citizens of civil society only as 'individuals', never as women, and yet, at the same time, the 'individual' is constructed from a male body so that his identity is always masculine (Pateman, 1988: 222–3).

I suggest that 'gender' should be reconsidered as a component of the 'binary oppositions' inherent to the conceptual system of Western thought. It should not be forgotten that women have been and still are subordinated (made inferior) as a sex. Women's subordination is indeed based on a form of biological reductionism but one which is a political construct in the sense that biology/nature/sex are postulated in (male) social and political theories and philosophy.

Nevertheless, revealing this and the masculine model of the 'individual' (Pateman, 1988: 224) does not mean that sexual difference should be discounted; equality and difference cannot be understood simply as alternatives. On the contrary, the abandonment of the masculine, unitary individual suggests that equality and difference can be understood as *incommensurate*, but at the same time *complementary*.

The notion of difference is in itself twofold. It can refer to *differences* between diverse individuals or to *sexual difference*. Speaking of differences between diverse individuals is possible in terms of the notion of substantial equality. As I pointed out earlier, the limit of this notion is in the fact that in terms of substantial equality (that is in terms of differences) feminine sexual difference still tends to remain intact. In other words speaking about *differences* doesn't necessarily direct attention to the bodily existence of human beings, but can also refer to differences in class, age, race and so on.

I suggest that the notion of sexual difference should be made operative within feminist theory in order to be able to recognize the primacy of the bodily roots of subjectivity and to reject both the traditional vision of the subject as universal, neutral or gender-free and the binary logic that sustains it. This means that the feminine should be reconnected to the bodily sexed reality of the female and the separation of the empirical from the symbolic, or of the material

from the discursive, or of sex from gender should be refused.
I agree with Rosi Braidotti (1989), who argues that sexual
difference is *ontological*, not accidental, peripheral or contingent
upon socioeconomic conditions. The notion of ontological sexual
difference does not deny the fact that one is socially constructed as a
female, but it suggests that the process of construction of femininity
also builds upon anatomical realities. The fact of being a woman is
neither merely biological nor solely historical, it is both: one is both
born and constructed as a woman (Braidotti, 1989: 101).

Affirmation of ontological sexual difference can be understood as
both a political and a theoretical strategy which assigns to women as
a collective movement the right and the competence to define our
vision, perception and assessment of ourselves (Braidotti, 1989:
102). Thus, it does not postulate any ethically superior female
subject, but it postulates an autonomous, self-determining female
subject, who is not only the reverse side of the 'male model'.

I am convinced that it is crucial also to feminist research to find an
autonomous way of defining female subjectivity and individuality.
In this respect the notion of ontological sexual difference may
function as a 'first principle' upon which feminist theorizing could
be based.

Note

* This chapter is a shortened and revised version of an article published in Keränen,
Marja (ed.) (1990) *Finnish 'Undemocracy'. Essays on Gender and Politics.*
Jyväskylä: Finnish Political Science Association.

References

Auvinen, Riitta (1977) *Nainen miehen yhteiskunnassa.* Helsinki: Sosiaalipoliittisen
yhdistyksen tutkimuksia no 25.
Auvinen, Riitta (1979) *Naisena ja tiedenaisena.* Espoo: Weilin & Göös.
Braidotti, Rosi (1989) 'The politics of ontological difference', in Teresa Brennan
(ed.), *Feminism and Psychoanalysis.* London: Routledge.
Cavarero, Adriana (1988) 'L'ordine dell'uno non è l'ordine del due', in Maria Luisa
Boccia and Isabella Peretti (eds) *Il genere della rappresentanza.* Rome:
Supplemento di Democrazia e diritto.
Dahlström, Edmund (1963) 'Analys av könrollsdebatten', in Edmund Dahlström
(ed.), *Kvinnors liv och arbete.* Stockholm: Studieförbundet näringsliv och
samhälle.
Eskola, Katarina (1968) 'Sukupuoliroolikeskustelu Suomessa', in Katarina Eskola
(ed.), *Miesten maailman nurjat lait.* Helsinki: Tammi.
Fredriksson, Ingrid (ed.) (1966) *Sukupuolten roolit. Puheenvuoroja naisen ja miehen
tasa-arvoisuudesta.* Porvoo: WSOY.
Haavio-Mannila, Elina (1968) *Suomalainen nainen ja mies. Asema ja muuttuvat
roolit.* Porvoo: WSOY.

Haavio-Mannila, Elina (1980) 'Naistutkimuksen kehitys Suomessa', in a report entitled 'Suomen Akatemian ja tasa-arvoasiain neuvottelukunnan naistutkimusseminaari 18–19.1.80 Helsingissä', published by Valtioneuvoston kanslian monisteita 1980:3, Helsinki.

Hakulinen, Auli (1980) 'Mitä naistutkimus on?' in a report entitled 'Suomen Akatemian ja tasa-arvoasiain neuvottelukunnan naistutkimusseminaari 18–19.1.80 Helsingissä', published by Valtioneuvoston kanslian monisteita 1980:3, Helsinki.

Koskinen, Pirkko K. (1983) *Naisoikeutta. Näkökulma työoikeuteen.* Jyväskylä: Suomen Lakiliiton Kustannus Oy.

Lampinen, Osmo (1984) 'Kahdenlaista tasa-arvoa?' in *Mies – nainen – ihminen. Tieteen näkemyksiä sukupuolten eroista ja tasa-arvosta.* Helsinki: Opetusministeriö, Valtion painatuskeskus.

Pateman, Carole (1988) *The Sexual Contract.* Cambridge: Polity Press.

Pietilä, Hilkka (1983) 'Uusi naisliike ja tasa-arvo', in Sirkka Sinkkonen and Eila Ollikainen (eds), *Toisenlainen tasa-arvo.* Pieksämäki: Kustannuskiila Oy.

Rantalaiho, Liisa (1988) 'Naistutkimuksen metodologiasta', in Päivi Setälä and Hannele Kurki (eds), *Akanvirtaan. Johdatus naistutkimukseen.* Helsinki: Yliopistopaino.

Räsänen, Leila (1984) 'Katsaus tasa-arvolainsäädännön kehitykseen vuosina 1970–82', in *Mies – nainen – ihminen. Tieteen näkemyksiä sukupuolten eroista ja tasa-arvosta.* Helsinki: Opetusministeriö, Valtion painatuskeskus.

Saarinen, Aino, Hänninen-Salmelin, E. and Keränen, M. (1987) 'Johdanto: Uuteen politiikan ja valtion tutkimukseen', in A. Saarinen, E. Hänninen-Salmelin and M. Keränen (eds), *Naiset ja valta.* Jyväskylä: Tutkijaliitto.

'Suomen Akatemian ja tasa-arvoasiain neuvottelukunnan naistutkimusseminaari 18–19.1.80 1980, Helsingissä', (Seminar on Women's Studies, Helsinki 18–19 January 1980, arranged by the Finnish Academy and the Council of Equality). Published by Valtioneuvoston kanslian monisteita 1980:3.

4
Equality, Autonomy and Feminist Politics

Jet Bussemaker

Of all the concepts of political theory that are being used in feminist thinking, equality is one of the most problematic. It has a great liberating and emancipatory force yet is limited and restrictive. The universal claims of equal rights and the assumption of an individualistic, rational, self-fulfilling agent that is embodied in the classical liberalism of social contract theories does not seem to fit very well with the existing social differences between men and women. Nevertheless, equality has been one of the important concepts of second-wave feminist thinking and feminist political strategy.

Since it has been adopted in government policies, we can start to evaluate the arguments for and against equality. On the one hand, the appeal feminists have made to equality has indeed had some effect, and extended the rights of women. On the other, it has not always realized the effects feminists wanted to achieve. Instead of more rights, the result often seems to be a situation in which women have more duties and fewer options. In other words, feminists may have made an appeal to equality, but this has not eliminated the problem of differences and uneven power relations between the sexes.

Using Dutch policy on the economic independence of women as my starting point, I shall discuss some of the problems of the concept of equality.[1] To explore these problems and take steps to alternatives I will look at the way the concept of equality is interrelated with other concepts, such as notions of the individual and autonomy. I shall – in regard to equality – pay special attention to the concept of autonomy, on the basis of the theories of John Stuart Mill. Although utilitarian thinking is partly responsible for the problems we are confronted with nowadays, and although Mill can be criticized for neglecting some major problems in the empowerment of women, I think he still has something to offer us, mainly on the conceptual level.

Equality in Dutch Policy on Economic Independence

From the start of the so-called second wave of feminism, women have been striving for equal rights and opportunities for men and women. Two (interrelated) conceptions of equality have been important in this respect: one in which equality is defined in terms of equal formal rights between men and women; and the other in which equality has been related to equal access to welfare and equal opportunities. The first conception is formal and legal, the second mainly material and social.

Equal formal rights are based on the philosophical supposition that men and women are born equal. Equality in this sense is a fundamental condition: as a result men and women should be equal before the law. Although this position has a long tradition, it was not totally taken for granted when the women's movement arose at the end of the 1960s. There still was inequality of formal rights with regard to labour force policy, incomes policy and family law, to give a few examples.

The material conception of equality was related to the popular, original social-democratic notion of 'equal chances'. Although this notion was not specially used in regard to the sexes, but mainly in relation to class differences between rich and poor, it provided the opportunity to translate the women's question into a respectable language. As Selma Sevenhuijsen has stated, this 'modern' conception of equality 'arose out of the contradictions of Keynesian welfare policies which, on the one hand, harboured an official family-oriented political programme, but on the other hand, promised individual work and welfare for every "citizen"' (Sevenhuijsen, 1986: 334). The two conceptions in which the inequality between the sexes has been formulated could be incorporated rather easily into Dutch policy.

In the development of thinking about equality between the sexes, incomes and labour force policy has played a crucial role. As long as participating in the labour market and the disposal of income and property is seen as the major way to be a full member of society and to enjoy (self-)respect, entering the labour market seemed to be the solution to the unequal position of women. Since 1974 it has been formal Dutch government policy to strive for an increase of women in the labour market.[2]

In feminist circles the notion of 'economic independence' was developed in the 1970s. This notion is not only related to the labour market but also to the system of social security, wage-related social insurance benefits as well as means-tested welfare benefits. The central idea behind this notion is that entering the labour market as such is not enough, and that women should have an income that is sufficient to live on. The notion of economic independence became, although formulated in a slightly different way, official government policy in 1985, when it was used as a central concept in the government's *Policy Document on Emancipation* (Beleidsplan emancipatie). The government has made it its objective to 'reach a situation in which every adult can build an independent livelihood, regardless of gender, marital status or living-arrangement'. This is to say that everyone must have the opportunity to 'provide for his or her own subsistence and take care of him – or herself'. The principle is that this situation must be realized by increasing the number of women participating in the labour market. If the opportunity to participate is missing, individuals must be able to claim social security benefits in their own right (*Beleidsplan Emancipatie*, 1985: 23).

We can see the two conceptions of equality in the notion of economic independence. The conception of formal equality means that forms of direct discrimination such as unequal pay for the same job, formal restrictions on women entering the labour market or formal differences between men and women with regard to rights for social security arrangements must be eliminated. A distinction on the basis of sex should not be allowed. The government has paid a great deal of attention to these types of formal inequality in the document on women's emancipation. Formal equality is formulated as equal treatment of men and women in access, payment and treatment in the sphere of paid labour and as eliminating inequality in rights between men and women in the system of social security.

The material conception of equality can be recognized in the attention paid to equal opportunities in access to the labour market and in the intention to eliminate indirect discrimination, including 'breadwinner' labels which, though neutral in appearance, usually mean that women are less able to qualify as such than are men.

In practice, however, these intentions have not come yet to fruition. There is, in my opinion, still a lot of indirect discrimination, especially in the sphere of means-tested benefits.[3] Discrimination between men and women in social security has been 'resolved' by a decrease in the rights of men and by an increase in thinking in terms of partners, which, as will be shown later, stimulates economic dependence. Besides the fact that this strategy has not eliminated indirect discrimination, it is executed in a way that Dutch feminists describe as 'equally bad is also equal'.

In the practical policy of the government, formal equality has been settled but material equality has not and indirect discrimination is still at work.[4]

But the problems that have arisen with material equality are not only caused by unwilling politicians or civil servants. Part of the problem is due to the formulation of the problem itself and to the way the conceptions of equality have been settled in the vocabulary of government policy.

Problems with Equality

Although the two conceptions of equality can be recognized in the policy document on emancipation, formal equality seems to have priority. In practice, the policy starts from the point that formal equality in labour and social security will lead to material equality in the long run. The problems that have arisen with regard to the consequences of measures for men and women – that they do not increase the economic independence of women – have not been defined in terms of (indirect) discrimination, but are seen as temporary difficulties. That is to say, it is expected that these problems will solve themselves in a few generations if both men and women can secure their own livelihood.

Although the emancipation document defines the relationship between the sexes in terms of power differences, the question of power does not form part and parcel of the policy on economic independence. Granting women equal rights does not, in fact, automatically lead to an improvement in their position. To grant to women the same formal rights that men already have is not a sufficient condition for material equality. The way rights are conceptualized not only forms an expression of relative power, but also seems to maintain, to affirm and sometimes even to increase the relative power relations between the sexes. This problem is hardly recognized in government policies.

This becomes clear from a recent part of the policy on economic independence, the so-called '1990 measure'.[5] The generation that reaches the age of eighteen in 1990 (and all after them) must try to provide for their own livelihood. That is to say, that as a condition for any (means-tested) welfare benefit, they must show their willingness to participate in the labour market. In practice this will only change the situation for couples; single people already have to be available for the labour market. For couples the measure will only have consequences when both do not have work or have an income under the level of social assistance. In the new situation, both must try to find paid work if they want to request social security welfare benefits. If only one shows his/her willingness to participate in the labour market, social assistance will be paid at the level for single people. In the old situation only one of a couple (the man) had to show his willingness, in order to make a request for the family rate of social assistance. As such, the new measure tries to stimulate the participation of women in the labour market. But there is one important exception in the new measure: namely, when the couple has children under twelve years old. In that situation the woman does not have to try to participate in the labour market. Because it is taken for granted that she will look after the children when they are young, policy-makers argue that caring responsibilities are taken seriously. But in practice it can mean an affirmation of the separation between 'men's work' and 'women's work'; when you have been out of the labour market for twelve years it will be difficult to find a satisfying job.

The problem of the combination of paid work and caring responsibilities could be resolved by increasing the possibilities for men and women to work part time and by a real improvement in child-care facilities. But instead of these possible measures, the choice has been made for a – temporary – exception for one of the parents of a couple who have young children, usually the mother, to participate in the labour market.

Equality in the sphere of caring is seen as a private affair that can only be altered by a change in mentality. Regulating caring responsibilities by state intervention is not discussed. The government tries to contribute to a change of mentality by advertising campaigns with slogans such as 'A girl who is bright, does not take her future light(ly).' This slogan has already been criticized because it formulates the problem of women entering the labour market as a problem of women at an individual level, and not as a power problem between the sexes. A new slogan for men has been made, although this is not part of the official campaign: 'A fellow who is clever, irons his own shirt ever.' But this slogan too has been criticized by feminists, who state that ironing their own shirt does not seem a very attractive thing to do for men. Are boys likely to feel addressed by this slogan? There is also criticism of the combination of the slogans because they could give the impression that girls are not prepared for the future, while boys are. But the situation is in fact the other way around. Girls are prepared for the future in the sense that they are aware of the difficulties of women's lives in contemporary society. Boys are not prepared as long as they think about the future in terms of jobs and careers. In the concrete situation, the '1990 measure' implies more duties for women, without compensating facilities or rights, which is likely to have adverse consequences for those who do not have much education and have a partner with a low income; that is to say, for those women for whom paid work is not a very attractive option.

Another problem with the concept of economic independence as it takes shape in the policy of the government is that it presumes that a woman lives together with a man and that in most cases they have or will have children. As far as problems in the combination of paid work and caring work are acknowledged, these relate to women who share a household with a man and – in most cases – children. The problems people have to put up with when they live alone, when they do not have a steady relationship or are single parents, are not considered in the government's emancipation policy. In this manner the policy of the government seems to affirm the idea that family life comes first and is the 'normal situation'.[6]

The same is true for the assumption of the values of paid labour. The idea about what labour is, means or ought to mean for an individual are not really discussed. Labour is defined as paid labour and is seen as valuable as such. A fundamental discussion about the relationship between labour and care, private and public responsibilities and between different forms of living arrangements cannot be carried on within the language of government policy.

Many of the problems with the policy of economic independence have to do with the centrality of the conceptions of equality and with the specific meaning attached to equality. Equality between the sexes has been seen as a respectable goal in the last fifteen years: an achievement that has been shared by socialist and radical feminists and by the government as well. But what sort of equality are we talking about: equality with whom and what?

Everyone agrees that discrimination against women in the social security system has to be banished and that women must have the right to participate in the labour market. But the real discussion about equality arises when this formal statement has to be transformed into concrete policies and the question is raised of when we can speak of equality, or when equality seems to confirm the existing material inequalities between the sexes, as is shown in the example of the Dutch 1990 measure.[7]

It is clear that formal equality is not a sufficient condition for women's liberation. But what about material equality? The Dutch policy on economic independence seems, at first sight, to be a respectable goal, which starts from material equality, not just formal equality. But on closer inspection its assumptions come from a discourse on formal equality, which is presumed to lead to material equality. This is an instrumental view in which equality as formal equal treatment and as material equality form one line; it starts from the assumption that equal rights and equal treatment will automatically lead to material equality. Ergo: the two conceptions have been fused into an idea of equality as a goal in itself, with the labour market as the standard.

I think that many problems which have arisen in the policy of economic independence are related to this instrumental view of equality and the assumptions about human nature that are incorporated in it. Equality, as formulated in Dutch policy, starts from the assumption of identical individuals. For both sexes the same rights and duties must be granted. Here the problem starts because the biological, social and material conditions are not the same for both sexes. The classical liberal language of individual rights and the notion of the self-sufficient individual seems to be inadequate to handle the problems of differences in conditions (Sevenhuijsen, 1986).

The concept of equality refers in theory to two things that are basically the same, or are at least commensurate. But as long as women are compared to men, but not men to women, the commensurateness seems to be hierarchical in the sense that one part of the equation (the position of men) is more highly valued than the other (the position of women). Equality in this sense takes the life of men as its standard.[8] It leaves women no other possibility than to try to participate in a world shaped by men, without changing it.

Rethinking the Interrelation between Concepts: Equality and Autonomy

What does this mean for the concept of equality? Should we reject it or can we use the valuable aspects, and supplement them with other concepts? Before we decide to reject thinking in terms of equality as such, because of the premises we do not wish to deal with, we have to explore the connotations equality has. Not only do we need to distinguish between different conceptions of equality, such as formal and material, but we also have to look at and discuss different levels at which equality is significant and can be meaningful, such as equality as an assumption, equality as a means or programme and equality as a goal (Komter, 1988). And even more than that, we cannot restrict ourselves merely to the concept of equality, but we also have to look at the way distinct conceptions of equality are interrelated with other concepts in the political vocabulary. The way we think about equality influences the meaning of other concepts we use, and vice versa: the meaning of equality differs, depending on the vocabulary in which it is being used. The way these concepts are interrelated and are linked to power relations between the sexes has to be re-explored. If we gain insights into these problems we shall be able to say more about the question of when and where it is useful and adequate to speak of equality and when and where it is not. Here I shall focus especially on the interrelation of equality and autonomy.[9]

The instrumental view of equality in the discourse on economic independence and women's emancipation by the Dutch government shows a special structure of argument that runs as follows: because men and women are fundamentally equal, they have to be treated equally and this will in the long run lead to equal positions between men and women; thus, it will end in an equality of result. Equality here is seen as a condition (moral value), a means and a goal in itself.[10] The definition of equality starts from the dominant, masculine norms. The only way left for women is to try to make themselves equal to men.

This view on equality goes together with a – mainly implicit – conception of autonomy, which can be found in the Dutch government's documents on emancipation. This *strong and positive* conception assumes abstract, self-sufficient individuals who are rational agents in an atomized world. It fits into a contractual concept of society, in which 'ungendered', individuals enter into contracts (Pateman, 1988). It is related to participating in the public world of paid labour and to the owning of property. The term 'independence' in Dutch policy documents on emancipation refers to this conception of autonomy. 'Autonomy' now seems to be possible for women also, but in a way that does not change the assumption that paid work is the only route to autonomy. The conceptions of autonomy and independence are, in government policy, defined in terms of separation, detachment and not needing others. According to the Dutch *Beleidsplan*, autonomy seems to mean that 'everyone must be able to take care of him or herself'; it is not clarified any further, but implicitly seems to refer to the labour market. Autonomy is mainly understood in economic terms in which the self is a rational and unitary thing. It takes the public sphere as the main reference, and leaves the private sphere as a sphere of non-intervention. Thus, despite its surface notions of individual equality, at a deeper level the policy does not change the assumption that society is built upon (mainly heterosexual) couples who have to share their duties and rights.

As an alternative I would like to state a different view of equality that starts from a *weak and positive* conception of autonomy.[11] This conception can be found in publications of one of the most feminist and progressive liberals, John Stuart Mill. According to this view, both equality and autonomy are of limited value.

Mill on Equality and Autonomy

Mill's utilitarian viewpoint makes it possible to state the woman's question in a rather sophisticated way, which sets aside some problems of abstract individualism of classical liberalism and the contractual concept of society. Mill is often criticized because he did not seriously question the family and the separation of spheres, which makes it hard to think through the implications of the sexual division of labour for women. He is also criticized for his great expectations of legal reform on women's emancipation. Nevertheless, he gives some clues for thinking out the relationship between equality and autonomy from a feminist point of view. These ideas can be useful when reflecting on some current difficulties with the concept of equality.

Mill's agnosticism makes it possible to see the relation between men and women as groups, as equivalent. He is radical in denying any natural inferiority of women and in discussing the problem of the distinction between natural and social causes (Mill, 1985: 229). According to Mill, we do not know if and to which degree men and women are different from each other. Mill states it as follows:

> Standing on the ground of common sense and the constitution of the human mind, I deny that anyone knows, or can know, the nature of the two sexes, as long as they have only been seen in their present relation to one another.

And further on he states even more clearly: 'What is now called the nature of women is an eminently artificial thing – the result of forced repression in some directions, unnatural stimulation in others' (Mill, 1985: 238).

This agnosticism opens the way to an egalitarian point of departure in the sense that it postulates a fundamental equivalence of psychological structure in all human beings (See Campos Boralevi, 1987: 163). Mill takes it for granted that women have interests, which must be taken into consideration, whatever sorts of differences may exist between the sexes.

The fundamental equality that is stated in this sense is equality as a moral principle: it expresses that all have to be treated as equally worthy of moral respect.

Some feminist authors have criticized this moral principle because it is itself based on the gendered liberal concept of rationalism, which is problematic for feminism.[12] The liberal view of rationality as morally and politically neutral has always excluded the life of women. But there is also another option, as Kathryn Jackson makes clear. She does not emphasize the ability to act as moral agents, but stresses the capacity to be the recipients of moral treatment. This implies that as moral agents 'we recognize and respect each person as someone who has a point of view and a set of goals, ends, etc. that matter fundamentally to her. Accordingly, moral equality could be derived from our status as the recipients of moral treatment, rather than as agents' (Jackson, 1989: 132). In this manner, Jackson gets round the difficulty of rationality in liberal thinking.

This equality of respect – equality as a moral value, as a starting point for the psychological structure of human beings – does not necessarily imply equal treatment; it intends to take people seriously as human beings and thus to take into account the different ways people are positioned in the world. It intends to take seriously each potential for development and to encourage this development. It also intends to take power differences into account. This may mean equal treatment, but can – depending on the context – also justify compensatory discrimination.

In this respect, we might use Mill's ideas to defend measures, when necessary by state intervention, that create a real equality of opportunity in the access sense (Tulloch, 1989: 198) like affirmative action[13] and measures that deal with the combination of paid work and home work for women.[14] As Tulloch states in her book on Mill and sexual equality, it is not simply a problem of women being denied access, but of opening up opportunities (Tulloch, 1989: 182). Although Mill did not plead for child-care facilities in *The Subjection*, it would not be contrary to his way of thinking, with respect to the current problems women are confronted with.[15]

But where we can use Mill's ideas to defend affirmative action (as an expression of equal opportunity in access), we cannot use his ideas to defend reverse discrimination (as an expression of equality of outcome, with an emphasis on quotas to be achieved); where we can defend child-care facilities (as a condition for equal opportunity), we cannot defend them with arguments only concerning women (which stress – often unintentionally – the 'natural' role of women in the welfare of children). That is to say, we can defend measures which consider women as group *members*, but we cannot defend measures which consider the special identity and special capacities of women and define women as a *group* (Tulloch, 1989: 190–7).

In *The Subjection* Mill states that 'nobody asks for protective duties and bounties in favour of women; it is only asked that the present bounties and protective duties in favour of men should be recalled' (Mill, 1985: 243). To plead for special facilities for women as women would be a reversal of first-order discrimination. If sex should not be given a negative weighting, it should not be given a positive weighting either; it does not constitute a competence qualification in itself (Tulloch, 1989: 191). Such a way of thinking embodies the same kind of thinking that produced the original first-order discrimination. So it is in danger of affirming the difference between men and women, that it wants to resolve.

Tulloch follows, and I think she is right in this, by saying that this position is precisely the position castigated by Mill: 'that of thinking in terms of groups rather than individuals. Such counter-stereotyping would be anathema to Mill, with his pluralist emphasis on variety and individual determination, rather than determination in advance or homogenisation' (Tulloch, 1989: 191).

This is an important point, because it emphasizes the limits of thinking in terms of equality as a goal. Equality as such, measurable in numerical data, is not a goal in itself, according to Mill, but a certain equality is necessary to reach freedom.

But this point also stresses the prominent role of individuality in Mill's work. In stressing individuality Mill comes to a conception of autonomy that goes beyond classical, contractual, liberal political theory.[16] For Mill autonomy is not an abstract, absolute value but it is influenced by the surrounding world of economic institutions, public opinion, existing hierarchical relationships and so on. This makes Mill's conception of autonomy an essential social and cultural contextualized value. Mill's question focuses on how individuals can develop their own conception of the good life in these circumstances. For Mill, autonomy requires a person to reflect upon him- or herself and on the influence of culture: that is to develop his or her character in a cultural context. To say that desires and impulses are one's own, is to say that one has a character. 'One whose desires and impulses are not his own, has no character, no more than a steam-engine has a character' (Mill, 1989: 189).

This development of character is sometimes specified as the development of the distinctive intellectual, moral, emotional and aesthetic potentials of an individual. Autonomy has, in this sense, a weak and positive meaning. Because of the cultural context, people can never be totally autonomous. Autonomy exists in degrees and we can do no more than strive for the conditions which are necessary to reach a specific level of autonomy.[17] This conception rejects an 'abstract self' as well as a fixed, 'real self': all people are individuals who are bound only by their specific situations and personal limitations.

This acknowledgement of the cultural context makes it possible to include hierarchical and power relations in the analysis. Mill knows that autonomy is not part of a power-free process of sorting out one's preferences, but is permanently being influenced by power relations. This is especially the case in respect of moral, controversial beliefs, for example with regard to lifestyles. Those in positions of power have, in the words of Richard Lindley,

> strong other-than-truth-centred motives for promoting conformity – for example in beliefs about acceptable life styles, and feasible alternatives. There is thus a danger that people will adopt life styles not because they represent truly their best options, but because they have not properly considered alternatives, and are carried along by the force of public opinion, or at least the opinions of influential individuals or groups. (Lindley, 1986: 50)

But if hierarchical and power relations play a role, how can people know what the good life is? Even more: does a conception of the good life mean the same for people who are positioned in society in a different way; that is, men and women? Liberalism is often criticized for its agnosticism regarding the human good, which makes it impossible to criticize the many historical examples of people who have apparently been content in a state of subordination. How then should we discuss the 'happy housewife', who seems to be in fact very dissatisfied (Jagger, 1983: 44)?

This criticism of agnosticism does not totally apply to Mill. Apart from his emphasis on the social and cultural contexts, he has not wholeheartedly adopted agnosticism in regard to moral questions. Mill makes a distinction between higher and lower goods and decisions. People who 'choose' the lower good do not choose voluntarily, according to Mill (1989: 261): before they devote themselves to the lower good, they have already become incapable of the higher.

Although how to distinguish between the higher and lower conceptions of the good remains a problem,[18] this point of view makes it possible to think about the conditions that are necessary to develop one's own conception of the good life, without prescribing exactly what a conception of the good life means for an individual.

The weak and positive conception of autonomy makes clear why an instrumental view of equality is not adequate. For Mill, equality is not a goal as such, in the sense that people end up in the same situation, but a certain equality is necessary to broaden the perspective of autonomy and plurality. According to Mill, equality as moral value is a condition for plurality, just as certain material conditions are necessary to develop one's own individuality. But equality defined in terms of (numerical) outcomes and 'being alike' has to be rejected because it cannot mean anything other than an adaptation to what is seen as the most common thing to do in a specific society.[19]

We might apply this remark to the current position of women, which leaves them no other choice than to do the most common thing for a woman (be a mother and a wife) or adapt to what is seen as the most common thing for men (participate in the labour market on given conditions). The second option will mean an imitation of masculine lifestyles and values for women. As long as equality takes the life of men as reference, it means the expectation of sameness through integration on male terms. That will be an assimilationist society in the normative sense (Tulloch, 1989: 196).

Instead of this option I would, with Mill, prefer a society in which plurality and heterogeneity have their place, a society in which differences are acknowledged and discussed at the same time. Such an option does not exclude different forms and arrangements of living, although it denies that there is one specific 'female' way of living or a specific 'male' or universal way. It denies that there is only one female identity. This means that we always have to question when and where and under what conditions differences between men and women are important, in what sense and in which context, and where they are not. As Joan Scott has stated, with regard to motherhood: 'There are moments when it makes sense for mothers to demand consideration for their social role, and contexts within which motherhood is irrelevant to women's behavior' (Scott, 1988: 47).[20]

In the same way, we have to take differences between women seriously. Not all women are mothers, nor are all women heterosexual, part of a fixed couple or anything else, and these identities are certainly in no way fixed and homogeneous identities. Not all women who have a child are always mothers, or want to present themselves as such. At certain moments it makes sense to stress some differences between women, at other moments these differences seem to be irrelevant, compared with other differences (between men and women as group members, or compared with other differences in the surrounding world).

Conclusion

The main advantage of a Millian perspective is the possibility it offers to think about equality from a perspective of autonomy and in terms of plurality, in which the context is acknowledged. To see the fruitful aspects of Mill, we cannot restrict ourselves to what he has written about women in the last century. If we only look at *The Subjection*, we can indeed criticize Mill for not really discussing the relation between the implications of a sexual division of labour and the separation of different spheres.[21] The main reason for this failure is that Mill himself did not see it as a serious problem. Apart from the anachronistic character to which this sort of critique easily leads, I do not think that it would be impossible to reflect upon these problems in the Millian framework. That is to say the conceptions Mill uses do not necessarily exclude a consideration of these problems.[22]

To use the worthwhile aspects of Millian thinking for current problems, we must see Mill's thinking in a broader perspective and not only focus on his texts on women. We also have to reckon with the historical context that has changed since the last century. Thus Tulloch defends state intervention in the problem of combining home and work, with the phrase that 'though it was not in the letter of Mill, it is not contrary to the spirit of Mill' (Tulloch, 1989: 198).

To think in the spirit of Mill would mean an approach which considers equal respect as a moral principle, related to cases in which this sort of equality is applicable, for instance with regard to social and political rights such as suffrage, the right to work and the right to freedom of expression. But equality cannot be formulated as the ultimate goal; this would lead to an equality of 'sameness' instead of an equality based on (the recognition of) 'difference'. Equality between men and women cannot be the goal in itself, but it may, in a specific situation and context, be a strategy to reach more autonomy. Since autonomy must be seen as a process instead of a static condition, it is necessary to be flexible in thinking about rights. Thus, autonomy can also mean striving for special rights in specific circumstances, on the grounds of dissimilarities. Saying in advance that either equal or special rights are the ones to pursue cannot deal with a conception of autonomy that is relative and contextual.

A relative and contextual conception of autonomy implies, as Jean Grimshaw states, a recognition of the dialectic of autonomy, a dialectic in which 'a constant (but never static or final) search for control and coherence needs balancing against a realism and tolerance born out of efforts to understand ourselves (and others) better' (Grimshaw, 1988: 106).

What does this all mean at the practical level and for the problems that have arisen in the policy on equality and economic independence? Although we cannot use Mill's ideas as a ready prescription, I do think we can use Mill at a more conceptual level, for his ideas on equality and autonomy force us to rethink the basic conceptions of government policy. They force us to think more precisely about what we want when we talk about equality, and how this is, or should be, related to autonomy.

It can help us to criticize a policy such as one the Dutch

government is pursuing, in which equality, once seen as a means of achieving economic independence, has become a goal in itself. The Millian conception of equality will mean considering and discussing the question of how far economic independence is a condition for autonomy, and in what way economic independence should be achieved, without losing autonomy. It is clear that a conception of equality as outcome, measured in percentages and numbers, such as dominates the Dutch policy, is not an adequate strategy from a Millian perspective. A policy that starts from an integrative programme of affirmative action (in the sense of equality in access), child-care facilities, flexible working hours and so on, would be a much better perspective from which to increase the autonomy of women. Such a policy would start from the question of what is seen as a conception of the good life by the individual, not by the government, as is the case with current Dutch policy on economic independence. It would also mean thinking in terms of plurality and differences, instead of sameness and being identical. Dutch policy on economic independence starts from abstract assumptions about sameness, which consider an integration of women on male terms. An alternative would be to start from assumptions of plurality, while considering one's personal autonomy and different conceptions of the good life. The last option would be in accordance with the spirit of Mill.

Notes

* The production and presentation of this chapter has been made possible by financial support of the Werkgroep Onderzoeks Zwaartepunt Vrouwenstudies, University of Amsterdam. The correction of the English language has been financed by the Stimuleringsgroep Emancipatie Onderzoek, Den Haag.

1. Let it be clear that I do not want to give a review of the Dutch policy of emancipation, but that I use a special case to illustrate some problems with a strategy based on notions of equality. I do not deal with other cases that embody equality problems, such as the history of the Dutch law on equal treatment between men and women, questions of affirmative action in the Netherlands and so on. Research on these cases may lead to other observations, although I doubt if it will lead to other conclusions.

2. It should be noted that the Netherlands had, together with Ireland, the lowest percentage of working women in the labour force of all the Western European countries. The percentage of women taking part in the labour force increased from 25 in 1970 to 37 in 1988 (CBS, 1988).

3. This problem refers to the question of what 'indirect discrimination' precisely encompasses. While feminist organizations speak of indirect discrimination, the EC Commission of the European Directives on equal treatment of men and women do not consider these arrangements indirectly discriminating. On direct and indirect discrimination on the Dutch system of social security and the policy of the EC, see Sjerps (1988).

4. In the Dutch discussions on equality the terms 'indirect discrimination' and 'material equality' are closely related, especially in the field of incomes policies, and more specifically with respect to social security policies. According to the dominant feminist view, 'indirect discrimination' is one of the main obstacles to material equality.

5. See *Beleidsplan Emancipatie* (1985) and the recommendations of the Emancipation Council (Emancipatieraad, 1987 and the Council for youth-policy, Raad voor het Jeugdbeleid, 1988).

6. This can also be illustrated by the development in some social security legislation. In order to achieve equal treatment of married and unmarried couples (heterosexual and homosexual) and men and women, new arrangements have been made that enforce the duty of maintainance. The duty of maintenance in marriage has been broadened to people who live together, or share a household.

7. Other examples are the abolition of the prohibition of night labour for women on the basis of arguments of equality, while nothing is done to enlighten the double load these women often have, and developments in family law (Sevenhuijsen, chapter 6 in this volume).

8. For an interesting view on hierarchy in a comparison of 'equal' things, see Dumont (1986: 247–8).

9. There are more concepts that need 'revision' from this perspective. With respect to autonomy, the concept of 'authority' is of special importance. I have no room to work this relation out, but see Mill (1989) and Kathleen B. Jones (1987). For contributions on autonomy and individualism see the collection edited by Heller *et al*. (1986).

10. For a critique of this kind of thinking about equality see Thornton (1986).

11. In some feminist thinking we can find a third conception of autonomy, which can be described as a *strong negative* conception. I do not see these ideas as very fruitful for feminist politics. For a critique on feminist conceptions of autonomy see Grimshaw (1986, 1988) and Jackson (1989).

12. See Jaggar (1983), especially chapter 3.

13. There are more arguments for affirmative action. It would also be possible to emphasize Mill's ideas of waste of talent and capacities when women do not use them for 'the general good'.

14. I do not focus in this chapter on discussions in the Netherlands between the content of and philosophies behind affirmative action, positive action and reverse discrimination. There is a specific problem with these terms, because they do not always mean the same thing in different languages. For the situation in the Netherlands, see chapter 7 by Joyce Outshoorn in this collection. For the philosophical assumptions in these debates see Verhaar (forthcoming).

15. In the same vein, Tulloch writes on Mill and feminization of poverty: 'Therefore, while it is true that Mill did not see poverty as discrimination to be corrected by government action, but as a disadvantage to be corrected by education, self-help, and co-operative associations, it is equally true that he would not have tolerated women being relegated to poverty by the perpetuation of a discriminatory status quo that has ensured their continued subjection just as surely as in Mill's own day' (Tulloch, 1989: 198).

16. Mill himself used the term 'individuality'; see chapter 3 in *On Liberty* (1989). Although 'autonomy' was not a term favoured by Mill, this book can be read as an argument for what we would now call (personal) autonomy, so I will speak of 'autonomy'. See also Lindley (1986: 44).

17. This implies that autonomy does not form a strict opposite to heteronomy. A

feminist approach should pay attention to the way these oppositions are configured. That also applies to oppositions such as dependence–independence, needing others and not needing others. Not all forms of dependence will be a threat to autonomy, although some can be (see also Grimshaw, 1986: 158).

18. This is especially problematic because Mill identifies higher conceptions with knowledge and rational challenging and thus returns to some problems with the concept of rationality, as I discussed earlier in the chapter.

19. Compare Mill's remarks on the tyranny of public opinion and tolerance: '. . . the man, and still more the woman, who can be accused either of doing "what nobody does" or of not doing "what everybody does", is the subject of as much depreciatory remark as if he or she has committed some grave moral delinquency' (Mill, 1989: 198).

20. But Scott stresses that binary oppositions can be of importance. She warns against a substitution of multiple for binary differences, 'for it is not a happy pluralism we ought to invoke'. According to Scott, the feminist position must always involve two ways: one in which the operation of categorical difference is criticized and one which looks forward to an equality that rests on differences (1988: 48). On motherhood, especially maternity leave, also see chapter 5, by Carol Bacchi, in this collection.

21. Although Mill discussed the separation of the public–private dichotomy of the individual and the state, he did not link his critique to the dichotomy of the family versus the civil sphere. A problem with Mill is his opinion that the private sphere is limited by marriage and that he affirmed the assumption that the common arrangement 'by which the man earns the income and the wife superintends the domestic expenditure, seems . . . to be in general the most suitable division of labour between the two persons' (Mill, 1985: 264).

22. This is not to say that other concepts cannot be useful in considering the problem between masculinity and femininity, with regard to the private–public dichotomy. For example, some of the notions of 'care' might be productive here, but not if this means rejecting thinking in terms of rights. For an integration of these concepts and for a critical approach to thinking in terms of care and moral theories see Benhabib (1987), Grimshaw (1986) and Tronto (1987).

References

Beleidsplan Emancipatie (1985). The Hague, Handelingen Tweede Kamer, zittings- jaar 1984–5, no. 19052, nos 1 and 2.

Benhabib, S. (1987) 'The generalized and the concrete other: the Kohlberg–Gilligan controversy and moral theory', pp. 154–78 in E. Kittay and D. Meyers (eds), *Women and Moral Theory*. New Jersey: Rowman & Littlefield.

Campos Boralevi, Lea (1987) 'Utilitarianism and feminism', pp. 159–78 in Ellen Kennedy and Susan Mendus (eds), *Women in Western Political Philosophy. Kant to Nietschze*. Brighton: Wheatsheaf Books.

Centraal Bureau voor de Statistiek (CBS) (1988) *Statistisch Jaarboek 1988*. The Hague: Staatsuitgeverij.

Dumont, Louis (1986) *Essays on Individualism*. Chicago and London: University of Chicago Press.

Emancipatieraad (1987) *Meisjes en jonge vrouwen; Advies*. 's-Gravenhage: Staats- uitgeverij.

Grimshaw, Jean (1986) *Feminist Philosophers: Women's Perspectives on Philosophical Traditions*: Sussex: Wheatsheaf Books.

Grimshaw, Jean (1988) 'Autonomy and identity in feminist thinking', pp. 90–108 in Morwenna Griffiths and Margaret Whitford (eds), *Feminist Perspectives in Philosophy*. London: Macmillan Education.

Heller, Thomas C., Sosna, Morton and Wellbery, David E. (1986) *Reconstructing Individualism. Autonomy, Individuality and the Self in Western Thought*. Stanford, CA: Stanford University Press.

Jackson, Kathryn (1989) 'And justice for all? Human nature and the feminist critique of liberalism', pp. 122–39 in Jean O'Barr (ed.), *Women and a New Academy. Gender and Cultural Contexts*. Madison: University of Wisconsin Press.

Jaggar, Alison M. (1983) *Feminist Politics and Human Nature*. Brighton: Harvester Press.

Jones, Kathleen B. (1987) 'On authority: or, why women are not entitled to speak', pp. 152–68 in J. Roland Pennock and John W. Chapman (eds), *Authority Revisited*. New York and London: New York University Press.

Komter, Aafke (1988) 'De constructie van dilemma's in het feminisme', *Tijdschrift voor Vrouwenstudies*, 9(2): 176–92.

Lindley, Richard (1986) *Autonomy*. London: Macmillan Education.

Mill, John Stuart (1985) *The Subjection of Women*. London: Dent (first published 1869).

Mill, John Stuart (1989) *On Liberty* (1859) pp. 126–250 and *Utilitarianism* (1861), pp. 251–321 in John Stuart Mill, *Utilitarianism and Other Writings*, ed. Mary Warnock. London, Fontana.

Okin, Susan Moller (1989) 'Reason and feeling in thinking about justice', *Ethics*, 99(2): 229–49.

Pateman, Carole (1988) *The Sexual Contract*. Cambridge: Polity Press.

Raad voor het Jeugdbeleid (1988) *Meisjes de helft van de jeugd*. 's-Gravenhage: Staatsuitgeverij.

Rhode, Deborah L. (1986) 'Feminist perspectives on legal ideology', pp. 151–60 in Juliet Mitchell and Ann Oakley (eds), *What is Feminism? A Re-examination*. New York: Pantheon Books.

Scott, Joan Wallach (1988) 'Deconstructing equality-versus-difference: or, the uses of poststructuralist theory for feminism', *Feminist Studies*, 14(1): 33–50.

Sevenhuijsen, Selma (1986) 'Fatherhood and the political theory of rights: theoretical perspectives of feminism', *International Journal of the Sociology of Law*, 14: 329–40.

Sjerps, Ina (1988) 'Indirect discrimination in social security in the Netherlands: demands of the Dutch women's movement', pp. 95–106 in Mary Buckley and Malcolm Anderson (eds), *Women, Equality and Europe*. London: Macmillan Education.

Thornton, Merle (1986) 'Sex equality is not enough for feminism', pp. 77–98 in Carol Pateman and Elizabeth Gross (eds), *Feminist Challenges. Social and Political Theory*. Sydney: Allen & Unwin.

Tronto, J. (1987) 'Beyond gender difference to a theory of care', *Signs*, 12(4): 644–62.

Tulloch, Gail (1989) *Mill and Sexual Equality*. Hemel Hempstead: Harvester Wheatsheaf.

Verhaar, Odile (forthcoming) *Prima inter Pares. Over de voorkeursbehandeling van vrouwen*. 's-Gravenhage: DCE.

Williams, Raymond (1988) *Keywords. A Vocabulary of Culture and Practice*. London: Fontana (first published 1976).

Wolgast, Elisabeth (1980) *Equality and the Rights of Women*. Ithaca and London: Cornell University Press.

5

Pregnancy, the Law and the Meaning of Equality

Carol Bacchi

The story I am going to tell is the story of women's encounter with the law, specifically with American anti-discrimination law, and the impact of this on feminism. America has been chosen as the central focus of the study because the themes I wish to illustrate are more apparent there. These are the ways in which feminist debates have been influenced by the interpretation of anti-discrimination law, and the problems created by the conventional conceptualization of discrimination and related concepts, in particular equality. These themes are important for feminists and reformers in other countries.

The starting point is the American equal treatment/special treatment debate. This is a dispute among American feminists which divides them into two contending factions. I say 'contending' because at this time they actively campaign *against* each other's reform proposals. One group favours the implementation of maternity leave legislation; the other wants maternity to be included under legislation covering short-term disabilities. The first group declares that they believe in 'positive action' (affirmative action in some countries) and that maternity leave fits under this rubric. The label 'special treatment' is usually affixed to them by their opponents (Krieger and Cooney, 1983). The second group is commonly identified as 'equal treatment', though they too have been searching for more precise words to describe their position. Wendy Williams and Christine Littleton have recently agreed to use the terms 'asymmetry' and 'symmetry' (Littleton, 1987: 1287 fn. 42).

Feminists in other countries do not divide today into factions over this issue,[1] but they are often confronted with an identical question: do women want 'equal' treatment or 'different' treatment? The implication of this question is that women should not want and cannot have both. The following case study therefore raises two questions. First, why do American feminists divide into these two camps when feminists elsewhere do not? And second, do women need 'equal treatment' or 'different treatment', *or* is there something wrong with posing the question in this way?

The Meaning of Discrimination

The answer to the first question lies in the history of anti-discrimination legislation in America, in combination with America's almost non-existent welfare state. The two factors operate in tandem. Here I will need to provide some detail on the evolution of anti-discrimination law in America, focusing in particular upon the way in which maternity has been treated.

First, it is important to recognize that at the present time American women have *no guaranteed paid or unpaid maternity leave*. There is nothing akin to British National Insurance or the Australian Arbitration system which managed to secure Australian women unpaid leave in an industrial award.[2] A few American states have maternity leave policies, but most women rely upon their employers to provide some sort of insurance, and employers are under no obligation to do this.[3]

The second important point is a more general one. In America as elsewhere the fundamental anti-discrimination principle is that *likes should be treated alike* (Fiss, 1977: 85). The common understanding of this notion is best exemplified in the history of racial discrimination. In America the Equal Protection Clause of the Fourteenth Amendment was introduced in 1868 to enable the federal government to strike down the ignominious Black Codes or Slave Codes which denied Blacks the opportunity to own property, attend schools or enter certain occupations.[4] Despite the anomalies of the separate-but-equal decisions over the next one hundred years which illustrate the susceptibility of the clause to the vagaries of judicial interpretation, 'equal protection' was interpreted to mean that 'those who are similarly situated be similarly treated'. And, after the Civil Rights Act was introduced in 1964, it was more or less accepted that 'people of different races are always similarly situated' (Goldstein, 1988: 88; Babcock *et al.*, 1975: 71; Freedman, 1983: 928). Race discrimination became the model for sex discrimination law in America (seen again in Title VII of the Civil Rights Act) and in Australia and Britain,[5] with the result that discrimination came to mean 'different treatment' of 'similarly situated people'.

The problem in applying this principle to male/female relations is that judges are often convinced that there are real and immutable 'differences' between women and men, that they are *not* therefore 'similarly situated', and that 'different' treatment as a result is not only *not* discriminatory but necessary. A few classic examples will illustrate the point. In 1873 Myra Bradwell was denied access to the

Bar to practise as a lawyer on the grounds that she was a married women and that '. . . the civil law, as well as nature herself, has always recognized a wide difference in the respective spheres and destinies of man and woman' (Goldstein, 1988: 71). The famous Brandeis brief which produced restricted hours regulations for women in 1908 used an elaborate differences argument to justify different treatment. The court in the end conceded 'that her [woman's] physical structure and a proper discharge of her maternal functions – having in view not merely her own health, but the well-being of the race – justify legislation to protect her from the greed as well as the passion of man' (Goldstein, 1988: 22). Brandeis had to argue 'difference' to obviate an equal protection challenge from men that they too needed protection against inhuman work conditions, a challenge employers would have fought strenuously.

In subsequent years an appeal to women's 'differences' was used to exclude them from all sort of activities. It became in effect the grounds upon which courts upheld nearly all cases of sex discrimination (Baer, 1978: 66). The merest suggestion of 'difference' seemed adequate in some cases to treat women unfairly. In 1948, when Ms Groesaert challenged a Michigan statute that prohibited a woman from serving liquor as a bartender unless she was 'the wife or daughter of the male owner', Justice Frankfurter dismissed the case in an almost cavalier fashion:

> The fact that women may now have achieved the virtues that men have long claimed as their prerogatives and now indulge in vices that men have long practiced, does not preclude the States from drawing a sharp line between the sexes, certainly in such matters as the regulation of the liquor traffic. (Goldstein, 1988: 102)

Again, in *Hoyt v. Florida* (1961), the Supreme Court upheld a statute which excluded women from jury service unless they volunteered, on the grounds that 'woman is still regarded as the center of home and family life', and she should therefore 'be relieved of the civic duty of jury service unless she herself determines that such service is consistent with her own responsibilities' (Goldstein, 1988: 107–8). The presumption here was that 'women's' homemaking role precluded them from certain citizenship responsibilities unless they insisted upon being included.

As Richard Wasserstrom says, sexism in our society is built into commonsense understanding of the way the world runs. It is so deeply embedded in ideological assumptions that we are inclined 'to take as appropriate even overt instances of sexist laws, e.g. that it is appropriately a part of the definition of rape that a man cannot rape his wife' (Wasserstrom, 1977: 602). The judiciary, aptly described as in the main a 'monopoly of elderly, white men from privileged backgrounds' (Gregory, 1987: 153) is more rather than less likely to hold these views, making the task of reform through the courts particularly difficult. To say this is not to deny the racism of those judges or to suggest that the effects of sexism are worse than the effects of racism. The point here is that the race/sex analogy is strained.[6] We are using 'borrowed language' which can work only in cases closely modelled on racial civil rights cases (Finley, 1986: 1164 fn. 197; 1142, fn.108).

This background has been traced in some detail in order to explain the determination of America's 'equal treatment' feminists to deny any identification of woman as different. If judges start from the assumption that women and men are *not* similarly situated in the way in which the peoples of all races are, feminists are almost automatically involved in the task of trying to prove that women *are* similarly situated. The judges' assumption that all distinctions between races are odious, but that some sex classifications are indeed beneficent also impels feminists to emphasize 'sameness'. Consequently, many American feminist lawyers concluded that 'Our legal structure will continue to support and command an inferior status for women so long as it permits *any* differentiation in legal treatment on the basis of sex' (Brown *et al.*, 1971: 873). They asked that 'sex' be made a 'suspect' classification under the Fourteenth Amendment. This would mean that, as with race, reference to group characteristics would be 'suspected (or assumed) to be "invidious" (based on unreasoning group antagonisms) until proven to be justified by a "compelling legislative purpose"' (Goldstein, 1988: 89). Those who felt that the Equal Protection Clause would never adequately protect women against this form of discrimination promoted a new Constitutional Amendment, the Equal Rights Amendment, which would 'obliterate sex as a functional classification within the law' (Babcock *et al.*, 1975: 256). In short, the history of anti-discrimination law made 'difference' a dirty word in the feminist vocabulary.

Pregnancy and the Law

As far as the treatment of maternity is concerned, the first feminist battles in America had to do with challenging *compulsory* maternity leave provisions. Before the 1960s many companies and public institutions had rules allowing them to compel a pregnant woman to leave her job at a set time and forbidding her to recommence work before a set date. These rules promised neither monetary compensation nor reinstatement. America's feminist lawyers set out to remove these arbitrary restrictions on a pregnant woman's right to work.

In 1973 Susan Cohen challenged the rule of the Chesterfield County School Board which specified that she *had* to go on leave at the end of the fifth month of pregnancy (Babcock *et al.*, 1975: 308–11). Cohen won her case at the District Court level on the grounds that pregnancy, although unique to women, was *like other medical conditions* and, therefore, failure to treat it as such violated the Equal Protection Clause of the Fourteenth Amendment. The decision was repealed in the Court of Appeals where it was argued that pregnancy was *not* like other medical disabilities *because it was natural*. It was also usually voluntary, the court maintained, and could therefore be planned. As to whether mandatory leave was an 'invidious discrimination based upon sex', the court ruled that such invidious discriminations are found only 'in situations in which the sexes are in actual or potential competition' (that is, similarly situated) and the fact that only women experienced pregnancy and motherhood removed all possibility of competition between the sexes in this area: 'No man-made law or regulation excludes males from those experiences, and no such laws or regulations can relieve females from all of the burdens which naturally accompany the joys and blessings of motherhood' (Babcock *et al.*, 1975: 309).

As a result of the campaign against mandatory leave, many feminist lawyers concluded that the wisest strategy to assist women was to insist upon their 'sameness' to men and to reject any identification of woman as unique since this identification was invariably used against them. Jacqueline Gutwillig, Chairperson of the Citizen's Advisory Council on the Status of Women, encouraged perhaps by the District Court's ruling in the Cohen case, decided that all that women had to do was to emphasize the *similarities* between pregnancy and other physical conditions and in that way prevent women from being singled out for treatment which disadvantaged them. To defend this position she had to argue *against* the proposition that pregnancy was 'a *special* condition warranting *special* arrangements' (Babcock *et al.*, 1975: 314, emphasis in original). As a corollary, this meant de-emphasizing the 'roles, behaviour patterns and mythologies' surrounding pregnancy (Wendy Williams in Kamerman *et al.*, 1983: 38). Produced in this climate, EEOC (Equal Employment Opportunity Commission) guidelines stated that all disabilities relating to pregnancy and childbirth should be treated *like any other temporary disability* (Baer, 1978: 160).

Subsequent court decisions demonstrated that feminists would have to battle to have this interpretation accepted. *Geduldig v.*

Aiello (1974) sustained California's disability insurance programme which at that time *excluded* all disabilities arising from normal pregnancy. The court ruled that the state had a 'legitimate interest' in maintaining the self-supporting nature of its insurance programme and, if pregnancy were included, it would be too expensive. As to whether such a policy discriminated against women, the decision stated simply that 'Normal pregnancy is no risk from which men are protected and women are not. Likewise, there is no risk from which women are protected and men are not' (Goldstein, 1988: 467). Expanding upon this intriguing logic the court explained that, while it was true that only women could become pregnant, it did not follow that every legislative classification concerning pregnancy was a sex-based classification. The disability programme, it argued, divided potential recipients into two groups – pregnant women and non-pregnant persons – and while the first group was exclusively female, the second included *some women* and hence treatment had not been sex-based.

An attempt by Martha Gilbert to use Title VII to claim sex discrimination because her pregnancy was excluded from General Electric Company's employee disability plan proved no more successful. The grounds for the decision (1976) were similar to those in *Geduldig*. Justice Rehnquist, writing for the majority, declared that pregnancy-related disabilities constituted an '*additional* risk, unique to women' and 'the failure to compensate them for this risk does not destroy the presumed parity of the benefits, accruing to men and women alike' (Goldstein, 1988: 472).

As a result of the *Gilbert* decision, feminists organized a concerted effort to secure an amendment to Title VII of the Civil Rights Act, stipulating that discrimination against pregnancy was indeed sex discrimination.[7] The Pregnancy Disability Amendment (PDA) to Title VII, passed in 1978, stated that

> The terms 'because of sex', or 'on the basis of sex' include, but are not limited to, because of or on the basis of pregnancy, childbirth, or related medical conditions; and women affected by pregnancy, childbirth or related medical conditions shall be treated *the same for all employment-related purposes* . . . as other persons not so affected but *similar in their ability or inability to work.* (Kamerman *et al.*, 1983: 41–2, emphasis added)

American women now had the right to require that employers treat pregnancy *no less favourably* than other disabilities. The limited commitment of the government to the health and welfare of the people and the unlikelihood of securing nationally funded maternity leave compelled feminists to try to use the existing law to gain for women the minimal protection which was available. The commonsense understanding of discrimination as treating likes unlike meant that the most successful strategy involved claiming that women were *like men* (that is, that pregnancy was a disability like other disabilities). Whenever women had been singled out as 'different', it had been used against them, as in the mandatory maternity leave laws. This then is the background to the equal treatment/special treatment controversy.

The Feminist Equal Treatment/Special Treatment Debate

Feminist groups had united in their campaign for the PDA. Divisions among them appeared only in the next stage of the evolution of maternity policy which concerned whether or not laws guaranteeing pregnant women certain rights and/or 'privileges' ought to be allowed or encouraged. The dispute revolved around two cases. In the first (1979) the Miller-Wohl Company of Great Falls, Montana, appealed against a judgement that the company had violated Montana's Maternity Leave Act (MMLA) by firing a recently hired sales clerk who discovered that she was pregnant and missed a few days of work due to morning sickness. The Miller-Wohl Company had a policy which denied sick leave to any employee for the first year of employment. Montana meanwhile was one of those few states which had a policy providing that it was unlawful to terminate a woman's employment because of pregnancy. Miller-Wohl claimed that Montana's MLA violated Title VII by discriminating *against men*. In a second similar case (1983) the California Federal Savings Association (Cal. Fed.) appealed against California's Fair Employment and Housing Act which requires a reasonable period of leave, not to exceed four months, for employees disabled by pregnancy or childbirth-related medical conditions (Krieger, 1987: 58, fn. 1).

These were the cases which sparked the equal treatment/special treatment debate, although there are hints that divisions in the feminist legal community appeared earlier.[8] A number of feminist groups including the National Organization for Women, the Legal Defense and Education Fund, the League of Women Voters and others, as *amici curae*, urged that the MMLA should either be *extended*, by guaranteeing other workers short-term disability leave, *or abandoned* (Williams, 1984: 371). An opposing contingent of California feminist lawyers strongly defended the MMLA in its original form. The dispute produced a series of conferences in 1982 and 1983 (Krieger and Cooney, 1983: 515 fn. 11). The Cal. Fed. case brought the disagreement to the awareness of a broader public (Hacker, 1986: 28).

The most obvious difference between the PDA, which all feminists supported, and laws like the MMLA, over which they divided, is that the former guaranteed that pregnant women should be treated *no less favourably* than men while the latter *singled out* pregnant women for favourable attention (Taub, 1982: 170). This is important, as is the fact that the grounds for that favourable consideration was the very characteristic, pregnancy, which had been invoked previously to rationalize discrimination *against* women. It is little wonder that feminists schooled in the campaigns to overturn mandatory leave laws were suspicious of a policy which now said that indeed pregnancy was a *unique* condition, requiring *special* treatment. It is equally understandable, of course, why any group of feminists would want to secure maternity benefits which women in other countries, even in Thatcher's Britain, have been able to take for granted. The points I wish to emphasize are that existing laws and conceptual systems forced feminists to divide into 'sameness' and 'difference' camps, that neither position is conceptually adequate to deal with family or women's needs, and that this case study holds lessons for feminists elsewhere.

The way in which the common understanding of anti-discrimination as treating likes alike impelled equal treatment feminists to try to assimilate women's circumstances to existing work rules has been established. Operating in free enterprise America, these women also feared that, if employers were required to subsidize maternity leave, either by direct payment or by restructuring and planning around pregnant absentees, they would have a financial incentive *not* to hire women (Babcock *et al.*, 1975: 315; Goodman and Taub, 1986: 23; Williams, 1982: 175).

On the other side special treatment advocates claim that comprehensive short-term disability programmes will be a long time coming, and that demands for coverage for maternity only will be easier to obtain since they require a less radical restructuring of workplace rights (Goodman and Taub, 1986: 23). They also point out that the disability approach is plainly inadequate. Women are required to produce medical certificates attesting to their inability to work, and doctors are reluctant to provide these for 'normal' pregnancies. Moreover, insurance companies have to be satisfied that the disability is real. This means that it is difficult to get coverage and whatever coverage one does obtain is for a limited time (Chavkin, 1986: 470–1).[9]

Tactically the equal treatment group fear that any identification of pregnancy as unique will encourage courts to reinvoke the *Geduldig* and *Gilbert* standard which allowed pregnancy to be treated less favourably (Krieger and Cooney, 1983: 533). Wendy

Williams, a strong and articulate equal treatment proponent, feels that a doctrinal approach which will permit the state constitutional freedom to create 'special *benefits*' for pregnant women is the same approach which allows 'pregnancy to be treated *worse* than other disabilities'. 'If we can't have it both ways,' she cautions, 'we need to think carefully about which way we want to have it' (Williams, 1982: 196).

Special treatment advocates are convinced that women will never achieve equal opportunities in the workplace *until* pregnancy is taken into account. Mary Segers insists that 'employers must regard sex as relevant if it is to become irrelevant'. In order for 'arbitrary discrimination' on the basis of sex to be removed from the workplace, 'reasonable discriminations' on behalf of the female sex need to be made in the areas of pregnancy, maternity leave, and child-care assistance (Segers, 1979: 323).

Since equal treatment feminists are convinced that identifying pregnancy as a unique condition will be used to disadvantage women, they tend to downplay the experience. Wendy Williams describes it as a 'purely physical event' (Williams, 1984: 355). Nadine Taub wants it to be considered 'the generative component to other creative abilities' (Taub, 1984: 382 fn. 5). Jacqueline Gutwillig readily accepted the analogy between childbirth and disability because 'for employment purposes' they shared similar characteristics – 'loss of income due to temporary inability to perform job duties' and 'medical expenses'. To those who claimed it was a 'normal physiological condition', she replied that she was certain that 'medical care, hospitalization, and death are not normally associated with this phrase' (Babcock *et al.*, 1975: 314).

The special treatment lobby on the other hand has no hesitation in claiming that pregnancy is 'unique' and 'special', and in stating their desire that motherhood be a 'profoundly human and enriching' experience (Finley, 1986: 1139; Law, 1984: 1007; Scales, 1981: 431). Their objections to the analogy with illness are ideological as well as strategic. Pregnancy may be 'special', but it is certainly *not* an illness.

It is possible to locate these approaches within historical developments in feminist theory. 'Equal treatment' women tend to be from the 'early Friedan' era.[10] They oppose the feminine mystique and the prospect of trapping women in their homes. Nadine Taub, for example, fears that special maternity leave might have the unfortunate side-effect of 'putting pressure on women to become mothers' (Taub, 1982: 170). Wendy Williams agrees that it would reinforce the 'traditional asymmetrical family model, with father as chief breadwinner and mother as childtender and housekeeper' (Williams, 1984: 377). Equal treatment theorists are reluctant to think of homemaking as a career and wish to facilitate women's engagement in paid labour. Special leave laws are opposed because symbolically they reinforce the idea of women as marginal workers. According to Goodman and Taub, women who made use of them only 'confirm this sterotype' (Goodman and Taub, 1986: 23).

Special treatment theorists represent a later development (mid-1970s and subsequently) which can loosely be labelled 'cultural feminism' (Echols, 1984). In part, cultural feminism grew out of a revulsion against the values of the public world to which women had been trying to gain access. It emerged from the countercultural revolution against bigness (the 'small is beautiful' movement) and competition (the 'rat-race') which made some women less eager to enter traditional jobs and institutions. There is a tendency in some of this literature to see women as representing a countervailing ethic based upon nurturance and co-operation (see for example Rich, 1976; Noddings, 1984; Ruddick, 1980). Some special treatment theorists, Elizabeth Wolgast, for example, are prepared to accept asymmetrical parental roles, and the home as woman's domain (Wolgast, 1980: 22, 32).[11]

It is important to recognize the genesis of both approaches and where they could lead us. The tendency among equal treatment feminists to downplay pregnancy is due, in part, to an acceptance of the prevailing work ethic which measures success by one's perform-ance in activities *outside the home*. There seems to be a willingness on the part of some of these American theorists to downplay the demands of family and personal living arrangements which might challenge that ethic.[12] It seems clear that their insistence simply upon entry into the system as it exists ignores the requirements for childbirth and child nurture.

The opposing special treatment tradition could on the other hand reinforce the notion that domestic responsibilities belong peculiarly to women. Although those who support this approach state carefully that they endorse parental leave and are concerned only about the period around the birth, there is still a tendency to equate women with pregnancy in a way many women today would object to. Portraying maternity leave as a response to woman's 'difference' tends also to lead to the conclusion that reproduction is woman's responsibility. This draws attention away from the inadequacies in the way in which work rules are set for men, and the problems associated with conceiving of the world as separated into public and private spheres.

Lucinda Finley makes the important point that, although preg-nancy is a 'difference' between men and women, this does not mean that 'pregnancy and its consequences affect only women'. *It almost invariably affects men and other people.*[13] Therefore policies labelled 'special treatment' for women are not in any sense a handout for women since they benefit men and children as well. Framed in this way women do not need *special* treatment; parents require appropriate consideration (Finley, 1986: 1169, 1174). Georgina Ashworth suggested using the word 'specific' rather than 'special' to remove some of that sense of women as petitioners or beggars (Ashworth interview, 12 April 1988). This reconceptualization can be used effectively against employer complaints that 'women' are unreliable because they go off to have babies, and court rulings that a disability policy cannot include 'pregnant women' because it is too expensive (see p. 76).

Moreover, designating women 'special' places them outside the social standard. Instead a way has to be found to insist that women's needs be *included* in the standard by which work and social rules are set. As Zillah Eisenstein insists, equality 'must recognize the specificity of the female body' (Eisenstein, 1988: 1 and *passim*).

Neither equal nor special treatment, therefore, adequately challenges the social order. There is a need for reproduction to be accepted as a *social responsibility* without transforming it into some form of national service or surrendering women's control over their fertility. There is also a need to challenge the assumption that people's public working lives have nothing to do with their private personal lives, and that their private personal lives should not be allowed to 'interfere' with their jobs. We need to expose the lie behind the public/private conceptualization so that both women and men can achieve a better balance in their lives between the demands and rewards of paid labour, and the demands and rewards of home life. Including women's sex-specific needs in the standard by which social and work rules are set marks a step in this direction.

The Meaning of Equality

The American equal treatment/special treatment debate, its causes, the inadequacies of the conceptualization on either side, and the proposed reconceptualization, are useful to feminists engaged in other versions of similar debates among themselves or against others. The case study clearly illustrates the problem of basing social legislation on the nebulous principle that likes be treated alike. Peter Westen demonstrates that the slogan is tautological and that it can be manoeuvred to argue any case, depending upon the criteria selected to identify 'likes' and/or the 'like treatment' they ought to be accorded. The particular rule behind the slogan is everything; the slogan on its own means nothing. Westen concludes that, on these grounds, 'Equality is an empty vessel with no substantive moral content of its own', and it should therefore 'be banished from moral and legal discourse as an explanatory norm' (Westen, 1982: 542, 547).

To the extent that equality is restricted to some notion of identical treatment regardless of particular circumstances, Westen is doubt-less correct. There have, of course, been numerous attempts to challenge this restricted view of equality, and this remains an option. Still, the way in which the Aristotelian idea is entrenched in Western political thinking and in the popular discourse is troubling. Feminists need to intervene at this conceptual level to highlight the way in which a limited notion of equality allows 'difference' to be set against it and sets restrictions on the possibility of genuine reform.[14]

Westen uses the example of affirmative action in race relations to illustrate the tragic consequences of applying the abstract rule, 'likes must be treated alike', while ignoring the substantive issues at stake. In *Sweatt* v. *Painter* (1950) the Supreme Court found that it was unconstitutional to exclude Blacks from a Texas law school on the basis of race. In *De Funis* v. *Odegaard* (1976) the court ruled that the University of Washington Law School could not deny admission to an otherwise qualified applicant solely because he was white, overthrowing the university's affirmative action policy. There was, the court said, a common principle: 'race is not a difference that is constitutionally allowed to make a difference'. This decision loses sight of one critical factor, however – that 'Texas sought to perpetuate racial segregation whereas Washington sought to end it' (Westen, 1982: 582–3).

The anti-discrimination principle, treating likes alike, is a laudable one and we certainly would not wish to abandon it. The problem is the way in which it has come to be interpreted. The original intent, as seen in the evolution of race discrimination law, was to make it illegal to single out a person because of some accident of birth and treat them badly. This intent became lost in the simple declaration that such people should not be treated 'differently'. The focus then has been upon classification rather than upon conditions (Littleton, 1987: 1282 fn.21). That is, the employ-ment of a gender or racial category triggers the analysis, ignoring whether the category has been invoked to the *benefit* or to the *detriment* of the person affected by the behaviour. Intuitively we know that this is not as it should be. Surely it is the unfavourable treatment and the harm which we wish to eliminate, not the singling out. It is the fact that the treatment is injurious, not that it is 'different', which forms the basis of the complaint. The word 'different' in this context seems entirely inappropriate. Catharine MacKinnon's contention that the focus in equal protection law should not be on the 'differences' or whether the 'differences' are 'arbitrary' rather than rational, but upon the basic issue of 'inequality', is unassailable (MacKinnon, 1979: viii).

Furthermore, focusing upon samenesses or differences diverts attention from the substantive issues, limiting the transformative potential of any analysis (Finley, 1986: 1162). The debate offers, as alternatives, assimilation to an existing standard or opting out of that standard, instead of questioning the standard (when in effect the existing standard may be the key to the problem). In other words, it is seen as discriminatory to treat any outgroup unlike the ingroup. The treatment of the ingroup becomes the norm and is unquestioned. In fact, it is the very treatment of the ingroup (men) which in many cases causes the problems for the outgroup (women). For example, by treating men as abstracted individuals without family commitments, women are left responsible for the 'personal' side of life, which then causes them to be disadvantaged. To quote Lucinda Finley:

> We could move further toward the goal of responding to social problems such as gender hierarchy if we focused not on sameness and differences, but on the conditions that have produced the problem, such as the separation of home and work and the consequent barriers for women and strictures for men. (Finley, 1986: 1169)

It follows that, if we focus upon the desired outcomes of legislation rather than upon the procedure, there is no conflict between demanding on the one hand that group characteristics be *ignored* and on the other that they be *considered*. In the first case people should *not* be treated in an injurious fashion because they belong to a particular subset of humanity. In the second, legislation *should* take account of the realities of people's lives. On the one hand employers will need to *cease* certain activities, such as preferring male to female employees because of assumptions about women's character or domestic responsibilities. On the other hand employers will be obliged to *undertake* certain activities, to encourage women where encouragement is appropriate, and to consider their particular requirements, given the fact of reproduction and the distribution of responsibilities in most families.

The American equal treatment/special treatment test case demonstrates that the issue at stake is the general working and living conditions of women and men, not whether women are the same as or different from men. It shows that feminists are forced to adopt these oppositional stances when government and employers refuse to accept social responsibility for basic human needs such as child-bearing and child nurture. It shows that, when working conditions are unsatisfactory for male workers, women are compelled to choose between 'equal' if inadequate treatment and an appeal to 'difference'. Constructing the problem as a choice between 'equal' and 'different' treatment diverts attention from these larger social issues.

The 'choice' between equal treatment and different treatment is therefore a false choice. It is a construct which has served to divert attention from needed social change. In the case of pregnancy, women are labelled 'different' and this construction is then used to avoid designing a workplace which accommodates people with children. Consequently, feminists should try to avoid this dichotomy. Despite its ubiquity in legal discourse, the task is to point out its limitations rather than to allow feminist arguments to be reduced to it.

Notes

* The ideas in this chapter are developed in the author's recently published book entitled *Same Difference: Feminism and Sexual Difference* (Allen & Unwin, 1990).

1. I specify 'today' because my research indicates that in Britain between the wars the feminist community was divided into analogous factions and over the same issue of how to treat maternity in the workplace. Briefly, one group, called 'equalitarian' or 'ultra' feminist, wanted pregnancy to be treated like any other 'disability'. A group which adopted the label 'New Feminists' preferred to emphasize women's 'special' needs. The dispute was resolved when in the early 1940s the Beveridge reforms introduced a basic amount of paid maternity leave. The point is that, while feminists sometimes appear to be divided over the issue of whether women are the same as or different from men, the debate dissolves when social institutions provide for basic human needs, including time off to care for children (Bacchi, 1990).

2. In Australia the breakthrough came in 1979 when the Australian Conciliation and Arbitration Commission granted a period of up to 52 weeks unpaid leave. Paid maternity leave is available only to some female public servants (Wulff, 1987: 14; Women's Bureau, 1985: 39).

3. California, Hawaii, New Jersey, New York, Rhode Island and Puerto Rico provide statutory benefits for working women at childbirth. A large number of private employers also offer some benefits, usually basic hospitalization insurance (Kamerman *et al.*, 1983: 4–5).

4. The Equal Protection Clause of the Fourteenth Amendment stipulates that no state shall 'deny to any person within its jurisdiction the equal protection of the laws' (Goldstein, 1988: 626).

5. In Britain the Labour government introduced the Sex Discrimination Act in 1975 and the Race Relations Act in 1976. Section 5 (3) of the former provides that like must be compared with like. In Australia the Whitlam Labor Government intended to follow the framework of its Racial Discrimination Act (1975) in sex discrimination legislation but lost office before it had a chance to do so. Australia's Sex Discrimination Act was finally introduced in 1984 (Gregory, 1987: 2; Ronalds, 1987: 14; McGinley, 1986: 420).

6. I tend to agree with Ruth Ginsburg that white women 'have not been impeded to the extent ghettoized minorities have', nor do most non-minority females encounter a 'formidable risk of "death at an early age"' (Ginsburg, 1978: 147). The race/sex analogy, as Bell Hooks points out, also makes Black women disappear from the analysis (Hooks, 1981: 141).

7. It is important to remember that America has no single Sex Discrimination Act and that feminists have relied in the main upon judicial interpretation of the Equal Protection Clause and of Title VII to establish sex discrimination.

8. Babcock, Freedman, Norton and Ross refer in 1975 (pre-PDA) to the dangerous line being developed by some feminists who 'supported special programs of aid to pregnant workers without realizing that their theory . . . could just as easily support discrimination against pregnant workers' (Babcock *et al.*, 1975: 315).

9. American College of Obstetrics-Gynaecology guidelines now specify that the traditional approach is 'to certify disability beginning two weeks before delivery and ending at six weeks postpartum', but they can only recommend this approach; they cannot enforce it (*ACOG Technical Bulletin*, 1980: 4).

10. I specify 'early Friedan' to refer to feminists inspired by Friedan's first book *The Feminine Mystique* (first published 1963).

11. There are important nuances in this debate which get lost when people are slotted into 'special treatment' and 'equal treatment' categories. In contrast to Wolgast, for example, some special treatment proponents insist that their goal is not to *exclude* women from the labour force, but to *include* them 'by removing barriers to their full participaton' (Segers, 1979: 333). Still, I would argue, designating women 'special' in their responsibility for procreation threatens to freeze traditional sex roles.

12. Again it is important to note exceptions to this generalization. For example, Nadine Taub's recommendation for paid nurturing leave for a range of family commitments indicates that some in this school see the limitations in simply demanding access to the existing system (Taub, 1984).

13. In a footnote Lucinda Finley explains that here she is talking about only the majority of relationships and does not wish to disparage lesbian or single mothers where, she argues, her model holds since other human beings are still affected by how society treats the pregnant woman (Finley, 1986: 1137 fn. 92).

14. Joan Scott argues this case in her important article 'Deconstructing equality-versus-difference: or, the uses of poststructuralist theory for feminism' (1988).

References

ACOG Technical Bulletin (1980) 'Pregnancy, work, and disability', 58 (May).
Babcock, B.A., Freedman, A.E., Norton, E.H. and Ross, S.C. (1975) *Sex Discrimination and the Law: Causes and Remedies*. Boston: Little Brown.
Bacchi, C. (1990) *Same Difference: Feminism and Sexual Difference*. Sydney: Unwin Hyman.
Baer, J. (1978) *The Chains of Protection: The Judicial Response to Women's Labor Legislation*. Westport, CT: Greenwood Press.
Brown, B.A., Emerson, T.I., Falk, G. and Freedman, A.E. (1971) 'The Equal Rights Amendment: a constitutional basis for equal rights for women', *The Yale Law Journal*, 80(5): 871–985.
Chavkin, W. (1986) 'Work and pregnancy: review of the literature and policy discussion', *Obstetrical and Gynaecological Survey*, 41(8): 467–72.

Echols, A. (1984) 'The new feminism of yin and yang', in A. Snitow, C. Stansell and S. Thompson (eds), *Desire: The Politics of Sexuality*. London: Virago.

Eisenstein, Z. (1988) *The Female Body and the Law*. Berkeley: University of California Press.

Finley, L.M. (1986) 'Transcending equality theory: a way out of the maternity and the workplace debate', *Columbia Law Review*, 86(6): 1118–82.

Fiss, Owen M. (1977) 'Groups and the Equal Protection Clause', in M. Cohen, T. Nagel and T. Scanlon (eds), *Equality and Preferential Treatment*. Princeton, NJ: Princeton University Press.

Freedman, A. (1983) 'Sex equality, sex differences and the Supreme Court', *The Yale Law Journal*, 92(6): 913–68.

Friedan, B. (1965) *The Feminine Mystique*. Harmondsworth: Penguin (first published 1963).

Ginsburg, R. (1978) 'Sex equality and the constitution: the state of the art', *Women's Rights Law Reporter*, 4: 143–87.

Goldstein, L. (1988) *The Constitutional Rights of Women: Cases in Law and Social Change*. Madison: University of Wisconsin Press.

Goodman, J. and Taub, N. (1986) 'For women only? The recurring debate over sex-specific laws', *New Jersey Law Journal*, 117(25): 1, 22–3.

Gregory, J. (1987) *Sex, Race and the Law: Legislating for Equality*. London: Sage.

Hacker, A. (1986) 'Women at work', *New York Review*, 14 August: 26–33.

Hooks, B. (1981) *Ain't I a Woman: Black Women and Feminism*. Boston: South End Press.

Kamerman, S.B., Kahn, A. and Kingston, P. (1983) *Maternity Policies and Working Women*. New York: Columbia University Press.

Krieger, L. (1987) 'Through a glass darkly: paradigms of equality and the search for a woman's jurisprudence', *Hypatia*, 2(1): 45–61.

Krieger, L.J. and Cooney, P.N. (1983) 'The Miller-Wohl controversy: equal treatment, positive action and the meaning of women's equality', *Golden Gate University Law Review*, 13(3): 513–72.

Law, S.A. (1984) 'Rethinking sex and the constitution', *University of Pennsylvania Law Review*, 132(4): 955–1040.

Littleton, C. (1987) 'Reconstructing sexual equality' *California Law Review*, 75(4): 1279–337.

McGinley, G.P. (1986) 'Judicial approaches to sex discrimination in the United States and the United Kingdom – a comparative study', *The Modern Law Review*, 49(4): 413–45.

MacKinnon, C. (1979) *Sexual Harassment of Working Women: A Case of Sex Discrimination*. New Haven, CT: Yale University Press.

Noddings, N. (1984) *Caring: A Feminine Approach to Ethics and Moral Education*. Berkeley: University of California Press.

Rich, A. (1976) *Of Woman Born: Motherhood as Experience and Institution*. New York: W.W. Norton.

Ronalds, C. (1987) *Affirmative Action and Sex Discrimination: A Handbook on Legal Rights for Women*. Sydney: Pluto Press.

Ruddick, S. (1980) 'Maternal thinking', *Feminist Studies*, 6(2): 342–67.

Scales, A. (1981) 'Towards a feminist jurisprudence', *Indiana Law Journal*, 56(3): 375–444.

Scott, J. (1988) 'Deconstructing equality-versus-difference: or, the uses of poststructuralist theory for feminism', *Feminist Studies*, 14(1): 33–49.

Segers, M.C. (1979) 'Equality, public policy and relevant sex differences', *Polity*, 11: 319–39.

Taub, N. (1982) 'A symposium on reproductive rights: the emerging issues', *Women's Rights Law Reporter*, 7(3): 169–73.

Taub, N, (1984) 'From parental leaves to nurturing leaves', *New York University Review of Law and Social Change*, 13(2): 381–405.

Wasserstrom, R.A. (1977) 'Racism, sexism, and preferential treatment: an approach to the topics', *UCLA Law Review*, 24: 581–622.

Westen, P. (1982) 'The empty idea of equality', *Harvard Law Review*, 95(3): 537–88.

Williams, W. (1982) 'The equality crisis: some reflections on culture, courts and feminism, *Women's Rights Law Reporter*, 7(3): 175–200.

Williams, W. (1984) 'Equality's riddle: pregnancy and the equal treatment/special treatment debate', *New York University Review of Law, Society and Change*, 13: 325–80.

Wolgast, E. (1980) *Equality and the Rights of Women*. Ithaca, NY: Cornell University Press.

Women's Bureau (1985) 'Maternity and parental leave'. *Information Paper No. 3.* Canberra: Department of Employment and Industrial Relations.

Wulff, M. (1987) 'Full time, part time, or not right now?', *Newsletter of the Australian Institute for Family Studies*, 19: 14–26.

6

Justice, Moral Reasoning and the Politics of Child Custody

Selma Sevenhuijsen

Legal rules concerning child custody have been a political issue in several Western countries for more than ten years.[1] At the end of the 1960s legal systems witnessed a fundamental change, usually called the modernization of family law, of which the instalment of equal rights within marriage and the liberalization of divorce were the most outstanding features. In the wake of these reforms legal marriage lost its dominating place in the regulation of parental rights and paternity in particular. The central issues in the change of family law have since been connected to the regulation of rights and duties between parents and children in situations without marriage. The political contests and debates in this field were initially focused on custody rules and access rights after divorce, and were extended towards parental rights over children of unmarried mothers, and towards issues connected to the regulation of legal parenthood in cases of surrogacy, artificial insemination and *in vitro* fertilization. The introduction of joint custody has been a main crystallization point in the developments towards a new regime in family law.

A common trend visible in the outcome of this process of change is that the autonomy of women as child-bearers and mothers is eroded. In some cases the state is the principal agent in this respect, for example when it counterposes the rights of foetuses against maternal rights, or when it acts to enforce maintenance duties from biological fathers in order to relieve its own budgets. A predominant trend in many Western countries is however, that the rights of men as fathers *vis-à-vis* mothers and children are strengthened. In public debate, in case law and in reform proposals there is a clear tendency towards a patriarchal reconstruction, in the sense of a strengthening of the legal position of fathers as bearers of rights towards women and children.

Equal rights reasoning is a crucial medium, by which patriarchal father-rights are (re)established. In legal discourse mothers and fathers appear as degendered 'parents', according to their genetic ties with specific children. In this way the equal rights argument can easily be connected to these 'persons', and the image can be upheld that the extension of equal rights is the culmination point of modernization and emancipation. The patriarchal element is none the less visible in the images of fatherhood which are connected to these reforms. Fatherhood is predominantly seen in terms of rights, and as an authoritarian and pedagogic principle, argued in terms of a functional need of society and of children, in the context of the guaranteeing of sexual identity and a specific form of sexual difference.

I will not go into the details of these changes (see Smart and Sevenhuijsen, 1989; Sevenhuijsen, 1986, 1989). Instead I am interested in the structure of the argument in the debate on child custody, and especially in the conceptual strategies of feminism. The issue is a perfect example of the limitations and pitfalls of equal rights reasoning for feminism. But it is also an example of the difficulties which confront feminist political theory when it tries to escape from the discourse of equal rights.

The most common argument recently used by feminists against equal rights reasoning in the field of custody politics and parental rights is that equal rights are used by father-rights movements, so that they are in a sense 'contaminated' for feminism. I think that this statement is an incomplete answer, because it uncritically accepts equal rights as a positive normative principle. It is an example of an instrumentalist attitude towards the law and towards rights, in which 'rights' are seen as entities, which are in principle neutral.[2] Instead of this attitude I propose an approach which analyses the foundations, hidden assumptions and moral value of equal rights reasoning. Equal rights reasoning should be interpreted as a discourse, in which power, knowledge and language are connected and grouped around concepts of rights. In this respect I am inspired by discourse analysis as introduced by Michel Foucault, especially by the way in which poststructuralist theories and methodologies are received among feminist political theorists (for example Fraser and Nicholson, 1988; Scott, 1988; Fraser, 1989). Feminist political theory thus conceived aims at analysing and rethinking the concepts and frameworks used in feminist politics, in order to reflect on the way a female/feminist citizenship is conceived.

For this reason I will start in the next part of this chapter to present some elements of a critical approach to equal rights theory as it is practised in the politics of family law and in feminist attitudes towards family law. I go on to consider whether theories of justice can give a positive perspective in avoiding the pitfalls of formal equal rights reasoning. Finally, I discuss the question of whether the debate on an 'ethic of care' (Gilligan, 1982; Feder Kittay and

Meyers, 1987) has the potential of opening new perspectives on the politics of custody.

Equal Rights Arguments

Since 1984 Dutch case law and legislation has supported the extension of equal rights principles to parental rights outside marriage (that is after divorce and in situations where a marriage never existed) by invoking Article 8 of the European Convention of Human Rights, which says that the protection of family life is a human right (see Holtrust *et al.*, 1989). This was preceded for ten years by a political and legal struggle of father-rights groups to extend equal rights principles and human rights reasoning to issues like alimony, access and joint custody.

Feminist legal politics and legal reasoning has been put in a complicated doctrinal situation and in a defensive position by this development. It has pressed liberal feminists, who have traditionally been strongly represented in the sphere of legal politics, to further argue their position on the relation between equal rights and equality as such. Liberal feminists have supported joint custody from the argument that men can be pressed to behave more responsibly towards children when they are accorded rights. This is an example of an educational or instrumentalist argument concerning the granting of rights. Rights are not grounded in a practice, or in an achievement, but in the hope of a future change in behaviour and identity. In this style of reasoning responsibility has the meaning of ascribed responsibility, or obligation, instead of actual or achieved responsibility.

In a more general sense liberal feminism supports equal rights reasoning from the background of an unreflected attitude about the relation between equality, difference and sameness, and the dynamics between them. In order to make this clear it is useful to take a critical look at the hidden assumptions of liberal feminist equal rights reasoning (see also Krieger, 1987; Thornton, 1986). First, equal rights strategies are based on the expectation that equal treatment and the granting of equal rights will lead to equality in outcome. This outcome can be thought of as an equal distribution of resources (as in the case of jobs and social security benefits), but also as an equality in characteristics or attitudes (as in the idea of moral reform by way of the granting of parental rights).

The second assumption is that there are no basic or 'fundamental' differences between men and women. Sexual difference is only recognized in two respects. First as a biological difference in reproductive capacity that can (or must) be counterbalanced by compensations and public provisions. And secondly as differences in attitudes and psychological make-up, which are predominantly seen as a result of sex role socialization or 'sexual stereotypes'. As such they should not be reckoned with, they even should be done away with as soon as possible. This is an extension of the general liberal doctrine that all persons are born equal, so they should be treated equally as well.

The idea that men and women are born equal, but are 'deformed' by culture, has always had a strong appeal for feminists, especially for those feminists of the second wave, who adhere to a socialization theory about sexual difference. As a consequence, a situation of differential rights is hard to reason for, because it might be that differential rights form part of the culture that keeps gender difference intact. This statement is of course speculative: as long as we can find instances of differential treatment, we can go on believing that differences in performance are caused by these differential treatments, and that a natural 'sameness' is somewhere hidden underneath (Thornton, 1986). When the sex–gender distinction is linked to a nature–culture dichotomy, support for equal rights appears as a *sine qua non* for feminist politics. The politics of motherhood is thus one-sidedly constructed in the perspective of the 'abolition' of gender as the main feminist goal.

Similar argumentational problems return, when one tries to frame special rights for women in the language of natural right theories. Equal rights reasoning mostly starts from an individualist stance, in the sense of characteristics and rights of individual persons. When trying to find a doctrinal basis for special rights for women, the argument that motherhood is a fundamental natural capacity of women seems nearby.[3] It is important to see that this dilemma is inherent in contractarian thinking as embedded in Western legal systems. The basic principle of contract theory is that law takes persons *as if* they are equal. In the public space of legal politics and the courts people meet each other as equal citizens. Unequal characteristics, whether considered of a social or of a natural character, are merely perceived as deviations from this 'fundamental' equality.

Modern political theorists have pointed out that this contractarian doctrine is a device for constructing a situation where male property-holders meet each other as equal citizens before the law. The public sphere as conceptualized in contractarian thinking supposes a private sphere outside politics, a family under the benign reign of the father, where the principles of contractarian thinking do not directly apply, or apply in a different mode.

The standard liberal feminist reaction to this idea of separate spheres has been to emphasize the fictional character of the borderline between public and private and to apply the legal doctrines of equality and equal rights to the private sphere as well. By implication other elements of contractarian thinking are also supposed to be applicable to gender relations, for example concepts of abstract individualism and rationalist thinking concerning legal politics. This means that a style of legal and moral reasoning, developed for the sphere of property relations, is transferred to the entire domain of relations between men and women.

The philosopher Janet Farell Smith has argued that dominant ideologies about the rights and duties of parenthood are influenced by a father-related property model (Smith, 1984). This property model of rights uses concepts like ownership, entitlement, interest and control. Rights are fundamentally interpreted as an entitlement to do or to have something, to exclude others from doing or having something, or as an enforceable claim. This property model has its roots in property law, but also in the patriarchal family and in patriarchal family law, where the main rights and duties of fatherhood were shaped around concepts like inheritance, the duty to provide and absolute control over women and children.

In another context the philosopher Onora O'Neill has stated that rights discourse is inherently stamped by a reifying language, which suggests 'that there is some good which the holder of a right is entitled to hold or possess, as though rights were a species of property right'. When taking (human) rights as a starting point, the correlation between rights and obligations is denied and rights discourse becomes a language of claimants who want to be entitled to something from which they feel excluded (O'Neill, 1986: 117–18).

This property-related style of reasoning is also visible in recent debates on the politics of child custody, especially in legal reasoning as inspired by fathers' rights movements. Children are perceived as entities to be possessed and the law has the duty to guarantee entrance to them against the interests of others, especially against malevolent mothers and radical feminists, who are supposed to be looking for a society of mother-right (Graycar, 1989). Whereas until recently care gave mothers a title to a *de facto* autonomy after divorce, arguments around care and the protection of privacy of women are becoming more and more marginal in legal discourse (Fineman, 1989). Here we see an important drawback of the introduction of gender–neutral categories in legal thinking and legal politics.

In practice this means that a legal system is established where men and women are *constructed* as equal right holders according to their genetic ties to children. The courts are then obliged to admit men as the bearers of rights in the sense of legitimate claims towards children. Considerations concerning the interests of women and children have at the best the status of side arguments or general formulas.

Arguments of Care and Justice

In reaction to new legal practices and to the deficiency of equal rights reasoning, feminists have developed an argument that can be characterized as a revisionist liberal argument. It states that it contradicts principles of justice to award rights to men as fathers, in a situation where women are the ones responsible for child care. This line of reasoning can be interpreted as a mixture of conventional justice arguments and Marxist ideas on the relation between labour and control. The conventional Aristotelean justice argument says that it is not just to treat unequal persons in an equal way. Equal rights and equal treatment should only be accorded to equal persons. Stated this way this argument contains all the risks of naturalist thinking concerning women-as-mothers. To circumvent these pitfalls the revisionist liberal argument states, in line with Marxist feminist reasoning about domestic labour, that child care is a socially constructed form of labour, and that its gendered character is the result of social circumstances.

This line of argument of revisionist liberalism has important advantages compared to equal rights reasoning. It supports the application of the so-called primary caretaker principle in custody conflicts and is sensitive to arguments about the interests of children and to situations in which men are the primary carers. In this way it is in many respects in accordance with crude measures of social justice: it promotes no fixed judgements against particular groups of persons, and it gives women a fair amount of protection in what is still predominantly a woman's job (Sandberg, 1989).

The question remains, however, whether revisionist liberalism has the potential of framing the issue of custody politics in a better *political* language. By this I mean a language which can include a feminist critique of rights discourse and a 'positive', less defensive perspective on child care in the public debate about the reform of family law. This question can be evaluated by confronting the revisionist liberal argument with the theory of distributive justice as formulated by John Rawls (Rawls, 1971).

Appeals to nature have no special place in the Rawlsian style of reasoning, which makes his theory attractive for modern feminists trying to escape the arguments about innate capacities and characteristics. Rules concerning the distribution of rights, goods, chances and so on have to be argued along rationalist lines, in accordance with the principles of justice. According to Rawls' first principles of justice everybody has an equal right to fundamental rights that are connected to freedom, like freedom of conscience and opinion, freedom of association and assembly, and the freedom of suffrage. These rights are of a political character, enabling everybody fully to participate in the concluding of the social contract. The second principle of justice contains the formulations that enable a choice between equal and unequal treatment. Social and economic inequalities are in accordance with justice on two conditions: that they favour those who are less 'well off', and that they are connected to functions and positions that are open to everybody by a system of fair, equal chances.

An attempt to apply these principles to the political debates on child custody as sketched above immediately shows the limitations of Rawlsian justice reasoning in this field. One should for example have to decide who are the ones who are initially 'less well off'. This depends to a large extent on the perspective and the standpoint of reasoning. One could argue that women never fully participated in the rights of parenthood, so that they have to catch up arrears in this respect. But it could also be argued that men were (until recently at least) the losers in custody issues, because women mostly got custody after divorce, or because women are favoured because they are the ones who bear children. In this perspective it would be fair when a larger proportion of men win in custody conflicts. The attribution of fundamental rights to men could be argued along this line as well.

This points to the problem that an application of the principles of distributive justice to the politics of child custody presupposes an answer to the question of what is at stake in custody politics. Is it simply the distribution of rights? Is it the distribution of children? Are children to be counted among the primary goods in the Rawlsian sense? In this context it is important to remember that Rawls himself does not see it that way. He talks about children as minors, who are represented by the head of the family, and he talks about them in the context of the transference of goods and morals between the generations (Kearns, 1983; English, 1977).

Stating it this way, it becomes possible to see that an extension of the Rawlsian language towards the politics of child custody has several disadvantages that were also connected to equal rights discourse, in so far as both perspectives are stamped by the language of property rights. Rawls' principles of justice are basically developed for reaching decisions on the distribution of freedom rights, material goods and social services. Applied to the revisionist liberal argument about the relation between care and parental rights this means that a number of comments can be made.

First, the level where the justice argument applies has to be specified. Individuals and collective aspects are often mixed. In this context we have to remember that Rawlsian arguments are developed for reaching collective decisions on broad rules of distribution. In political debate feminists indeed use the argument on a collective level, in the sense that the law should not be changed as long as mothers are the main carers. In my opinion this is a poor argument because it does not specify when the moment has arrived when change *is* acceptable. Should we approach this issue in a quantitative manner, for example when a certain percentage of men is responsible for the daily care of children? I think on the contrary that the care argument is more useful in individual cases of conflict, in the sense that it is just for children to remain with the parent who is the primary carer, and that this person should have the possibility/right to make the main decisions as well.

This argument is based on two considerations. One is that decisions concerning children are heavily interwoven with the lifeplan and the lifestyle of the one who cares for them. The other is that motherhood is still in many respects an oppressive institution, when in its name irrationality and precariousness are ascribed to women. Autonomy is a counterclaim to a discourse that perceives motherhood as a state of being which necessitates that women should be supervised or ruled. Motherhood and rights are still predominantly seen as antinomous entities under patriarchal conditions. The question which 'rights' women can derive from actual or potential mothering should remain on the political agenda from this perspective.[4]

Secondly, the revisionist liberal argument does not give many specifications about what counts as care, because it equates care with work. The relations between parents and children are however governed by many aspects that cannot be covered by a labour-related concept of care. Emotional bonds are based on more than primary care, and they take many forms. So if arguments of rights for women as carers are to serve as a protection against claims of others, in this case men as fathers, they have to be connected to a well-developed theory of why the care of women in a sense overrules other considerations, and which rights are at stake. Rights of access, for example, should be distinguished from legal rights of decision-making on school choice, place of residence, use of health services or rights of decision-making concerning pregnancy and abortion. Care is in itself far too broad a term to give specifications about collective decisions on the distribution and the character or rights.

A third observation is that a conceptual apparatus that is completely non-naturalistic or disembodied is deficient in this field, because it excludes reasoning about reproductive differences between women and men. Here we see the drawbacks of the nature–culture dichotomy at its sharpest. Using the concepts of Rawls it is immediately clear that the 'functions and positions' towards childbirth are bodily differentiated. On the one hand it is possible to design a Rawlsian scheme of compensatory inequalities in order to reach more equality with respect to child care, that is public child care, shorter labour days, maternity/paternity leave for both parents. On the other hand it is important that feminist theory does not concentrate *too* much on a moral language of equality. In any case, equality should be differentiated from 'sameness'.[5] When this is overlooked feminism runs the risk of forgetting that mothering is a lived identity and in many respects a specific 'female' experience, especially as it is organized under the present social conditions. Issues concerning pregnancy and childbirth clearly affect men and women differently, unless one puts all hope on a rationalistic ideal of equality in which genetic engineering introduces male pregnancy.

And last but not least: the application of the Rawlsian language gives little specification as to what is *un*just in the present politics of custody. The issue remains framed as a problem of distribution that can be solved by universal, abstract reasoning. The Rawlsian discourse is relatively closed to claims of specific groups in specific contexts that something is experienced as unjust. The universalist pretensions of Rawls' theory of justice and the epistemological device that supports this (the veil of ignorance) exclude claims from specific groups by labelling them as 'particularistic'. Or as the feminist philosopher Seyla Benhabib has stated: the form of moral deliberation of Kantian justice reasoning excludes thinking in terms of difference(s) because it presupposes a 'generalized other' that is identical to the moral actor (Benhabib, 1987). Not only differences are excluded from deliberation; the ideal of abstract reasoning also excludes power as a relevant concept. The application of contractarian discourse gives the illusion that these issues concerning parenting can be decided in a power-free space. Thus we lack a conceptual apparatus for perceiving and analysing law as a strategic field of power relations (Sevenhuijsen, 1986).

My main conclusion from these considerations about distributive justice is that it makes little sense to extend the application of the Rawlsian principles of justice towards family law and family politics.[6] In this respect I agree with the argument of justice theorists like Michael Waltzer that different spheres in society should be governed by different principles of justice and by different styles of moral reasoning (Waltzer, 1983).

The Ethics of Care and Responsibility

It is in this context that the debate on women and moral theory and on the 'ethic of care' can give new perspectives on the politics of custody, provided that it is carefully read in order to undo it from misleading elements.

Carol Gilligan's work has aroused a great deal of controversy among scholars from a wide variety of disciplines. In her psychological research she has interviewed women in order to extend Kohlberg's theory on the development of moral judgement (Gilligan, 1982). Gilligan criticizes Kohlberg in that he takes a male model as a starting point and as a norm. This model confirms the Kantian idea of autonomy and individuality as well as the corresponding idea that mature moral reasoning refers to finding an equilibrium between conflicting rights and rules. According to Gilligan's account women differ from men in that they develop a morality of care and responsibility instead of a morality of justice. The morality of care is described as the ability to find an equilibrium between connectedness and empathy on the one hand and the feeling of an autonomous self on the other.

The morality of care differs in three respects from what Gilligan perceives as a morality of justice (Tronto, 1987: 85–6). First it revolves around different moral concepts: responsibility and relations instead of rights and rules. Secondly, it is tied to concrete circumstances rather than being formal and abstract. And thirdly, the morality of care can best be described not as a set of principles, but as an activity, the 'activity of care'.

Gilligan's contribution to moral theory and to the development of a feminist ethics is best evaluated by putting it in a larger framework of political and moral theory. The concept of a 'different voice' has not in the first place to be connected to gender difference, but to a different style of moral reasoning and to a different epistemological conception about the sources of moral reasoning, that can be traced back to the moral theory of the Scottish enlightenment.

The philosopher Anette Baier has listed several differences between Kant's and Hume's moral theories, in order to answer the question 'whether Hume is the women's moral theorist' (Baier, 1987).[7] For Hume morality is not a matter of obedience to a universal law, but of cultivating specific character traits, in particular a corrected sympathy instead of a law discerning reason. The source of moral reasoning is not to be found in universal rules, but in instrumental reason, self-interest, custom and historical chance. The best moral stance is to participate in a community and to communicate opinions and feelings. Morality depends more on context-bound opinions than on universal reason. Desires and emotional needs are not excluded from moral reasoning, although they have to be corrected by reflection, self-control and social discipline. Baier contrasts Hume's moral philosophy with Kantian theory in its version of what problem morality is supposed to solve. For Kantians and other contractarians the main problem is that of the relation between freedom and autonomy on the one hand and obedience to political and legal authority on the other. For Hume the tensions to be solved are intrapersonal as well as interpersonal. It is the problem of contradiction, conflict and instability in any one person's desires, over time as well as conflicts between persons. Morality points to the issue of how to minimize oppositions of interests, how to arrange life, so that sympathy, and not hostile comparison will be the principle relating our desires to those of our fellows. Where in the contractarian model morality regulates and arbitrates interests that are opposed, in a Humean view morality's main task is to rearrange situations so that interests are no longer opposed.

Although I would not recommend homogeneity and consensus as a general model for feminist politics, I think that this style of reasoning can give important openings for the inclusion of a feminist perspective on child care and custody in public debate. This supposes that one can agree with the statement that child custody has at this historical conjuncture too much the character of a contested issue. When we take into account the context, in which rights are claimed by fathers' rights movements, we can see that this claim is predominantly based on a concept of possessive power. Rights are placed in position to enforce contacts with children and control women's lives. One of the most urgent tasks is, I think, to pursue the goal of making children a less contested issue, and at the same time protecting the interests, dignity and personal rights of the women who mother them, without overlooking the idea that the relations between men and children should be recognized and changed as well.

Thinking in terms of virtues might make it possible to develop a normative language, which can frame the problem in such a vein that the interests of men, women and children are no longer seen as so fundamentally opposed. Of course this goal is a moral statement in itself. It is based on a conception of the needs of children, which attaches a positive value to the experience of clarity, stability and trust in children's lives. I think it is not in children's interest to be a bone of contention and an object of legal conflict. And it is based on the above-mentioned view that it contradicts principles of group justice to take away children and/or rights of decision-making from women in situations where they have been and are the primary carers.

In this context it might be better to see care as an attitude and not in the first place as an activity. The ethic of care in Gilligan's sense refers to the ability to make a moral judgement, in which the needs of the moral actor are balanced with the ability to perceive the needs of others and the moral obligation of not hurting them. I will give some examples of possible implications for custody politics of this style of moral reasoning.

First, in cases of potential conflicts of attitudes and interests attention should be paid to the way in which the problem is framed. The experience of a bond with a child does not necessarily have to lead towards the claiming of a right to have contact or lead a daily life with the child. Empathy and the ability to imagine oneself in the perspective of another person can as well lead to the conclusion that enforcement of rights and contacts can cause hurt or damage in other respects. This consideration applies in individual cases, as well as in collective debate. The public debate on access and child custody is heavily influenced by the patriarchal idea that bonding needs rights and enforcement. Contextual moral reasoning rejects a style of moral reasoning that delimits ethics to a choice between rights of individuals and sees instead the diagnostics and framing of the problem as an integral part of moral activity. This implies that critical reasoning about the character and the provenance of images of motherhood and fatherhood with which the issue is assessed forms a legitimate and indispensable part of public debate.

Secondly, reasoning in terms of virtues can facilitate a public debate on the question of what counts as *good* care, or what is a careful attitude towards children and their parents. This implies the necessity of thinking about the character as well as the roots of virtues and moral reasoning. Gilligan's formulation of the ethic of care points to the idea that the 'different voice' need not necessarily be solely characterized by empathy and compassion, but that it is the relation between connectedness and a feeling of an autonomous self that corresponds to a 'feminine' model of moral maturity. This can correct the idea that women are better carers because of their psychological make-up that is to be found in mainstream social theory as well as in some strands in feminist thinking. Contrary to this idea the point should be stressed that moral attitudes towards children are not necessarily rooted in gendered identities or in the practice of daily care, but can be developed by all kinds of contact with children, as well as by the experience and training of moral reasoning.

These considerations point to the need of developing a moral language on child care, which starts from concrete situations and takes into account the way in which women and men frame their attitudes about connectedness and autonomy, responsibilities and rights. In this respect feminist moral theory can be connected to research strategies in women's studies, based on interviewing women on their moral dilemmas and moral views as mothers. Gilligan's ideas can be used as hypotheses in such research. If she is right in her statement that women frame their moral views primarily from the viewpoint of relations, and if we agree that a public moral language on the virtues of parenthood can be developed, then we should start listening to women's 'storytelling'.

At the same time it is urgent to do this in such a way that gender-bound stereotypes are avoided (Code, 1988). This is only possible by making careful comparisons with men's reasoning about the same subjects, and by being open-minded about the possibility that moral reasoning about connectedness is less gender-bound than feminists often tend to believe. It is an urgent task for feminist moral theory to develop an ethics of sexual difference, which acknowledges on the one hand that women are embodied beings, supplied with an employable epistemology, but on the other hand uses women's knowledge as an instrument of change, refusing to accept it as an innate characteristic. The model that corresponds to this feminist moral attitude is that of a situated knowledge and contextual ethical reasoning (Haraway, 1988). This style of reasoning denies Woman as other or the dream of an essential female subject, but supports the articulation of heterogeneous and fragmented subjectivities of women. Mothering as it is constructed and lived in the present cultural and political situation is one of its elements.

Concluding Remarks

By presenting equal rights reasoning, justice arguments and the ethics of care as separate parts of my argument I do not want to give the impression that these styles of reasoning are mutually exclusive. This idea of exclusion is supported by writers on justice theories, who present universalist and particularist theories of justice as opposites and by universalists who employ stereotypical ideas about a supposed inherent conservatism of 'particularism'. Instead of marrying itself to one of these positions, feminist thinking on justice should keep at a distance. Universalist thinking is important because it gives an ideal of general norms and values and a shared language to which feminist politics can speak. Its style of moral reasoning and its rigid norms about a disembodied rationality exclude, however, many of the diverse experiences, considerations and injustices that feminism tries to take as a foundation for political activity.

Finally, the crucial point in the context of the politics of custody is that ways should be found to integrate contextual and relational moral reasoning as a legitimate concern in public debate on the rights and duties of parenthood. Concepts of care, needs, responsibility and connectedness will have to be confronted, or where possible integrated, with the language of interests, obligations and rights. In this respect the dichotomy that Gilligan and many of her followers perceive between the languages of responsibility and rights clearly has to be questioned (see for example O'Neill, 1989). This implies first that mothers should be taken seriously in their considerations and their knowledge about children and care. It also implies that a connection should be made between their considerations and the public language of moral virtues, and the moral diagnoses that underlie reasoning in terms of rights. Concepts like autonomy and self-determination could in that way be embedded in a relational language instead of being the starting point for theorizing about rights and responsibilities. It might be possible, for example, to frame the necessity of compensation for a lack of autonomy in terms of rights, for example by re-examining the concept of privacy from the perspective of women (Allen, 1983).

It is to be hoped that by such a conceptual strategy feminism can develop a sound alternative to the disadvantages of the language of abstract individualism with its image of human beings as atomistic individuals. This is important if feminism is to develop a viable politics in which the interests of women with children are not submerged under a universalist idea of equal rights with the male right-holder as an implicit or explicit point of reference.

Notes

* This chapter forms part of an ongoing research project and thought process on gender, care and ethics, especially in the field of parenthood and family law. I would like to thank the members of workshops in Paris, Leeds, Warwick, Manchester, Enschede, Madison and Utrecht for their fruitful discussions about earlier versions, and Ian Forbes and Aafke Komter for their detailed and thoughtful comments.

   1. In this chapter I concentrate on child custody as it relates to the divisions of parental rights and duties between parents in situations without marriage. This

means that I refer only obliquely to the state as an agent in child protection. Besides this I abstract from differences between jurisdictions and from exact legalistic meanings of the term 'custody'. The concept of 'custody' is used in a loose way to indicate the field of rights and duties of parenthood, in situations where marriage is broken up by divorce or where legal marriage never existed.

2. For a more elaborated critique of rights reasoning in feminist legal politics, see Smart (1989).

3. This problem is reflected in the controversies over equal versus special rights that have plagued American feminism in connection with the issue of maternity benefits and protective legislation. These ideological controversies can flower under a social and legal system where arguments about rights are the starting point, instead of arguments connected to needs and welfare. See Scott (1988) and Bacchi, chapter 5, in this volume.

4. In this respect I agree with Onora O'Neill that practical ethical reasoning should have the potential of criticizing and moving beyond existing political structures. It should be able to develop a conceptual structure that addresses the aspects of social organization that one wants to change, giving at the same time ideas and standards for change (O'Neill, 1986: 27–54).

5. This implies for example that a more equal distribution of child care between men and women should be argued by an appeal to fairness and the potential for women to do paid work, rather than by dreams of eliminating gendered character structures.

6. This implies a critical attitude towards proposals of feminist justice theorists like Susan Moller Okin to extend distributive justice to family politics and to the family as an institution which creates gender divisions (Okin, 1987). A (justified) critique that Rawls excludes the distributive mechanism in the family does not lead to the logical conclusion that all aspects of family life and family politics could and should be included in the Rawlsian paradigm.

7. In this chapter I will not go into the meta-theoretical aspects of the debate on gender and morality, because I concentrate on applied moral reasoning.

References

Allen, A.L. (1983) 'Women and their privacy: what is at stake?', pp. 233–49 in C. Gould (ed)., *Beyond Domination. New Perspectives on Women and Philosophy*. Totowa, NJ: Rowman & Allanheld.

Baier, A.C. (1987) 'Hume, the women's moral theorist?', pp. 37–55 in E. Feder Kittay and D.T. Meyers (eds), *Women and Moral Theory*. Totowa, NJ: Rowman & Littlefield.

Benhabib, S. (1987) 'The generalized and the concrete other. The Kohlberg–Gilligan controversy and feminist theory', pp. 77–95 in S. Benhabib and D. Cornell (eds), *Essays on the Politics of Gender in Late-Capitalist Societies*. Cambridge: Polity Press.

Code, L. (1988) 'Experience, knowledge and responsibility', pp. 187–204 in M. Griffiths and M. Whitford (eds), *Feminist Perspectives in Philosophy*. Basingstoke: Macmillan Education.

English, J. (1977) 'Justice between generations', *Philosophical Studies*, 31: 91–104.

Feder Kittay, E. and Meyers D.T. (eds) (1987) *Women and Moral Theory*. Totowa, NJ: Rowman & Littlefield.

Fineman, M. (1989) 'The politics of custody and gender: child advocacy and the transformation of custody decision making in the USA', pp. 27–50 in C. Smart and S. Sevenhuijsen (eds), *Child Custody and the Politics of Gender*. London: Routledge.

Fraser, N. (1989) 'Talking about needs: interpretive contests as political conflicts in welfare-state societies', *Ethics*, 99: 291–313.

Fraser, N. and Nicholson, L. (1988) 'Social criticism without philosophy: an encounter between feminism and postmodernism', *Theory, Culture & Society*, 5 (2–3): 373–94.

Gilligan, C. (1982) *In a Different Voice. Psychological Theory and Women's Development*. Cambridge, MA: Harvard University Press.

Graycar, R. (1989) 'Equal rights versus fathers' rights: the child custody debate in Australia', pp. 158–89 in C. Smart and S. Sevenhuijsen (eds), *Child Custody and the Politics of Gender*. London: Routledge.

Haraway, D. (1988) 'Situated knowledges: the science question in feminism and the privileges of partial perspective', *Feminist Studies*, 14(3): 575–99.

Holtrust, N., Sevenhuijsen, S. and Verbraken, A. (1989) 'Rights for fathers and the state: recent developments in custody politics in the Netherlands', pp. 51–77 in C. Smart and S. Sevenhuijsen (eds), *Child Custody and the Politics of Gender*. London: Routledge.

Kearns, D. (1983) 'A theory of justice – and love; Rawls on the family', *Politics. Journal of the Australasian Political Studies Association*, 2: 36–42.

Krieger, L.J. (1987) 'Through a glass darkly: paradigms of equality and the search for a woman's jurisprudence', *Hypatia*, 2(1): 45–61.

Okin, S. Moller (1987) 'Justice and gender', *Philosophy and Public Affairs*, 1: 42–72.

O'Neill, O. (1986) *Faces of Hunger. An Essay on Poverty, Justice and Development*. London: Allen & Unwin.

O'Neill, O. (1989) 'The great maxims of justice and charity', pp. 297–312 in N. MacCormick and Z. Bankowski (eds), *Enlightenment, Rights and Revolution*. Aberdeen: Aberdeen University Press.

Rawls, J. (1971) *A Theory of Justice*. Cambridge, MA: Harvard University Press.

Sandberg, K. (1989) 'Best interests and justice', pp. 100–25 in C. Smart and S. Sevenhuijsen (eds), *Child Custody and the Politics of Gender*. London: Routledge.

Scott, J. (1988) 'Deconstructing equality-versus-difference: or, the uses of poststructuralism for feminism', *Feminist Studies*, 14(1): 33–50.

Sevenhuijsen, S. (1986) 'Fatherhood and the political theory of rights: theoretical perspectives of feminism', *International Journal of the Sociology of Law*, 14(3/4): 329–40.

Sevenhuijsen, S. (1989) *The Portrait on the Wall. International Trends in Gender Politics and Child Custody after Divorce*. London: Institute of Education.

Smart, C. (1989) *Feminism and the Power of Law*. London: Routledge.

Smart, C. and Sevenhuijsen, S. (eds) (1989) *Child Custody and the Politics of Gender*. London: Routledge.

Smith, J. Farell (1984) 'Parenting and property', pp. 199–212 in J. Trebilcot (ed.), *Mothering. Essays in Feminist Theory*. Totowa, NJ: Rowman & Allanheld.

Thornton, M. (1986) 'Sex equality is not enough for feminism', pp. 77–98 in C. Pateman and E. Gross (eds), *Feminist Challenges. Social and Political Theory*. Sydney, London and Boston: Allen & Unwin.

Tronto, J.C. (1987) 'Beyond gender difference to a theory of care', *Signs: Journal of Women in Culture and Society*, 4: 644–62.

Waltzer, M. (1983) *Spheres of Justice. A Defence of Pluralism and Equality*. New York: Basic Books.

PART 2

POLITICAL PROCESSES AND PUBLIC POLICIES

7

Is This What We Wanted? Positive Action as Issue Perversion

Joyce Outshoorn

In the course of the 1980s affirmative action, or positive action, as it is usually called in the Netherlands, became one of the focal points in public policy on women. Judging by the number of conferences, symposia and reports it was seen by many as the new magic formula to solve the 'woman question'. The underlying assumption was that access to the labour market is the problem for women, and this assumption fitted in well with the major demand of the women's movement for 'economic independence', which most feminists thought was best achieved by paid work. It also fitted in well with government policy which tended to define the issue as purely a problem of access to wage labour. Former hot topics such as 'role change', consciousness-raising, education, sexual violence and individual entitlement to state benefits seem to have disappeared from public debate. It raises the question of how a topic such as positive action achieved agenda status, seeming to determine the whole of the 'woman question' and crowding out other political demands of the women's movement. What is the previous history of the demand for positive action? Who are its proponents? For which problem is it being propagated as a solution?

In this chapter I shall address these questions, using the agenda-building or agenda-setting approach as a frame of reference. I shall briefly outline this approach, after which I will trace the route of positive discrimination, the original demand, to the political agenda and its policy outcomes. I then shall make the case that positive action in its Dutch version is threatening to take the place of positive discrimination and force other demands of the women's movement off the agenda.

The Agenda-building Approach

The decision-making process around positive discrimination and positive action can be analysed by utilizing the agenda-building approach. This approach emphasizes the processes of selection of issues over which a group of decision-makers, the national government, take decisions. The approach is not an explanatory theory but a frame of reference one can use to order the policy process and to trace the various forms issues take. In policy analysis the approach is often used in conjunction with a model conceptualizing the political process as a series of stages separated by a number of barriers which a demand will have to overcome in order to achieve some sort of policy outcome. Many authors by now have contributed to this approach.[1] The model I shall employ in this chapter is one I developed in a study of the abortion issue in the Netherlands (Outshoorn, 1986a). The model has six stages with five barriers. In the first stage there is as yet no problem. If something is going to become one, it is necessary that wishes for change are articulated and transformed into political demands. Conditional for this conversion process is that the government is perceived as responsible for doing something about the problem. The then ensuing issue has to reach the political agenda, which can be defined as the set of issues at any given time which the decision-makers acknowledge it is their task to do something about (Outshoorn, 1986a:70). Only after this can a decision be taken; deliberation on the issue can take a very long time. In the Netherlands it is not so difficult to get an issue on the political agenda, but much more difficult to get the authorities to make a decision. Once there is a decision, it has to be implemented. Only then is it possible to evaluate the policy's effectiveness in redressing the problem and only then can one address the question of whether the outcomes were intended by the claimants of the original demand.

The model shown in Figure 7.1 may seem to imply that demands are always generated from outside government and its various departments or agencies. However, as has been pointed out by many policy analysts (for example Hall *et al.*, 1975; Cobb *et al.*, 1976; Kok, 1981) most demands are generated within the government bureaucracy itself.

In the case of positive action this possibility should not be ruled out at the outset. Logically speaking there are several routes to the political agenda (see Figure 7.2).

In my version of the approach I do not proceed from the premiss that demands are 'given'; central to the analysis are the processes of definition and redefinition of the issue. The agenda-building approach then becomes a method to trace the life-cycle of issues.

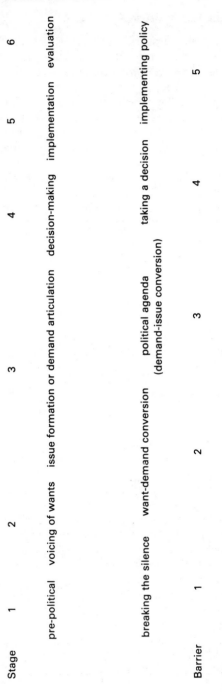

Figure 7.1   *A barrier model of the political process*

Source: Outshoorn (1986a:72)

	public discussion before agenda status	no public discussion before agenda status	outcome
Authorities do not consider acting	1	2	not on political agenda
Authorities do undertake action	3	4	on agenda
Authorities refuse to take action after consideration of issue	5	6	on agenda (from which it disappears)

Figure 7.2   *Routes to the political agenda*

Source: Outshoorn (1986a:69)

Setting the Agenda

Looking at the 'woman question' in focus, one can situate the first stage, the *pre-political* one, in the period prior to 1967. It is characterized by consensus about 'women's place': that was in the home. The welfare state built after the Second World War defined men as breadwinners and women as housewives and constructed this division explicitly into its social security and incomes policy. Implicitly this was also done by the employment policy of the period (Keynesian full-employment goals were full employment for men) and by defining certain areas as inappropriate for state intervention. Part of the post-war consensus was also the assumption that women had achieved equal status.

Granting married women full equal status as legal subjects in civil law and abolishing the Act on the compulsory dismissal of women as civil servants or teachers at the point of marriage in the mid-1950s were seen as the completion of this evolution. The women's movement and feminism were seen as relics from a distant past. On the eve of the outburst of the new wave of feminism in the mid-1960s there was actually quite a debate among women on abolishing separate women's organizations in politics as no longer necessary.

To date there has been no convincing explanation of the rupture in this consensus at the end of the 1960s. Factors such as demographic trends, developments in the labour market and the breakdown of traditional morality around marriage, sexuality and reproduction obviously form part of the conditions in which renewed demands on women's status could be articulated. The publication in 1967 of the famous article by Joke Smit on the 'discontent of women' (Smit, 1967) breached the first barrier, here operational- ized as an ideological barrier: the dominant consensus on women's status. She voiced the *wants* of a new generation of women trapped as housewives.

With the (re)creation of a social problem around women's status a lively public debate followed, new organizations emerged, new spokeswomen came to the fore who formulated the first political demands. These demands were notable for their scope; the new feminist groups tackled a remarkable amount of topics and de- veloped several conflicting definitions of women's position.

In translating these topics into political demands Man-Vrouw- Maatschappij (MVM – Man-Woman-Society), the first new orga- nization that the second wave of feminism spawned in 1968, played a major part. The group was set up as a pressure group to influence public policy on women. In the period up to the late 1970s it was one of the few groups which was oriented towards the traditional politic- al arena. MVM developed its ideology from then current American sociology; Helen Hacker's idea of women as a minority group, analogous to Blacks and other people of colour, served as a basic idea for MVM's concept of women's status (Hacker, 1951; Outs- hoorn, 1987). Women were seen to be in an inferior position, manifested in many areas of social life. Such a second-rate position is internalized at an intra-psychic level; women also see themselves as inferior. (Later this idea became known as 'internalized oppres- sion'.) This early view of women's status was very broad and gave rise to a large number of demands, including a heavy emphasis on consciousness-raising and the challenging of dominant perceptions of women. Widely current were ideas on non-sexist child-raising, breaking down sex stereotyping, creating more opportunities for girls in education, abolishing discriminatory practices in the labour market, adjusting school times, setting up child care, providing sex education and contraception, and legalizing abortion.

Defining women as a minority group was not the only way in which women were conceptualized. Many socialists were members of MVM and they were familiar with the traditional socialist view of the 'woman question'.

The socialist conceptualization went much farther than the equal rights view implicit in the minority group definition by emphasizing substantial equality and stressing the importance of paid work for women's liberation. Just as many women in the first wave of femin- ism had seen wage labour as basic to women's status, many now too stressed its importance to women's liberation. This was also the case for the much publicized 'younger sister' of MVM, Dolle Mina, which burst into life in 1970. It demanded part-time work for both women and men, so that they could share child care.

In 1973 MVM celebrated its first jubilee and it utilized the occasion to confront the government with the demand for a new policy on women. In the keynote speech the chairperson called for explicit anti-discrimination measures, by which she meant a quota system in employment, being under the impression this was part of remedial action in the United States. There had already been a group within MVM working on anti-discrimination policy, including several members of the Dutch Labour Party, which was aware of the Swedish and American attempts at equality policy for women. The demand for positive discrimination, in the form of quotas, however, remained an MVM issue; the women's section of the Labour Party did propose a preferential hiring scheme for women, but that was in 1975, and the demand was addressed to employers, not to the government. The socialists seized upon the idea of quotas in a very different way when they decided on setting up quotas for the representation of women in politics.

A rule was adopted, which said that 25 per cent of electoral candidates and party officials should be women.

On the Political Agenda

The 'woman question' attained *agenda status* at the national level in 1974, when the cabinet Den Uyl (a Socialist–Christian Democrat coalition) set up a Committee on the Status of Women (Emancipatie-kommissie), acknowledging the role of government. This was the effect not only of the pressure that MVM exerted on the cabinet, but also of the UN Women's Year in 1975, which forced the cabinet to make some sort of gesture. Taking up the 'woman question' was facilitated by the ideological compatibility of the demands with the left-wing programme of the cabinet: a more equal distribution of income, property, power, knowledge and political participation. As has been noted by others (Dijkstra and Swiebel, 1981:45) the cabinet placed the responsibility for developing a policy on women on two non-governmental bodies, the already mentioned Committee on the Status of Women and a National Committee for the International Women's Year. The first committee gave national policy its basic philosophy. Many of its members were recruited from MVM and the Labour Party and their ideas heavily influenced future policy.

There was also pressure on the government to act from the European Community (EC) by way of the Directives on Equal Pay,

Equal Treatment and Equal Treatment in Social Security (Sjerps, 1987). The members of MVM who were appointed to the committee took the idea of positive discrimination, which was part of the larger issue of women's status, along with them. In the most important document the committee produced in its five-year existence (Emancipatiekommissie, 1976:12,14) 'temporary' preferential hiring was listed as one of the new policy instruments. This demand was legitimized by pointing to the experiences with similar practices in the United States. The document of the committee became the basis of the first government paper on women's policy (Emancipatie, 1977). Positive discrimination was once again named as one of the potential policy instruments, the issue now being framed as a means of enabling women to achieve equality with men. With this government paper the *demand* for positive discrimination itself can be said to have achieved agenda status in 1977.

For this relatively smooth state of affairs several explanatory factors can be advanced. One is the strategic location of the members of the new women's movement organization MVM within the committee and in the Labour Party (de Wildt, 1980; Dijkstra and Swiebel, 1981; Sloot, 1986). Another can be seen to lie in the ideological compatibility of the demand of positive discrimination with the ideology of the welfare state, which in the Dutch situation assumed that something extra could and should be done for the less privileged, so legitimacy seemed assured (Sloot, 1986).

This needs to be qualified somewhat. Seeing women as a separate category needing special treatment is a much older idea dating from a period before the welfare state; it was indeed basic to the formation of the modern democratic state in which women were at first not seen as bearers of citizens' rights, being excluded from the suffrage, military service and not having the status of full legal subject in civil law. In addition, right from the outset (the late 1880s) social policy differentiated along gender lines when the first labour legislation regulated women's labour but not men's.

A third factor – like the second factor an issue characteristic making for easy access to the political agenda – is that the demand could be quantified easily, and matters which can be translated into figures have a better chance of making it to the political agenda than other issues (Outshoorn, 1986a: 64–6). Fourthly, the demand is very specific and concrete; at first glance it does not seem complicated and it is easy to formulate in the terms of the dominant political discourse of the day. The Socialist Christian Democrat cabinet employed as its slogan the 'redistribution of knowledge, power and income', and positive discrimination was clearly a matter of redistribution of jobs.

Some critics of the demand, such as Sloot (1986) have held the women's movement responsible for the issue modification taking place after it achieved agenda status. In his view, the movement confined the women's issue to the right to employment, a reduction he explains in a sociological vein by pointing to the fact that the women making up MVM had found themselves blocked in their career aspirations (Sloot, 1986: 180–1). This last observation is not erroneous but is beside the point. By neglecting the fact that the original demand for paid work was part of a whole parcel of demands, the extent of issue modification is considerably exaggerated. The definition of the women's issue in the paper of the Committee on the Status of Women also implied much more than the demand for the right to work. Seen from the point of view of one of the mainstream traditions of nineteenth- and twentieth-century feminism in which wage labour is seen as a necessary condition for women's liberation, broadening the issue to encompass other demands can with justification also be seen as issue modification. (When the new liberation movement of the 1970s started tackling sexuality, many socialists at first saw this as perverting the 'real' issue!) When MVM defined wage labour as crucial, it was perfectly in keeping with this tradition; there is no question of reduction here. The idea of quota was firmly set within this older tradition.

In the government paper (Emancipatie, 1977) which formed the basis for equality policy for women, the demand for positive discrimination was formulated in terms of 'temporary preferential hiring', the 'temporary' making it sound less threatening. The paper emphasized that government would use this instrument with 'reserve' and declared itself against the use of quotas in the Civil Service. Important to the later debate was that the definition of the issue of positive discrimination on the political agenda was not gender-neutral; it was about preferential treatment as a method to redress the wrongs of women, to bring them to a par with men.

Looking at this agenda-setting process, it can be determined that the route to the political agenda taken by the issue of positive discrimination is what I have called the fourth one in Figure 7.2 (p. 107). The issue achieved agenda status (the decision-makers decide to do something about it) without any public debate taking place. Being part of a larger package of measures, very few people noticed it. A point to be noted is that the idea of preferential hiring for women in the Netherlands preceded the application of the idea to ethnic minorities and Blacks, contrary to the situation in the US, where it was the other way round.

Taking a Decision

Once on the political agenda, nothing much happened to the issue of positive discrimination for quite a time. If one wants a decision to be taken, issue maintenance, not only in the minds of the public, but also in those of the decision-makers themselves, is crucial (Outshoorn, 1986a: 79–80). The definition of the issue also has to be maintained during the *decision-making stage*.

Public debate had hardly taken place before 1977; after this date this remained the case, so there was little political pressure on the decision-makers from that direction. In addition, a new government of another political persuasion came to power in 1977 (Liberal/Christian Democrat). Although it adopted the 1977 paper of the preceding cabinet as its policy, which meant the women's issue as a whole remained on the agenda, there now was a greater emphasis on political education as an instrument towards equality than on other policies. Despite the lack of public debate, the idea of positive discrimination also remained alive. Two factors may account for this fact. First, there was a debate on a related issue, quotas for the representation of women in political parties. As already mentioned, the women's organization of the Labour Party managed to get a resolution passed in 1977 by the party congress for 25 per cent women candidates on all lists. This led to some debate about the representation of women in public life and in the Civil Service: no longer would a token woman suffice on candidates' lists or in committees. Furthermore, from the first parliamentary debates on women's policy onwards, it became obvious that politicians liked the idea of quotas for women, it being a potential policy which can be quantified and evaluated easily. Under-representation of women became the fashionable topic; a resolution was passed by parliament almost unanimously in 1976 (Sloot, 1986:188), calling for positive discrimination for women in the national Civil Service. This had the undesirable side-effect that debate on substantive policy was pushed to the sidelines, but the resolution did spur further action on preferential hiring.

Secondly, civil servants at the department responsible for women's policy (Culture, Recreation and Welfare) kept the issue going within the department. A section for women's policy was set up in 1977. The civil servants of this section were partly recruited from the former staff of the Committee on the Status of Women, and one may suppose that they took their ideas along with them. They had the backing of the parliamentary resolution of 1976 and faced the necessity of implementing the Second Directive of the EC on equal treatment for the Netherlands. This gave ample opportunity for issue maintenance. The issue stayed on the agenda, but became subject to some surprising skirmishes during the decision-making stage.

The Second EC Directive of February 1976 allows for the possibility for preferential treatment (Van der Weele, 1983:99–106). The official advice the Committee on the Status of Women gave to the government on a draft bill for an all-inclusive anti-discrimination law also included this possibility, but gave it an extraordinary twist. The whole tendency of this advice was gender-neutrality, as though forgetting for whom positive discrimination was intended in the first place: women were mentioned only in the examples given in the text. Both the laws on equal treatment (to adjust Dutch law to the Second Directive) passed by parliament in 1980 adopted this gender-neutral language, in stark contrast to the wording of the Second Directive itself.

Nobody in parliament commented on this discrepancy during the debate. The draft anti-discrimination bill of 1981 intending to complement the two bills on equal treatment also contained the possibility of positive discrimination, and once again it was framed in gender-neutral language. As this draft became very controversial (it also contained clauses opposing discrimination against lesbians and gays) the government had to come up with separate amendments of the 1980 laws to close some of the more obvious loopholes. These correctives reverted to speaking about women but now the possibility for preferential hiring had almost disappeared. All these incidents kept the issue alive throughout the 1980s. At present there is still no overall anti-discrimination Act although it is still on the political agenda. The correctives to the 1980 Equal Treatment Acts were finally passed in 1989 by parliament and became operative in 1990; they do allow for preferential hiring of women, but the clauses allowing for preferential hiring have yet to be implemented. This raises the question of what happened to positive discrimination since its agenda status in 1976.

The parliamentary resolution of 1976 first had to be implemented in the personnel policy of the national Civil Service. For this task an interdepartmental committee was set up; in its documents the gender-neutral modification of the issue can be traced. It started by saying that men too should be eligible for preferential treatment; later committees adopted this idea. Fortunately, later Civil Service policy was influenced by the Emancipation Council, the committee which succeeded the Committee on the Status of Women in 1981. Among its members were several women from the professionalized parts of the women's movement and these were well aware of equality policy in the US. The council managed to stop the modification of the issue as a gender-neutral concern by stressing that the whole idea of positive discrimination was intended to improve women's position on the labour market. This renewed emphasis on women can be traced in their various pieces of advice to the government on personnel policy and in various drafts of the proposed 1981 anti-discrimination bill. As already mentioned, this was also the case in the amendment bill on equal treatment of 1984, but now again the idea of preferential hiring had disappeared from the plan. When the Department of Internal Affairs, responsible for the Civil Service, finally came up with an affirmative action plan in 1983, the original definition of preferring women had been restored. Several departments resorted to a very mild form of preferential hiring by asking women specifically to apply in their personnel advertisements.

With these decisions accepting a (very mild) form of preferential hiring the issue entered its next stage, that of *implementation*, but the issue had undergone change. No longer is it about the possibility for quotas or a stricter form of preferential hiring; it has become a vague intention of hiring women in the Civil Service. It is also a limited result, as decisions only cover the national Civil Service. From later government publications one can gather that part of the action plan has been implemented in the various departments of the national government, but that its effects appear to be very limited (De Jong *et al.*, 1986).

A New Issue

A certain shift in the debate about positive discrimination had been discernible at an earlier stage. It can be located in the Emancipation Council, which started to use 'positive action', as synonymous with positive discrimination. In this emerging view, preferential hiring or quota could be seen as part of a much broader policy on recruitment, selection and career planning for women. It was inspired by the Dutch perception of affirmative action in the US, which was not totally unknown in the Netherlands as several corporations already had such plans in operation. As these were part of American multinationals they had had to adapt to US standards. This view on affirmative action also emerged in the Social Economic Council[2] which in 1981 published an early paper on equal treatment. In this paper equal treatment was seen as part of 'socially responsible' corporation policy. This paper was women-inspired, emerging from the committee on Women and Work (which had influential women members), which in turn had been inspired by the Equal Opportunities Commission in the UK. No mention was made, however, of preferential hiring.

The term 'positive action' had already been employed in the Netherlands in 1982 by economists working on the participation of women in the labour force. The Emancipation Council also euphemistically came to speak of 'temporary' preferential treatment and no longer made mention of quotas.

The idea of quotas had become a topic of some public debate in the early 1980s. With media reports from the United States on preferential hiring circulating, quotas were entering the public mind; indicative of this are national surveys on public opinion which usually reflect current debate. Quotas were not a popular idea; 73 per cent of a nationally representative sample was opposed to them (Sociaal en Cultureel Planbureau, 1982:247). It seems plausible that this unpopularity gave rise to the need to redefine the issue, a terminological change as a tactical redefinition. Positive discrimination became positive action.

To account for the changed labelling of the issue by the Emancipation Council, three other causes for this redefinition can be discerned. First, there was an EC report on positive action in 1982 (Vogel-Polsky, 1982). Secondly, the already mentioned amendment of 1984 to the Equal Treatment Acts of 1980 included a plea for affirmative action, framed within an eloquent call for private initiative, concerted action by trade unions and employers' organizations, and careful incremental implementation. Thirdly, the Council of EC Ministers came along with a recommendation on positive action for women in 1984 (EC, 1984).

The new redefinition of the issue can be distilled from these and similar documents. As one proponent of positive action has it, positive action is 'a policy aimed at achieving equal opportunity for women and men in practice', and an 'active policy on job-description, criteria for selection, information, training of personnel-managers and staff, extra training for women in traditionally male positions' (De Jong, 1983:133). If all of this succeeds, quotas or even preferential hiring are no longer necessary, they form a measure of 'last resort'. Surveying the life-cycle of the original demand, its reversal is complete: the interest group of MVM saw quotas as essential, as it considered regular personnel management unable to solve the problem of women's disadvantage on the labour market; now the regular state of affairs in personnel management suddenly comes to be presented as the solution of the problem which somewhere along the way became reduced to the issue of more women in higher employment. Analysing the various texts and documents on positive action programmes, one notices that quotas 'can' be part of such a plan; letting go of them altogether then becomes a very small step. Precisely this is what one sees happening in the most recent policy statements of the national government. They may sometimes turn up as target figures to be attained by organizations when setting up a positive action plan.

Modifying the Issue

The year 1982 is an important watershed in Dutch politics. A new coalition government between Liberals and Christian Democrats (named the first cabinet-Lubbers after its prime minister) then came to office and the political climate took a definite turn to the right. This transformed the context of national policy on women, with its roots in the ideology of the welfare state now under discussion. The interim cabinet of Socialists and Christian Democrats of 1981–2, which held power for only nine months, had reallocated the responsibility for policy on women from the Department of Culture, Recreation and Welfare to the Department of Social Affairs and Employment. This move accentuated the character of the women's issue as redistributive and as one in which paid work is seen as a necessary condition for women's liberation. It also initiated the first steps in a new basic policy formulation, which survived the interim cabinet and was approved of by the first cabinet-Lubbers in 1985. The next year parliament gave its approval to the new official policy document, which had as its basic theme economic independence for women. But under the second cabinet of Lubbers, also a coalition of Christian Democrats and Liberals, implementation of this new policy on women stagnated, scoring mainly on the symbolic level (Keuzenkamp and Teunissen, 1990).

In the debates on the restructuring of the welfare state, a restrictive social security and incomes policy, a non-Keynesian employment policy, the lack of policy in the area of child care, the classic demands of the women's movement remained on the political agenda but were not met. It is in this situation that positive action becomes a redefinition of the original issue, not only as issue modification of the original demand of quotas, but of the whole policy on women.

Positive action is an issue which was generated within certain parts of the national government. It is an example of administration setting its own agenda, which in Figure 7.2 (p. 107) is called the fourth route (government undertakes action, agenda status without public debate). Until 1985 there was little discussion on this issue; when the Minister of Social Affairs and Employment came up with an information leaflet *The Right Woman in the Right Place*, the media, the managers and the movement at large discovered the issue. The demand for positive action did not emerge from the women's movement, but originated from professionals in several networks such as the Emancipation Council, the Committee on Women and Work in the Sociaal–Economische Raad (Social–Economic Council), and various civil servants of the Department of Social Affairs and Employment, including those responsible for national policy on women. The women's movement in the 1980s had up to then mainly addressed such issues as the revision of the social security system, economic independence, women's nightwork and the reduction of overall working time. It only got into the act after 1985.

That the issue of positive action is a success in the traditional political arena and that it landed on *the political agenda* in 1986 (with the already mentioned information leaflet of the Department of Social Affairs) is not surprising. Avoiding the stigma of the politicized concept of positive discrimination and sounding more up to date than the somewhat faded 'emancipation policy', as public policy on women is known in the Netherlands, the label is well chosen. The issue seems concrete and specific; it is in accordance with regular procedure and can be legitimized in terms of the current political discourse on less state intervention. No sanctions, no obligations, but a matter of negotiations between the 'social partners' of labour and private enterprise; at the level of the firm and in collective bargaining people can give shape to their 'own responsibility'. The pragmatic character of the issue makes it attractive to politicians who like to convey that they are alert and active. At the local level the issue is easily picked up as it gives lower government the illusion that it can form and pursue its own policy independent of central government. The issue also fits the rising career feminism of women within large organizations and corporations who discover the barriers in their own careers. Almost cynically one can add that positive action creates job opportunities for labour sociologists, legal experts and feminist management consultants; this perhaps partly accounts for its popularity among the professional part of the women's movement.

For 'femocrats' at the local or provincial level it is a godsend, enabling them to give meaning and content to their often poorly delineated tasks by setting up a positive action plan for civil servants. It also fits in with those feminist activists who seize on the issue to revive the flagging spirit of the movement. Its increasing popularity can definitely be related to the fact that many in this heterogeneous movement can agree on it: a consensus around the lowest common denominator.

At the end of the 1980s, positive action has tended to push other aspects of the 'woman question' off the agenda; equality policy for women threatens to be reduced to it; a modification of the original issue of women's status. Two arguments can be advanced to prove the point. First it can be deduced from recent policy papers. The most recent one from the Department of Social Affairs and Employment addresses positive action as the 'best opportunity' to improve women's position on the labour market, positive action here being defined as: 'an active and planned approach . . . in systematically unearthing barriers for women' and in finding 'which conditions offer the best chances for improvement' (Nota, 1987:2). Not that any concrete measures have followed from these; those are left to the 'social partners'.

Secondly, it can be inferred from the lack of progress on other issues in women's policy. Without sufficient child-care facilities, jobs, a decent incomes policy including women's own right to social security benefits, further implementation of policy on sexual violence, reduction of working hours so that men may at last start sharing housework and child care, and effective legislation on equal treatment, positive action in its current definition is a palliative. It does not contribute to the redistribution of paid work and housework, one of the oldest demands of the women's movement, it does not make for a redivision of the 'roles' of men and women. In addition, it is a demand which only aids women already employed (except in the case of hiring policy) and in practice it is only meaningful to the better educated at the higher echelons of the job pyramid. Positive action can be no replacement for an employment policy creating new jobs and can only partly counter sex segregation in the labour market. Its decentralized character, calling for negotiations between trade unions and employers, shifts the problem to an arena where women are hardly represented. It also involves long-term 'trench warfare' which requires organization and, as is well known, this is precisely what women on the whole lack.

Conclusions

If one looks at the life-cycle of the issue of positive action, one can discern that there has been a creeping process of issue modification. This can take place along several lines. It can emerge by broadening a demand, diluting the original content, or by a reductive process in which the original demand loses its scope. An issue can also be redefined in new terms, leading to the disappearance of the old issue. These phenomena are inherent in the policy process and it would be mistaken to see modification as the result of the conscious intention of the actors involved. One of the advantages of the agenda-setting approach is that it can show that modification is usually the result of a process in which many take part but which few can really control. The issues discussed here are no different in these respects.

Positive action was not one of the original demands of the women's movement. Early feminist ideals were consciousness–raising, role change, equal opportunity in education, adequate child care, jobs, availability of contraception and the legalization of abortion. Later in its history a whole new series of demands was developed in the domain of sexual violence and incomes policy. In the early feminist view positive discrimination, which stood for quotas and preferential hiring of women, was only one of the instruments to achieve equality on the labour market. The protagonists of the demand were MVM and the Committee on the Status of Women; it then found its way on to the political agenda. Later proponents were civil servants and the members of the Emancipation Council; only after 1985 could the issue bank on the interest of the women's movement. The life-cycle of the issue progressed from being part of a nearly all-encompassing view on women's status in society to a separate demand in terms of the redistribution of paid and unpaid work; quotas and preferential hiring were part of it. These two demands then became subject to redefinition in terms of positive action in which the idea of quotas has disappeared altogether and the idea of state intervention has been abandoned. In combination with the fact that public policy on other aspects of the 'woman question' is making no progress, positive action is a meagre response to the original demands of the women's movement. In this longer-term view issue modification occurs by way of reduction. If this tendency persists, one can justifiably speak of issue perversion.

As yet, it is too early to say whether the new Christian Democrat/ Socialist cabinet which took power in 1989 will continue to push positive action as the summum of equality policy. The official policy goal is to achieve economic independence through job creation and by removing barriers to access to the labour market. Child care is on the agenda, and the anti-discrimination bill has been promised for next year; positive action, parental leave and the reduction of working hours are all mentioned in the founding document of the cabinet (Regeerakkoord, 1989:5). At the same time, the government is professing less state interference and more responsibility for other social actors. Against this background positive action without quotas will remain tempting to politicians, administrators and the private sector as a form of symbolic action, fitting in so well with neo-liberal equal opportunities discourse. In the long run it may continue to undercut more effective measures for improving women's position.

Notes

* This chapter is based on an earlier version written for the Dutch public policy journal *Beleid en Maatschappij* (Outshoorn, 1988).

1. For a review of the literature, see Outshoorn (1986a, 1986b).

2. This council is the top-organization representing the 'social partners' – trade unions and employers' organizations – and advising the government on social and economic policy. The 'social partners' make up two-thirds of its membership: the other third are experts appointed by the Crown and are formally independent. It is the most important 'corporate structure' in the Netherlands, but many observers are of the opinion that its importance has declined progressively since the early 1970s.

References

Cobb, R.W., Ross, J. Keith and Ross, M.H. (1976) 'Agendabuilding as a comparative approach', *American Political Science Review*, 70(1):126–38.

Dijkstra, T. and Swiebel, J. (1981) 'De overheid en het vrouwenvraagstuk: Emancipatiebeleid als mode en taboe', pp. 42–65 in *Socialisties-Feministiese Teksten 7*. Amsterdam: Feministische Uitgeverij Sara.

EC (1984) *Recommendation of the Council of 13 December 1984 on the Promotion of Positive Action for Women*, Publicatieblad (Journal) of the EC, L331/3–4, 19 December.

Emancipatie (1977) *Proces van verandering en groei. Nota over het emancipatiebeleid*, Handelingen Tweede Kamer, zittingsjaar 1976–7, 14496, no.1–2, 18 May.

Emancipatiekommissie (1976) *Aanzet tot een vijf-jaren plan*. Rijswijk: Emancipatiekommissie.

Hacker, H. (1951) 'Women as a minority group', *Social Forces*, 30:60–9.

Hall, P., Land, H., Parker, R. and Webb, A. (1975) *Change, Choice and Conflict in Social Policy*. London: Heinemann.

Jong, A.M. de (1983) *Gelijke behandeling en het personeelsbeleid. De positie van de vrouw in de arbeidsorganisatie*. Deventer: Kluwer.

Jong, A.M. de, van Doorne-Huiskes, J., Maan, M. and de Olde, C. (1986) *Positieve actie 2. Verslag van de besluitvormings– en uitvoeringsfase van he PAVO-project*. The Hague: Ministerie van Binnenlandse Zaken.

Keuzenkamp, S. and Teunissen, A. (1990) *Emancipatie ten halve geregeld. Continuiteit en inening in het emancipatiebeleid*. The Hague: Ministerie van Sociale Zaken en Werkgelegenheid.

Kok, W.J.P. (1981) *Signalering en selectie. Rapport over een onderzoek naar de agendavorming van de rijksdienst*. The Hague: Staatsuitgeverij. (Achtergrondstudie no. 3, Cie. Hoofdstructuur Rijksdienst, Ministerie van Binnenlandse Zaken.)

Nota (1987) *Positieve actieprogramma's voor vrouwen in arbeidsorganisaties*. Ministerie van Sociale Zaken en Werkgelegenheid, 30 November.

Outshoorn, J. (1986a) *De politieke strijd rondom de abortuswetgeving in Nederland 1964–1984*. The Hague: VUGA.

Outshoorn, J. (1986b) 'The feminist movement in the Netherlands and abortion policy in the Netherlands', pp. 64–85 in D. Dahlerup, (ed.), *The New Women's Movement. Feminism and Political Power in Europe and the USA*. London and Beverly Hills: Sage.

Outshoorn, J. (1987) 'Power as a political and theoretical concept in "second wave" feminism', pp. 25–34 in M. Leijenaar *et al.*, *The Gender of Power, A Symposium*. Leiden: Department of Women's Studies.

Outshoorn, J. (1988) 'De verwording van een politieke eis:positieve actie en het "vrouwenvraagstuk"', *Beleid en Maatschappij*, 15(4):216–26.

Regeerakkoord (1989) *Resultaten programmatische besprekingen informateur Lubbers*. Handelingen Tweede Kamer, zittingsjaar 1989–90, 21132, 9, 26 October.

Sjerps, I. (1987) 'Indirect discrimination in social security in the Netherlands: demands of the Dutch women's movement', pp. 95–105 in M. Buckley and M. Andersen, *Women, Equality and Europe*. Basingstoke: Macmillan Education.

Sloot, B.P. (1986) *Positieve discriminatie. Maatschappelijke ongelijkheid en rechtsontwikkeling in de Verenigde Staten en Nederland*. Zwolle: Tjeenk Willink.

Smit, J. (1967) 'Het onbehagen bij de vrouw', reprinted pp. 15–43 in J. Smit, *Er is een land waar vrouwen willen wonen*. Amsterdam: Feministische Uitgeverij Sara, 1984.

Sociaal en Cultureel Planbureau (1982), *Sociaal en Cultureel Rapport*. The Hague: Staatsdrukkerij.

Vogel-Polsky, E. (1982) *Study on Positive Action Programmes as Strategies to Integrate Female Workers and Other Hard-to-place Groups into the Labourmarket*. Brussels: EC.

Weele, J. van der (1983) *Wet Gelijke Behandeling van mannen en vrouwen*. Deventer: Kluwer.

Wildt, J. de (1980) 'Emancipatiebeleid en de rechtspositie van vrouwen met betrekking tot de arbeid', in *Ars Aequi*, X29(7):3–88–399.

8

Agendas and *Egalité Professionnelle*: Symbolic Policy at Work in France

Amy Mazur

While equal employment policy for women in some industrialized democracies, like Great Britain, has tended to centre on gender discrimination in hiring and firing (Meehan, 1985), policy in other countries, such as Sweden, has addressed gender inequities at work in terms of full employment (Ruggie, 1984). Still other countries, like the USA, have opted to use affirmative action quotas (Ratner, 1980).[1] In France, however, equal employment or 'égalité professionnelle'[2] has neither been integrated into general employment policy, nor successfully enforced by the court system in discrimination cases. Furthermore, positive discrimination quotas have been rejected in favour of a voluntary system of preferential hiring and training similar to the approach of the Netherlands (see Outshoorn, chapter 7 in this volume).

The French *égalité professionnelle* policy (EPP) could be described as symbolic regulation in the 1972 equal pay and the 1975 equal treatment laws and as symbolic redistribution in the 1983 égalité professionnelle law.[3] In this chapter, I will examine the question of why policies followed this trajectory with an analytical framework that suggests links between policy formation and outcome. The central argument will be that the dynamics of agenda setting affected the way each law was formulated and implemented. (The impact of these laws on private sector employment, but not on public sector jobs, will be analysed.) Before analysing EPP, it is first necessary to discuss the policy formation model in terms of its application in this chapter.[4]

Analytical Framework

Kingdon's (1984) model for the pre-decision policy process in the US federal government provides a plausible explanation for how issues get placed on the decision agenda.[5] In the policy formation game, according to Kingdon, there are three separate streams of processes: problem recognition, policy proposition and politics. The independent dynamic of each stream can either move an item up the government agenda or prevent an item from gaining government agenda status. The probability of a policy alternative gaining decision agenda status is at its highest when the three streams are joined at critical junctures.[6]

A proposal actually achieves decision agenda status only when a window opens in the policy system and a policy entrepreneur, a person willing to invest resources in certain issues (Kingdon, 1984: 188), joins the three streams together and pushes a pet proposal from the government agenda through the open window to the decision agenda. An item is more likely to rise to the top of the decision agenda when all three streams are skilfully packaged together (Kingdon, 1984: 184). Windows can either open as a result of changes in the political stream (a significant shift in public opinion or a change in government or parliament) or in the problem stream (the appearance of a pressing problem) (Kingdon, 1984: 182–3). Whereas some policy proposals may have been floating in the 'primeval policy soup' for years, only the proposals which meet the political needs of the moment rise to the top of the decision agenda (Kingdon, 1984: chapter 6).

I have selected this model to examine EPP for two reasons. First, recent discussions of the state of comparative public policy analysis have pointed to the lacuna in studying how policy formation affects policy outcomes (Hancock, 1983; APSA, 1987). As E.E. Schattschneider suggests, 'The definition of alternatives is the supreme instrument of power' (1975: 66). Although Kingdon is only interested in explaining why agendas change over time, his model can also inform us about the linkages between policy formation and outcome. Given that the better a policy is packaged the higher its decision agenda status, we can assume that the higher the placement of a proposal on that agenda the stronger the government support. Taking this proposition a step further, the better a policy proposal is coupled with the two other streams and pushed through the open policy window, the more likely it is not just to retain its original intent throughout the formulation process (ministerial, social partner and parliamentary scrutiny). But, once passed into law, such a well-packaged policy will also generate 'policy feedback' in the implementation stage or, as Theda Skocpol has stated,

> In the first place, through the official efforts to implement them, policies transform the capacities of the state, affecting possibilities for future efforts at policy implementation. In the second place, social policies affect the social identities, goals and capabilities of the groups that subsequently struggle or ally over policy-making. (Skocpol, 1988:22)

Secondly the concept of 'organized anarchy' that Kingdon attributes to the US policy system (fragmented decision-making, poor information distribution and policy actors with rudimentary knowledge of their role in the process) also captures the essence of the French policy system as revealed in this chapter. Although the conventional wisdom about the French state posits a centralized policy mechanism (see Crozier, 1970), much recent research suggests a more fragmented policy system in which decision-making and implementation are disjointed (see Suleiman, 1987; Thoenig and Dupuy, 1985; Bodiguel and Quermonne, 1983). Therefore the portability of this model suggests a comparative approach to the analysis of French public policy. This is especially important given that most French politics specialists tend 'not to write about France in a comparative perspective' (Schain, 1988: 64).

Symbolic Policy at Work

From the cues of this model, I will examine the dynamics of the pre-decision, formulation and implementation stages first for the 1972 and 1975 laws and then for the 1983 law. In this analysis I will show how the manner in which policy entrepreneurs joined the three policy streams and pushed them through open policy windows determined the symbolic nature of all three laws. Symbolic policy outcomes occur when the demands of unorganized interests for change in the status quo are met in a policy settlement that 'is mostly meaningless in its effects on resource allocation' (Edelman, 1965: 24). While the winners are elected officials and powerful interest groups that defend the dominant distribution of resources, power, values, and so on, the losers are inevitably the least powerful groups.

Symbolic Regulation in the 1972 Pay Equity Law

Kingdon argues that policy actors must redefine conditions as public problems before they can be part of the government agenda (1984: 118). In France, in the mid-1960s women's inferior position in the workforce shifted from being an accepted condition of economic growth to a public problem. Although left-wing trade unions had attempted to draw attention to women's low status in the workforce in the 1950s (Jenson, 1984), this problem was not placed on the government agenda until the Committee on Women's Work (CWW) was created in 1965. As an advocate for women's rights at work within the government, led by a core group of bureaucrats or 'state feminists' (Nielsen, 1983), the CWW brought together representatives from trade unions, women's groups and employers' organizations along with experts to discuss problems related to women in the workforce. Starting as a study group, the consultative body was upgraded to a committee in 1971, receiving a budget, one full-time staff member and the right to publish all reports (Lévy, 1988).

The CWW explained women's low position in the labour force in many different ways, but the problem which came to the forefront of its work in the late 1960s was inequality in pay. Indeed, as the president of the CWW asserted in an interview, addressing direct pay discrimination was the first politically feasible step to dealing with the larger problem of gender inequality. The policy proposals suggested in a seminal state feminist report on wage discrepancies demonstrated the array of solutions floating in the 'primeval policy soup' (Guilbert, 1971). Policy suggestions ranged from raising salaries in feminized sectors of industry and including those sectors in collective agreements to extending professional training opportunities to women, adopting job equality measures in the public sector, removing family considerations from employment decisions about women and improving day care facilities (Guilbert, 1971:32–4). The core of these suggestions, however, was pay equity. Not only did three proposals single out the regulation of employer pay practices, but the first draft of an equal pay bill was included in the report.

At the end of the 1960s a new awareness began to develop about pay inequity between the sexes. While the CGT and the CFDT, the major working-class trade unions, sponsored rival conferences on equal pay in 1967, public opinion polls showed that equal pay for equal work was the most popular measure to improve women's status (*Express*, 8 May 1972 and *Nouvel Observateur*, 16 November 1970). Obstacles in the political process, however, prevented proposals in this area from reaching the decision agenda until 1971.

From 1962 to 1969, with Charles De Gaulle in the presidency and Gaullist loyalists dominating key political and administrative positions, the government refused to pursue public policy in favour of women's rights. Gaullism not only embraced women's traditional role as mothers, but women as a cheap source of labour were essential to the economic growth promoted by De Gaulle (Rueff-Armand, 1960). Moreover, there was little articulated political pressure for a better response to the rising demands for women's rights. While on one hand women as voters were perceived as pro-Gaullist, giving 62 per cent of their vote to De Gaulle in 1965 (Mossuz-Lavau, 1985), the left-wing parties were unable to organize a unified and successful political opposition. So the state feminists in the CWW could not push their proposals from the government to the decision agenda until the events of 1968 opened a political policy window.

The instability generated by the uprisings challenged De Gaulle's leadership and the basic tenets of the Gaullist philosophy. After De Gaulle's resignation in 1969, the new president, Georges Pompidou, named Jacques Chaban-Delmas, a Gaullist reformer, prime minister. Chaban-Delmas pursued a controversial programme of social reform ('La Nouvelle Société') which, without explicitly including women's rights, provided a framework for social regulation.

Although the Left failed to win a majority in parliament in 1969, centre-right parties became an important part of the right-wing coalition. As a result, a prominent centrist, Joseph Fontanet, was appointed Minister of Labour in June 1969. The combination of the Nouvelle Société programme and Fontanet's interests in social justice created the opportunity for the state feminists to couple their well-designed proposal for a pay equity bill to the political stream. In 1971, Fontanet upgraded the CWW and named Claude Du Granrut general secretary.[7] Immediately following her appointment, Du Granrut convinced the Labour Minister to present the state feminist equal pay bill to the Council of Ministers before the window snapped shut in July 1972 when the reformist prime minister was forced to resign and Fontanet was moved to another ministry.

Not only was the pay equity bill low on the decision agenda before the government reshuffle in 1971, but the new Minister of Labour, Edgar Faure (a socially conservative Christian Democrat) had little interest in the regulation of employer pay practices to benefit women workers. The impetus for social reform also disappeared with the appointment of an unknown Gaullist hardliner, Pierre Messmer, as prime minister. This conjuncture of political events caused the state feminist version of the equal pay bill to be stripped of its original intent by more powerful interests in state and society in the formulation process before it even reached parliament.

In the original bill pay equality had been defined as the same pay for work of equal value rather than the same pay for the same work. (Trade unions had traditionally pursued equal pay for equal work between the sexes to defend men's jobs from low-paid women's work: Cook, 1985.) Since implementing equal value requires a thorough re-evaluation of the job classification scheme (Ratner, 1980) and, to many French policy-makers at that time this meant the invasion of the sacrosanct sphere of the employer, the final law clouded over the issue by including both terms – equal pay and equal value. Neither did the law stipulate how the government would go about defining equal value. As one state feminist put it, 'the battle over equal value was lost in the formulation process'.

Another lost struggle was the one over the burden of proof. Despite demands from feminist activists in the unions as well as in the CWW, employers' interests were favoured once again in this conflict, with the responsibility of proof left to the defendant.

The centrepiece of the state feminist bill, the creation of an independent authority along the lines of the Equal Opportunity Commissions in the USA and Great Britain, was also axed from the 1972 law. For advocates of pay equity such an office was essential not just to oversee discrimination cases, but also to guide the reassessment of job classification systems, the negotiation of new collective agreements and the definition of future policy efforts in this area. Despite the importance of such a commission, the Direction des Relations de Travail (DRT), the powerful administrative authority of the work inspectorate which enforces the labour code, had shown sustained opposition to the creation of any tripartite commission or ombudsman that would challenge its authority in this domain (interviews with members of the CWW and the DRT).

Once presented to parliament, given that the bill had been denuded of any real regulatory impact, the law was passed in one reading in both houses with no opposition and no amendments. Since the bill did not strictly regulate either management or labour, there was no lobbying effort against the laws. During the short debate, the 'symbolic use of politics' was displayed by both sides. While right-wing senators and deputies, such as Solanges Troisier, congratulated the government on defending the cause of women, Michel Rocard (then a deputy of the Unified Socialist Party – PSU) made a long campaign-like speech on women's rights. The communist and socialist groups tried to restore some of the bill's original authority but a proposal to establish an ombudsman was defeated by the right-wing majority. One socialist deputy, Jacqueline Thome-Patenôtre bitterly accused the National Assembly of adopting a meaningless bill (for National Assembly debates see *Journal Officiel*, 21 November 1972: 5551–70; for the Senate, 13 December 1972: 3057–69).

Promulgated on 22 December, 1972, law no. 72–1143 officially established the principle of equal pay for equal work and work of equal value in the private sector. Henceforth the state would refuse to sign any contracts and collective agreements with clauses that discriminated between men's and women's salaries. Firms which employed women were obliged, under penalty of a fine of up to 1000 francs, to post the text of the law. As part of the Labour code, government work inspectors were empowered to enforce equal pay at company level, but no separate authority was set up to administer the law.

Symbolic Regulation in the Equal Treatment Law of 1975

At the same time as women were becoming a permanent fixture of wage labour even in times of economic crisis (INSEE, 1986), a new model for women as autonomous individuals capable of free choice was slowly replacing the old traditional model of women as mothers (Lévy, 1988: 134). Although the modern model had been advanced by feminists since the end of the nineteenth century and had been the major premiss of the action of the EPP community since the 1950s, it was not until the late 1970s that French society at large began to accept that women's experience could extend beyond the home. Not only had the increase in the number of working women caused this shift in public opinion, but the rise of a youthful third-wave feminist movement in the 1970s put into question traditional family-oriented roles for women. The Paris-centred and radical nature of the fragmented feminist movements (Duchen, 1986; Batiot, 1986) meant that the Mouvement de Libération des Femmes (MLF) did not produce any formal organization that sought to directly change the government agenda of EPP.[8] Nevertheless, the rise of third-wave feminism in the 1970s drew political attention to women's rights at work and the new feminist ideas indirectly influenced individual women in political parties, trade unions and academia who were active in the EPP community. The shift in voting patterns in the second electorate away from conservative parties – for example in the 1974 presidential elections the gap between men and women voters for left-wing candidates dropped from 12 to 7 per cent (Mossuz-Lavau, 1985) – also contributed to the importance of women's rights as a political issue in the mid-1970s.

Valéry Giscard d'Estaing, as leader of a centre-right cadre party, was able to capitalize on these changes. In his campaign speeches for the presidential election in 1974, he supported legalizing abortion and promoting women's rights at work. Winning the election by a mere 1.4 per cent against his socialist opponent, Giscard was under pressure to appeal to more progressive interests in French society. Policy on women's rights became an important symbol for the president's progressivism. To promote this image, he appointed Françoise Giroud, a prominent journalist and known left-wing sympathizer, to a newly created State Secretariat on Women's Status. Unlike the state feminists, Giroud had no expertise and little professional interest in this area. None the less, as a state secretary she had the power to propose legislation in the Council of Ministers. When Giroud was given three slots on the parliamentary agenda for legislation on women's rights at work, she had to depend on a piecemeal understanding of the causes of women's inferior position in labour and an overloaded staff in the preparation of draft legislation.

The 1975 equal treatment bill was the result of a political window that favoured quick action to show that the president was fulfilling his promises on women's rights, but a policy entrepreneur was markedly absent. Instead, the overworked Giroud rushed together a bill proposal to take advantage of the open policy window that in the long run, according to some critics, did more to favour discriminatory practices in employment than to strike them down. The bill sought to regulate discrimination in the hiring and firing of pregnant women rather than general sex discrimination. Neither the CWW nor the normal social partners (labour and management) were consulted in drawing up the proposal. As a consequence, the bill bore no relation to any policy proposals that had been floating in the policy soup. Because of the manner in which the proposal was pushed through the open policy window, the equal treatment bill, flawed from its inception, was rendered virtually meaningless in parliament. Reflecting its low position on the decision agenda, it was the third of three government bills for women workers discussed in the National Assembly in a single late-night, marathon session. (The first two were on women in the Civil Service.) Unsatisfied with the vagueness of the bill, both the communist and socialist groups proposed amendments that would prevent contracts from being broken during the period of pregnancy and for eighteen months afterwards. The right-wing deputies, representing management interests, strongly opposed a law that would dictate employment decisions. A contested vote on the socialist amendment forced the opposition camps to agree on a compromise amendment which introduced the notion of 'legitimate motive', whereby employers would be excused from sanctions if they provided due cause. In the last minutes of the session, using her government prerogative, Giroud successfully introduced an amendment that extended the protected categories to family situation and gender. This action further diluted the bill's coherent authority to regulate gender discrimination. The law was finally passed by both houses two months later with little fanfare (for the National Assembly debates see *Journal Officiel*, 22 April 1975: 1930–43; 16 June 1975: 4246–9; for the Senate see 4 June 1975: 1241–9; 29 June 1975: 2320–1).

Implementation of the 1972 and 1975 Laws

In the absence of an administrative authority charged with implementation, the CWW tried to identify the most blatant cases of discrimination in its monthly newsletter. In one instance, the committee officially denounced the national employment agency (ANPE) for discriminating against women in its own job listings. Yet without funding or authority and overloaded with concerns for other policy areas, the CWW was unable to enforce effectively either pay equity or equal treatment. In 1976 the Minister of Labour, Michel Durafour, requested the CWW to report on the implementation of the 1972 law. The highly critical report asserted that the state's role had been insufficient in enforcing the law. For example, departmental work inspectors had only handled twenty cases, in only half of which action was either pursued in a court or in the firm.[9] The report also underlined the problem of measuring 'equal work'. The biases of a corps of work inspectors which was predominantly male was certainly influential in the low success rate of the actual cases pursued (CWW, 1976: 7–10). No similar report was commissioned for the 1975 law.

Another problem related to enforcement was the conservative nature of the French court system (which is still a problem today). In an analysis of eighteen discrimination cases brought before the courts from 1973 to 1981, Colette de Marguerye (1983), a court lawyer, maintained that the judges' attitudes tended to favour the freedom of choice of the employer over the individual right of women to equal pay and treatment. In many cases, if a lower court decided in favour of the plaintiff, employers would appeal to a higher court; in all of these cases the lower court decision was overturned. De Marguerye also claimed that at the top of the judicial hierarchy, conservative gender bias underscored many decisions against solid discrimination cases. The nature of the legal system in France must also be factored into an explanation of the dearth of cases. Not only is judicial review a recent practice in French law, but class action suits are rare (Katz, 1986). Both legal procedures are central to the successful enforcement of laws which target direct discrimination.

In addition to the failure of these laws to 'transform the capacities of the state', they did not 'affect the social identities, goals and capabilities' of interest groups and organizations in society (Skocpol, 1988: 22). Unions rarely encouraged women to lodge complaints against employers. In interviews, many younger trade union activists in the CFDT, CGT, CFTC and CGT-FO said that they had not heard of the 1975 law. The fading traditional women's associations (CNPF, CILAF, UFF and UFCS) neglected to inform the public about the new rights for women workers, and no new feminist legal aid societies or watchdog organizations emerged. In 1979 Gisèle Halimi, feminist lawyer and president of Choisir,[10] lost the only equal treatment case she ever defended, partly because the judge invoked the legitimate motive clause. When asked recently why pay equity and equal treatment never became feminist causes in the 1970s in France, Halimi replied, 'One cannot write a book about a lost battle.'

Symbolic Redistribution in the 1983 Law
In the late 1970s and early 1980s a new generation of feminist-influenced labour sociologists produced a multitude of studies that showed the permanence or 'l'irreversabilité' of female labour and the gendered nature of the two-tiered labour force (for example Huet, 1982; Bouillaguet-Bernard *et al.*, 1981). Following the lead of these feminist experts, other members of the EPP policy community turned their attention to the mechanisms of indirect discrimination and occupational segregation. The State Secretary of Women's Employment (Baudoin, 1979) and the women's sections of the Parti Socialiste (PS, 1980) and the CFDT (CFDT, 1979) all maintained that whereas outright acts of discrimination were made illegal by the 1972 and 1975 laws, inequities still existed in fact. Therefore, a new policy was necessary to address the more complex causes of discrimination in the structure of the labour force.

Solutions to the problem of occupational segregation had been circulating in the EPP policy community since the publication of the Guilbert report in 1969 (see p. 125), but the use of quotas was firmly rejected by the state feminists (CWW, 1979), the tripartite Baudoin Report (1979) and the Constitutional Council[11] on the grounds that the potential to discriminate against women, (by setting a ceiling that could be eventually surpassed) as well as against men (by automatically excluding men from certain positions) outweighed the benefits of a quota system. Instead, solutions in the policy proposal stream revolved around different versions of *égalité professionnelle*. Gender discrimination would be attacked at company level through work committees (*comités d'entreprise*) monitoring employer efforts to promote women within the enterprise. The key to *égalité professionnelle* would be the analysis of the sources of gender inequities in each firm. Preferential training and hiring programmes could then be designed to deal with each firm's particular problem. *Egalité professionnelle* provided a framework in which gender discrimination could be addressed through redistribution of job and training opportunities from men to women.

With the rise of a strong Socialist Party and the looming 1981 presidential elections, the centre-right government was under a great deal of pressure to appeal to an electorate increasingly interested in social change. Furthermore, middle-class, well-educated women under the age of twenty-five were voting for left-wing candidates as much as, if not more than, their male counterparts (Mossuz-Lavau and Sineau, 1983). It was in this politically charged atmosphere that the State Secretary of Women's Employment, Nicole Pasquier, who was close to prime minister Raymond Barre, coupled the problem definition and proposal streams to politics in 1980. Following the recommendations of the Baudoin report, Pasquier's office drafted an *égalité professionnelle* law which was approved in the Council of Ministers; however, the election of François Mitterrand in May 1981 to the presidency and the dissolution of the National Assembly prevented the bill from making it to parliament. (Several critics in the EPP policy community suggested in interviews that the bill would not have been approved by the Council of Ministers if there had been any possibility of it ever reaching parliament.)

Not only had Mitterrand been the first politican to come out in favour of the legalization of abortion in 1965 (*Nouvel Observateur*, 17 November 1965), but he had understood early on the importance of incorporating women's rights at work into his campaign platform. Although the women's section of the Socialist Party (PS) had to struggle to get official party recognition, PS feminists, under the leadership of Yvette Roudy, obtained the inclusion of measures on women's rights in the party platform (PS, 1978). In the run-up to the 1981 elections, Mitterrand attended a presidential debate sponsored by Choisir, which no other candidate attended, and received the endorsement of Psych et Po, a major group in the radical feminist movement.

Fulfilling his campaign promises, Mitterrand appointed Yvette Roudy Junior Minister for the Rights of Woman.[12] In addition to having a seat on the Council of Ministers, the office had a much larger budget than gender-specific offices of the past. In the flurry of reforms placed on the overloaded parliamentary agenda, two slots were given to the ministry. A political window was clearly open for Roudy to use her new powers as well as her expertise as a PS feminist to get an EPP bill proposal on the decision agenda. Roudy took as a starting point a bill drafted for a PS-sponsored conference on women's employment (PS, 1980). Compared to the manner in which proposals for EPP had been brought through open policy windows in the past, decision agenda placement for the 1983 law seemed quite favourable; however, as the formulation process unfolded in the following two years of government and sectoral consultation it became clear that the Roudy bill actually had very low decision agenda status.

The historic rise of the Left to power produced not only a staggering number of bill proposals, but an entire cluster of laws, the Auroux Laws, related to workplace reform preceded formulation of the EPP legislation. (The Roudy bill was actually meant to complement the laws. To this end, many articles had a similar company-level approach.) Involving the same complex sectoral and ministerial consultation, the Auroux laws first monopolized the attention of the social partners, then taxed the patience of parliamentarians. When Roudy's turn came several months later the mainstream policy-makers and social partners were not just bored with the topics, but many felt the government's efforts were being replicated (interviews with Roudy's personal staff). For example, both the Auroux laws and the Roudy bill asked that an annual report on working conditions be presented to work committees. (In the Roudy law the report was to be gender specific.)

Internal documents on the formulation of the bill showing the major changes effected to the original bill demonstrate the low commitment to *égalité professionnelle* inside and outside the government. While the Minister of Finance slashed the original budget of the bill by half, the Minister of Labour refused to grant enforcement powers to the body that would be in charge of overseeing the law. As in the past, the DRT did not want to be policed by an outside authority. Moreover, the Minister of Justice voiced doubts over some of the innovations in legal procedure, pointing out that many judges would resist the more unorthodox propositions.

Trade unions and employers also had problems with the original bill. While the CNPF (the major employers' association) objected to the degree of responsibility placed on the employer, the CGT (the communist-affiliated working-class trade union) opposed a clause that would wipe out all articles in the Labour code that specifically protected women workers. (The traditional CGT position had been that protection should be extended to men rather than taken away from women.) The CGT and the CFDT (the other main working-class trade union) further opposed an article in the original bill which gave feminist groups the right to defend discrimination cases. While employer grievances were glossed over, trade union demands were met. Even though feminist groups organized a letter-writing campaign to get the clause on feminist representation reinserted, the unions won because in this particular policy game trade union interests outweighed feminist interests.

With an absolute left-wing majority composed of communist and socialist deputies in the National Assembly, the bill was approved in a first reading in the lower house. Only ten deputies were present for the debate (*Libération*, 12 June 1982). Efforts by the minority right-wing deputies to propose an amendment that would reduce employer responsibility in analysing the situation of women in the firm were blocked. The Senate, representing employer interests, also tried to introduce curtailing amendments that would reduce the impact of the law. Along with the provision of a state subsidy for the equality plans, the Senate objected to the obligation of the employer to make an annual report. Senators from the opposition managed to prolong debate on these amendments through a series of tactics used frequently by the right-wing opposition to undermine socialist reforms. These efforts, however, did not succeed; after four readings in each house and a joint commission review, the *égalité professionnelle* law was adopted. (For the National Assembly see *Journal Officiel*, 6 December 1982: 7978–8019; 13 June 1983: 2460–8; 27 June 1983: 3252–5; 30 June 1983: 2390–2; for the Senate see 11 May 1983: 805–17; 21 June 1983: 1809–18; 26 June 1983: 2066–71).

The final law (no. 83–635, 13 July 1983) reflected at the same time an effort to address past weaknesses of EPP and the compromises of the formulation process. With regard to individual discrimination cases, the burden of proof was shifted to the employer. A more sophisticated definition of equal work was elaborated, including the idea of equal worth. Unions, but not feminist associations, were given the right to defend such cases. The legitimate motive clause from the 1975 law was eliminated from the Labour code. If an employer was brought before a court for an offence, the judge could allow the employer to present specific measures which would address the causes of the discrimination instead of invoking the normal penalties (a fine of up to 20,000 francs or two months in prison). Henceforth collective agreements were not to include any protectionist clauses (Article 19), but the stipulation was not retrospective.

Firms were obliged to prepare an annual report comparing the situation of women to that of men in the workplace, which was to be presented to the work committees.[13] From the annual report firms could formulate a programme of professional training and preferential hiring for women employees. These *plans d'égalité* would be negotiated and signed by management and union representatives from the firms. If approved, the government would fund 50 per cent of the cost of each plan (decree no. 84–136, 22 February 1984). A tripartite advisory body, Conseil Supérieur de l'Egalité Professionnelle (CSEP), attached to the Ministries of Labour, Professional Training and Rights of Woman would participate in the definition and the application of public policy in this area. Rather than having any real enforcement power, the council's role was limited to consultation and discussion. The overall tone of the law was highly voluntaristic. As one administrator told me, 'the state cannot decree *égalité professionnelle'*.

A multi-media promotional campaign launched by the Women's Ministry in 1984 gave an energetic start to EPP; two years later, the resistance expressed by important institutional actors and social partners in formulation began to surface in implementation. A study conducted for the ministry in 1985 showed that the annual reports tended to be incomplete and poorly updated (CREDOC, 1986). The incomplete reports were often either ignored or summarily discussed in work committees (Laufer, 1984; Alezra *et al.*, 1987). Indeed, it became clear that, without incentives or penalties, management and union representatives were not devoting the time necessary to analyse the position of women in their firms. The *plans d'égalité,* also dependent on the analysis of the annual reports, were far less successful than originally expected. In 1985, according to a source close to the minister at the time, Yvette Roudy had predicted that 300 plans would have been signed by 1986. As of June 1989, only 20 plans had been completed with only half of those receiving a government subsidy (GRAF, 1989). Much more complicated than expected, the negotiations necessary to draw up a training programme took as long as two years (interviews with CFDT representatives). After the initial campaign, many firms were not aware of the possibility of financing. Several of the subsidized plans were used to restructure the organization of firms, further showing the lack of interest in goals of gender equality.

With regard to policy feedback, without any administrative authority the CSEP has become a forum for discussion rather than incentive; symbolic gestures rather than concrete action. Behind the CSEP, it is the Mission pour l'Egalité Professionnelle (MEP), attached to the office charged with gender-specific policy, which in reality guides state intervention. The MEP not only controls the agenda of the CSEP, it also formulates all of the collective opinions and makes the final decision on equality plan funding. Staff cutbacks in all unions, due to the crisis in union membership, have meant that union delegates are generally overloaded with committee responsibilities. Union representatives on the CSEP consequently have tended to be apathetic about the work of the commission (interviews with staff members of the MEP). In 1984 the Women's Ministry placed pressure on the DRT to sensitize work inspectors to the law. In addition to an administrative circular (MDF/DRT, no. 4, 2 May 1984) which gave orders to all departmental directors to be aware of instances of gender discrimination, a member of Roudy's cabinet worked closely with the DRT on enforcement. As a part of this effort, *égalité professionnelle* correspondents were placed at department level to work with labour inspectors. These efforts were brought to a standstill by the change in government majority following the legislative elections in March 1986, and even beforehand their impact on administration had been limited. For instance the national school for the work inspectorate never provided specific training on enforcement of the Roudy law (interviews with work inspectors).

Under 'cohabitation' from 1986 to 1988, Jacques Chirac reduced the women's ministry to a Delegation on Women's Status attached to the Ministry of Social Affairs. Although the administrative services of the Women's Ministry remained intact, the new delegate, Hélène Gisserot (a magistrate and higher-level administrator with no party affiliation) lacked the political capital or governmental authority of her predecessor. Despite efforts by Gisserot to continue *égalité professionnelle* programmes, EPP was by no means a priority of the Chirac government. From 1986 to 1988 the CSEP only met once and general budget cuts reduced the agency's staff to two. As members of the agency asserted, without a strong voice from the government, social actors are even more reluctant to participate in the voluntary *égalité professionnelle* measures.

Since the re-election of François Mitterrand to the presidency and a return to a socialist government under Michel Rocard in 1988, EPP has not received renewed attention. A new State Secretary of Women's Rights, Andrée Michel, responsible in title for gender-specific policy, in reality has done little to promote women's rights at work. Instead a handful of academics and policy advocates sprinkled in administration struggle to draw attention to the merits of *égalité professionnelle*. A recent conference jointly sponsored by the State Secretary and the National Business School (HEC) in March 1989 invited firms to a day-long information session and discussion of the *plans d'égalité*. Most of the firms which participated were more interested in the plans to restructure their workforce than in promoting gender equality. A 1988 European Court decision sanctioning France for violating a 1977 employment equality directive was still officially unanswered as of June 1989. Finally, no feminist organizations have taken up the cause of *égalité professionnelle*. Staff of the MEP as well as experts who have closely followed this policy all express their disappointment in the outcome. With no policy feedback in state and society, *égalité professionnelle* remains relegated to symbolic policy.

Conclusion

In France, although state feminists in gender-specific offices have brought a certain degree of governmental attention to *égalité professionnelle* in the agenda-setting process, it appears that the marginalization of these offices from mainstream policy formulation channels means that policy remains unsynchronized with adjacent policy efforts. For instance, at the same time that the Women's Ministry was attempting to implement *égalité professionnelle*, the Ministry of Labour was promoting part-time work as a solution to high unemployment and the Ministry of the Family increased family allowances for larger families. Both efforts, wtihout gender equality in employment, narrow women's choices about work and family. Indeed, this conflict between gender-specific policy and other policy areas accentuates the unorganized and anarchic nature of the French policy system.

Linking the outcome of the agenda process to policy outcome indicates a recipe for symbolic policy. When a policy proposal comes out at the bottom of the decision agenda, it will get short shrift in the formulation process and will not provoke significant policy feedback. As the French case shows, there are different explanations for why problem recognition, policy proposition and politics are not effectively bundled together. While in 1971 the state feminist proposal received low agenda status because the policy entrepreneur wielded little authority over the government in power, in 1975 an ineffective equal treatment bill was put forward because the policy entrepreneur had little expertise in the policy area. In 1982, even though the policy entrepreneur had expertise and power, more powerful interests inside and outside government diminished the bill's importance in the wider scheme of social reform. Symbolic policy, at least in France, has an important role of drawing political attention to an issue that normally would not gain decision agenda status; however, the outcome of such policy can only be incremental at best.

Notes

My thanks go especially to Elizabeth Meehan, Selma Sevenhuijsen, Joyce Outshoorn and Andrew Appleton.

1. According to Ratner (1980), equal employment policy means any policy (legislation, decree, programme, etc.) which targets direct or indirect discrimination based on gender, race, religion or age in hiring, firing, professional training and promotion.

2. *Egalité professionnelle* uniquely focuses on women workers in large part due to

the absence (until recently) of a significant minority citizen population, hence any significant demands for minority rights at work.

3. In France, *égalité professionnelle* did not become the general term for equal employment policy until after the adoption of the 1983 law. Before that *égalité professionnelle* referred to the particular redistributive approach incorporated into that law. This chapter will use the abbreviation for *égalité professionnelle* policy – EPP – to refer to the general policy area, and the complete term – *égalité professionnelle* – to refer to the specific redistributive approach.

4. The research for this chapter comes out of twelve months of field work in France, from 1988 to 1989, for a doctoral dissertation in Politics and French Studies at New York University. I conducted 60 open-ended interviews with policy actors involved with EPP in administration, government, parliament, women's associations, feminist movements, trade unions, employer unions, political parties and the academic community. Although the names of the interviewees cited have not been included, they are available on request. I also consulted personal archives, ministerial files, trade union and interest group documentation, parliamentary papers and press articles.

5. Inspired by certain aspects of rational decision-making, incrementalism (Lindblom, 1959) and Cohen, March and Olsen's garbage can theory (1972), this model captures the contradiction between the randomness and predictability inherent in the policy process in Western industrialized polities.

6. A government agenda is the list of items that receives serious government attention and the decision agenda is a sub-list of items from the government agenda which can be decided upon for future enactment (Kingdon, 1984: 3–4).

7. Du Granrut was not only a member of the same party as Fontanet, but, prior to her appointment, she had worked for him on education policy and thus had the clout necessary to successfully take advantage of the open policy window.

8. Within the MLF there was one group which attempted to organize working women at a grass-roots level, the Marxist Luttes de Classes, but this group was more interested in consciousness-raising among workers than changing company-level policy (*Rouge*, 13 June). Women's groups at the grass-roots level affiliated with the CFDT also organized women workers. But again, protest and reflection, rather than provoking policy change, were their primary goals (Maruani, 1979).

9. In the UK, in 1976 and 1977, industrial tribunals had heard 2493 claims and 472 equal treatment claims (Mazey, 1988: 70).

10. A reformed-oriented feminist group, Choisir was founded by Halimi to promote the legalization of abortion. After the abortion laws were passed Choisir's efforts to go beyond its single-issue orientation failed.

11. A landmark Constitutional Council decision in November 1982 struck down a law that had stipulated that only 75 per cent of municipal election lists could be of the same sex.

12. While feminists in the MLF pressed the ministry to use the term 'women's rights', the socialist government favoured 'rights of woman' after the French term for human rights – *droits de l'homme*. The feminists argued that whereas 'rights of woman' implied some distant vision of womanhood, 'women's rights' represented women as a collective. In the end, the socialists won this struggle over political meaning. Ironically, the title of the ministry changed to 'women's rights' in 1986 under the Rocard government after the office was demoted.

13. In the first year of implementation, only those companies with 300 or more employees had to present the report. The following year firms with 50 or more employees were obliged to participate.

Abbreviations

ANPE	Agence Nationale Pour l'Emploi
APSA	American Political Science Association
CFDT	Confédération Française Démocratique du Travail
CFTC	Confédération Française des Travailleurs Chrétiens
CGT	Confédération Générale du Travail
CGT-FO	Confédération Générale du Travail-Force Ouvrière
CILAF	Conseil International de Liaison des Associations Féminines
CNPF	Conseil National du Patronat Français
CREDOC	Centre de Recherche pour l'Etude de l'Observation des Conditions de Vie
CSEP	Conseil Supérieur de l'Egalité Professionnelle
CWW	Committee on Women's Work
DRT	Direction des Relations de Travail
EEP	Equal Employment Policy
EPP	Egalité Professionnelle Policy
GRAF	Groupe de Recherche sur l'Activité des Femmes
HEC	Haute Ecole de Commerce
INSEE	Institut National de la Statistique et des Etudes Economiques
MEP	Mission pour l'Egalité Professionnelle
MLF	Mouvement de Libération des Femmes
PS	Parti Socialiste
PSU	Parti Socialiste Unifié
UFCS	Union des Femmes Civiques et Sociales
UFF	Union des Femmes Françaises

References

Alezra, Claudine, Laufer, Jacqueline, Maruani, Margaret and Sutter, Claire (eds) (1987) 'La Mixité du travail. Une Stratégie pour l'entreprise'. *Cahier Entreprises*, 3 (June).

APSA (1987) 'Paradigm problems and new directions in comparative public policy'. Round table at APSA meeting, 3–6 September, Chicago, Illinois.

Batiot, Anne (1986) 'Radical democracy and feminist discourse: the case of France', pp. 85–102 in D. Dahlerup (ed.), *The New Women's Movement*. London: Sage.

Baudoin, Jacques (ed.) (1979) *Les Discriminations et les disparités du travail féminin*. Paris: Documentation Française.

Bodiguel, Jean-Luc and Quermonne, Jean-Louis (1983) *La Haute fonction publique sous la cinquième république*. Paris: PUF.

Bouillaguet-Bernard, Patricia, Gauvin-Ayel, Annie and Outin, Jean-Luc (1981) *Femmes au travail prosperité et crise*. Paris: Editions Economica.

CFDT (1979) *Conférence: Travail des Femmes et Action Syndicale*. Reports and speeches published by the Confederation.

Cohen, Michael, March, James and Olsen, Johan (1972) 'A garbage can model of organizational choice', *Administrative Science Quarterly,* 17 (March): 1–25.

Cook, Alice (1984) 'Introduction', pp. 3–36, in A.H. Cook, V.R. Lorwin and A. Kaplan Daniels (eds), *Women and Trade Unions in Eleven Industrialized Countries.* Philadelphia: Temple University Press.

CREDOC (1986) *Evolution 1984–1985 des rapports sur la situation Comparée des hommes et des femmes dans l'entreprise.* February.

Crozier, Michel (1970) *La Société Bloquée.* Paris: Seuil.

CWW (1976) 'Bilan de l'Application de la loi sur l'égalité de rémunération entre hommes et femmes'. Report to the Minister of Labour, January.

CWW (1979) *l'Avis sur la Question des Quotas.* Report to the Minister of Labour.

de Marguerye, Colette (1983) 'Les Juges français et la discrimination sexuelle', *Droit Social,* 2 (February): 119–30.

Duchen, Claire (1986) *Feminism in France from May 1968 to Mitterrand.* London: Routledge & Kegan Paul.

Edelman, Murray (1965) *The Symbolic Uses of Politics.* Urbana, IL: University of Illinois Press.

GRAF (1989) *Les Plans d'Egalité Professionnelle. Etude-Bilan. 1983–1988.* Paris.

Guilbert, Madeleine (1971) *Les Disparites entre salaires masculines et féminines.* Report of the Sub-Commission on Employment Conditions of the CWW.

Hancock, Donald, M. (1983) 'Comparative public policy: an assessment', pp. 283–308 in A. Finifter (ed.), *Political Science: The State of the Discipline.* Washington DC: APSA.

Huet, Marguerite (1982) 'La Progression de l'activité féminine est-elle irreversible?', *Economie et Statistiques,* 145 (June): 3–17.

INSEE (1986) *Femmes en Chiffres.* Paris: La Documentation, Française.

Jenson, Jane (1984) 'The "problem" of women', in M. Kesselman (ed.), *The French Workers Movement.* London: Allen & Unwin.

Katz, Alan N. (1986) 'France', pp. 105–24 in A.N. Katz (ed.), *Legal Traditions and Systems: An International Handbook.* Westport, CT: Greenwood Press.

Kingdon, John W. (1984) *Agendas, Alternatives and Public Policies.* Boston, MA: Little, Brown.

Laufer, Jacqueline (1984) 'Egalité Professionnelle. Principes et pratiques', *Droit Social,* 12: 736–46.

Lévy, Martine. 1988. *Le Féminisme d'Etat en France. 1965–1985: 20 ans de prise en charge institutionells de l'égalité professionnelle entre hommes et femmes.* Doctoral dissertation presented at the Institute for Political Studies, Paris.

Lindblom, Charles E. (1959) 'The science of muddling through', *Public Administration Review,* 14 (Spring): 79–88.

Maruani, Margaret (1979) *Les Syndicats à l'Epreuve du Féminisme.* Paris: Syros.

Mazey, Sonia (1988) 'European Community action and women', *Journal of Common Market Studies,* 1 (September): 64–84.

Meehan, Elizabeth (1985) *Women's Rights at Work: Campaigns and Policy in Britain and the United States.* New York: St Martin's Press.

Mossuz-Lavau, Janine (1985) 'Le Vote des femmes en France (1944–1984)', pp. 209–21 in D. Gaxie (ed.), *Explication du vote: un Bilan des études électorales en France.* Paris: Presses de la FNSP.

Mossuz-Lavau, Janine and Sineau, Mariette (1983) *Enquête sur les femmes et la politique en France.* Paris: Presses de la FNSP.

Nielsen, Ruth (1983) *Equality Legislation in a Comparative Perspective, Towards*

State Feminism. Copenhagen: Women's Research Center in Social Science.

PS (1978) 'Manifeste du PS sur les droits des femmes', *Le Poing et la Rose*, supplement to 68 (February).

PS (1980) *Actes du colloque du Pré St. Gervais*, 18–19 October.

Ratner, Ronnie Steinberg (1980) 'The policy and problem: overview of seven countries', pp. 1–52 in Steinberg Ratner (ed.), *Equal Employment Policy for Women*. Philadelphia: Temple.

Rueff-Armand (1960) *Les obstacles à l'expansion*. Report prepared for the Fourth Plan (government plan which sets general objectives for the French economy). Paris: La Documentation Française.

Ruggie, Mary (1984) *The State and Working Women*. Princeton, NJ: Princeton University Press.

Schain, Martin (1988) 'Book review of Meny's *Politique Comparée, French Politics and Society,* 6: 64–6.

Schattschneider, E.E. (1975) *The Semi-Sovereign People*. Hinsdale, IL: Dryden Press.

Skocpol, Theda (1988) 'Comparing national systems of social provision: a polity centred approach'. Paper presented at APSA Meeting, 1–4 September, Washington DC.

Suleiman, Ezra, N. (1987) *Private Power and Centralization in France: The Notaries and the State*. Princeton, NJ: Princeton University Press.

Thoenig, Jean-Claude and Dupuy, François (1985) *L'Administration en miettes*. Paris: Fayard.

9

Equality or Marginalization:
The Repeal of Protective Legislation

Jennifer Jarman

This chapter examines the use of Britain's equal opportunities legislation as a justification for repealing some sections of the 'protective' legislation which had been on the statute books. It is fairly routine to make minor revisions to other statutes to remove contradictory or overlapping provisions after the enactment of a new piece of legislation. But the implications of the Equal Pay Act and the Sex Discrimination Act for the existing protective legislation were quite substantial. Two very different sets of conceptions with respect to women workers had to be reconciled. The first is that female workers are intrinsically 'different' from male workers and that this difference necessitates separate legislative provisions for the two genders. The second conception is that female workers are intrinsically similar to male workers and so legislative provisions should treat the two genders in the same way. This chapter elaborates on these two conceptions of male and female worker. It then links each conception to a particular historical approach to employment policy for women. It explores the way in which protective legislation constructs the woman worker as 'different' and the way in which equal opportunities legislation constructs the woman worker as 'equal' to a man.

These two conceptions came up for discussion when the Equal Opportunities Commission undertook to review Britain's existing protective legislation and make recommendations about its repeal, in accordance with the European Community Directive of 9 February 1976. On the face of it, this would seem an obvious step towards treating women in a way more in keeping with 'progressive' views about their capabilities. If one considers the repeal in terms of the employment trends and policies of the late 1970s and 1980s, however, a more negative interpretation emerges. This chapter concludes with an assessment of the outcome of this particular conflict between principles of 'difference' and 'equality' for the situation of men and women workers and its consequences for future strategy on women's employment policy.

Protective Legislation and Difference

The Health and Safety of Apprentices Act (1802) was the first piece of protective legislation passed in Britain. Over the next thirty years a series of measures was legislated with respect to employment practices utilizing the labour of children. State intervention to police women's employment conditions was first raised by Michael Sadler in 1832. His arguments are discussed here because they came to be widely supported and repeated by middle-class reformers. Sadler recommended that protection should be extended from children and young persons to include women for three reasons: 'the differential physical ability of women to endure factory labour; the effect of this on child-bearing ability; and the morality of factory women' (Mockett, 1988: 2).

One of the assumptions behind the advocacy of protective legislation was that women were physically weaker (as opposed to equal to or stronger) than men. While this assumption was not strongly contested in the nineteenth century, its validity has been debated at length in recent years (see Barrett, 1980). A second concern about the effect of employment on child-bearing ability emerges from a more general nineteenth-century concern about the health of the working class and in particular high mortality rates of young children. It was argued that factory work for women had a negative impact on working-class health in several ways. First, pregnancies were more dangerous because factory women were not getting adequate care and rest. Secondly, young children were neglected or left in the care of unsuitable or irresponsible child-minders. Thirdly, general health and sanitary conditions in the home were lowered because working women did not have time to maintain them. These problems were real. But the 'solution' marginalized women. 'Protection' of women took the form of limiting their labour force participation with the supposed aim of increasing the general health of the working class.

A third concern, about the morality of factory women, is more difficult to interpret. The 1842 Children's Employment Commission (which also investigated working conditions for women below ground in coal mines) contains allegations that working women were more promiscuous than their house-bound counterparts. Humphries suggests that one possible reason for middle-class reformers' concern about working-class morality was an attempt to enforce broad social standards of sexual fidelity of women to their husbands. Sexual faithfulness of middle-class women ensured a more simple inheritance process as husbands could be certain that they were in fact the fathers of their own children. While this might not have had much relevance for miners and their children, the argument goes that these middle-class preoccupations were imposed on the working class. Humphries also suggests that at this time there may have been concern about the maintenance of the family as an institution in order to ensure the reproduction of the working class (Humphries, 1981: 26). While the latter explanation is somewhat functionalist, there can be no doubt that issues of morality were influential in the discussions around protective legislation.

The fact that it was a man, Sadler, who first proposed protective legislation for women reflected the political reality that women were not as organized as men either in terms of trade unions or in broader politics. The participants in the debate were primarily male reformers, male legislators, male government officials and male trade unionists. The involvement of these men fitted with nineteenth-century notions that an appropriate male role was the chivalrous one of male protector of women (Davidoff and Hall, 1987).

How working women felt about the prospect of being 'protected' is difficult to determine given that they were not members of parliament, Royal Commission members or prominent elsewhere in the public debate. The position of working-class men is clearer in the historical record. Male trade unionists saw that women workers depressed men's wages both by competing with men for jobs and by being forced to accept lower wages on the grounds that women needed less money. The male trade unionists often lobbied to get women out of their occupations and places of employment (see Lewenhak, 1977). While there were male trade unionists who did *not* seek to exclude women, this was not a widespread attitude.

That there were splits in the interests between men and women has been contested by Jane Humphries (1981). She views developments such as the family wage as 'the (imperfectly realized) historically specific goal of working-class men and women struggling in a hostile environment for a better life' (Humphries, 1981: 4). This 'fight from behind women's petticoats' view relies on the existence of factories in which there were processes which were interdependent on male and female labour. Thus restrictions on women's hours would mean restrictions on men's hours at the same time.

Opposition to protective legislation came primarily from capitalists. They were concerned about the lower productivity that would result, the effect of this on Britain's ability to compete internationally, and the reduction in the value of fixed capital as a result of not being able to keep equipment running as long (Mockett, 1988: 8). Nevertheless, their opposition was insufficient to prevent a number of Acts of protective legislation from being placed on the statute book from the 1802 Act onwards.

By 1961, the legacy of the lobby for protective legislation was a series of Acts which governed hours of work (1936), working conditions (1961), the prohibition on children working in factories (1936), the prohibition on women working in certain occupations particularly in underground mines (1954), and the existence of Sunday work provisions (1961). (Some of these restrictive practices had been introduced much earlier and merely updated in the years specified.)

To reiterate, protective legislation rested on a view of workers as inherently differentiated on the basis of gender. It assumed that all women workers were mothers and wives, and that these roles were more important than their role as workers. It did not emphasize the financial *return* of jobs as being particularly important, as it was expected that women would be receiving support from elsewhere. In the nineteenth century, legislation was developed without much participation by women. In the twentieth century there was more participation. However women's needs, particularly the need for financial independence, were not uppermost in the minds of the policy-makers.

Equal Pay Legislation and the Concept of Equality

Although a demand for legislation to enforce at least equal *pay* practices can be traced back to the nineteenth century, equal opportunities legislation has only received widespread support since the Second World War. 'Equal pay for equal work' became policy for the Civil Service in 1955. The first large-scale application of equal opportunities policies occured in 1970, when the Equal Pay Act 1970 was passed, covering both the public and private sector. Further legislation covering discrimination in employment, education, housing and provision of goods and services became enforceable in the Sex Discrimination Act 1975.

Unlike the case of protective legislation, women themselves first demanded equal pay legislation. The earliest documented case of this was in 1833, when a group of female power-loom weavers went on strike for equal pay with male workers (Lewenhak, 1977: 31). In more recent times, the lobby that culminated in the first large equal pay policy was headed by two women Conservative Members of Parliament (Meehan, 1985: 43). The passage of the Equal Pay Act 1970 has been partly attributed to the work of the Secretary of State for Labour, Barbara Castle (Meehan, 1985: 54). Equal opportunities legislation was supported by women's interest groups which were concerned with the inability of women to compete in the market-place on the same basis as men. The argument was pre-

sented as an issue of justice for women, and also as an issue of the
economic ability of women as individuals to support themselves in
the labour market, thus decreasing their marginality in society.

The passage of these Acts signalled that the underlying assumptions about workers which influenced public policy in the period of
the passage of protective legislation had changed dramatically: 'The
Government's general view is that much of the legislation protective
of women at work had its origin in the view that women were
"particularly vulnerable and unable to protect their own interests"'
(*Equal Opportunities Review*, 1988: 32).

The intent of these Acts was predicated on very different notions
of the role and capabilities of men and women from those underlying protective legislation. Women's physical abilities were
assumed equal unless shown otherwise, or at least of lesser concern
in an economy which had increasingly shifted towards the provision
of white-collar jobs. Women's health and the health of working-
class families and children were no longer a concern in the way that
they had been in the nineteenth century. Family responsibilities
were no longer seen as being threatened by the existence of a
working wife or mother, and so for the purposes of employment
legislation, the woman's family role was no longer seen as relevant.

Equal opportunities legislation, at least at the level of rhetoric,
reflected a concern for the economic status of women. This concern
was entirely lacking or at least relegated to a minor role in discussions of a protective legislation. When Barbara Castle introduced
the Equal Pay Act into the House in 1969, she stated as its purpose:
'to make equal pay for equal work a reality, and, in so doing to take
women workers progressively out of the sweated labour class'
(House of Commons, 1970). Her intention was to remove (or reduce) the marginality of women.

The general principle of equal opportunities legislation is that
male and female workers should be treated on the same basis in the
workforce. If men and women do the same work, they should be
paid equally. If men and women apply for the same jobs, the one
with the set of individual worker characteristics closest to the adver-
tised job description should get the job, and so on. The ideology of
the 'family wage' should not be upheld – male or female, workers'
family roles should not bear upon the employment relationship.

In order to establish that employers are making non-sexist decisions about workers, equal opportunities legislation resorts to
measuring individuals on the basis of their 'human capital' characteristics, and in this way imposes judgements about what sorts of
characteristics are acceptable for an employer to make wage payments. Under the terms of the British Equal Pay Act these charac-

teristics include 'effort, skill, and decision'. One difference between the post-Second World War and the pre-war situations is that women were more fully integrated after 1945 into the policy process – in trade unions, women's interest groups and to a limited but still important extent in parliament. A second difference in the later period is that equal opportunities legislation is based on a broader conception of women's social role. It is no longer assumed that all women are wives and mothers and that this role impinges in a major way on their ability to work formally.

The 1970s Review of the Protective Legislation Provisions

In 1975 the Equal Opportunities Commission and the Health and Safety Commission was given the duty to review provisions of the Health and Safety at Work Act 1974, in which men and women were being treated differently, and to make recommendations about whether or not these were inconsistent with the new Equal Pay Act 1970 and the Sex Discrimination Act 1975. The main motivation for this action was the EEC Directive of 9 February 1976 which specified that protective legislation contrary to the principle of equal treatment must be reviewed by February 1980.

But a second motivation was present. The government also reviewed this legislation as a result of pressure from business interest groups such as the Confederation of British Industries. The Confederation of Business Industries had in fact lent its support to the passage of the Equal Pay Act 1970 on the condition that Section 6 of the Factory Act 1961 be rescinded as contravening the principle of equality for men and women workers.

The review covered three pieces of protective legislation: the Factory Act 1961 Part Six, the Hours of Employment (Conventions) Act 1936 and the Mines and Quarries Act 1954. Section 86 of the Factory Act restricted women's daily working hours to nine, and weekly hours to forty-eight. It specified that women (but not men) must be given half-hour breaks after every four and a half hours worked. There was a prohibition on nightwork by women: women were not to start work before 7 a.m. or finish after 8 p.m. In this way women's participation in rotating shift systems was also prevented. Section 93 of the Factory Act prevented women from working on Sundays. In Sections 88 and 89, women's overtime was restricted to not more than six hours a week, or one hundred hours in any calendar year.

There were numerous exceptions to these provisions in certain industries, occupations, religious affiliations of the firm owner and employee and so on. The provisions of the Factory Act 1961 did not cover 'service' jobs, nurses, office workers, waitresses, cooks, bus conductors and shop assistants or cleaners in factories, women managers or supervisors. At the time of the 1979 review, however, it was estimated that it probably did apply directly to 1.3 million women, or 17 per cent of the entire female workforce.

One of the major findings of the commission was that employers could use these protective legislation provisions to discriminate against women workers. Employers could refuse to hire women because they would not be able to do nightwork, even though exemption orders could easily be obtained. Similarly they might refuse to promote women to supervisory or management positions because the women had not had the experience of working on night shifts. The Employment Appeal Tribunal decision *Young v. United Biscuits Ltd* (1977) illustrates one instance where an employer actually did discriminate. The tribunal found that although United Biscuits failed to file for an exemption order (so that they could hire a woman), the fact that they did not do so and instead refused to hire the woman was not illegal (Equal Opportunities Commission, 1979: 31). Arising from this was the concern that preference for men over women by employers was being structured by the law and reinforced by the courts.

To some extent these problems arose through a lack of information about the possibilities for exemptions allowed in the Factory Acts. Employers could apply to receive an exemption order, but they argued that these were difficult to obtain, and the process was excessively bureaucratic and irksome (Equal Opportunities Commission, 1979: 20). The commission found that this was not the case: of 947,000 full-time women manual workers in productive industries, 200,000 were working on permanent exemption orders in 1979.

The commission also found that the protective legislation had an impact on the wage differential between men and women workers. 'Nightwork and shiftwork establish job segregation and pay differentials. . . . Nightwork and shiftwork provide pay premia over and above the normal wage because they involve work during unsocial hours' (Equal Opportunities Commission, 1979: 33). Nightwork premiums average 25–30 per cent of the basic hourly rate of pay, so denying women access to these nightwork premiums contributes to differentials in wages between men and women.

In order to collect evidence about women's views on the repeal of Section 6 provisions, the commission conducted a survey. It found that women, especially women with young children, were willing to do nightwork because their husbands could provide child care in the evenings. The survey did not ask women whether they thought this an optimum way of dealing with the problem of looking after young children when mothers worked.

The commission expressed the view that an employer's right to require a nightwork obligation of employees, or the contractual right to vary employees' hours of work could be a source of indirect discrimination which was not fully covered by the Sex Discrimination and Equal Pay Acts. While these Acts, and the hours of work legislation, remained as they were, women would continue to receive unfavourable treatment in relation to pay and job opportunities. The commission used this willingness by women to undertake nightwork to conclude that the protective legislative provisions should either be repealed or extended to men.

The Trades Union Congress (TUC) voiced its opposition to the repeal of protective legislation: 'In particular, the prohibition on nightwork should not be removed until unions and workers were prepared to accept such a change and equal pay was generally applicable' (Equal Opportunities Commission, 1979: 17). The insistence that equal pay should become a general provision was based on the old fear of the development of the female labour force as a low-paid group of workers who could be used to undercut male wages. The TUC particularly favoured the retention of nightwork restrictions from 10 p.m. to 7 a.m. Nevertheless the nightwork restriction was repealed.

The Labour Force Context

Although it would seem acceptable that these restrictive provisions be removed from female workers in order to allow them to compete on equal terms with male workers, I would like to consider the impact of this change in legislation in the light of the changes in labour market practices in the 1970s. I will briefly discuss general employment trends and then draw conclusions.

Between 1971 and 1987 the number of employees in employment remained at roughly the same level of just over 21 million workers (although there was a slight increase in the period 1971–6, which was then reversed). While the number of employees may not have increased, there have been major structural changes. In the period 1971–87, the manufacturing sector lost 1.8 million workers, of which the majority were men. The service sector during this period expanded by 1.5 million workers, the majority of them women. So a major shift in the labour force occurred in terms of the ratio of men to women. While the service sector was providing many new jobs, these jobs did not have the same characteristics as jobs that were being lost in the manufacturing sector. The primary difference is that the jobs lost in the manufacturing sector were full-time and those gained in the service sector were part-time.[1] This partly explains why women rather than men filled the new jobs: men refused them because they were not enough to sustain a 'head of household' role, and women accepted them as sources of supplementary income.

While the number of employees in employment remained virtually the same, unemployment rose by 2.1 million from 1971 to 1987, according to official statistics. Other sources estimate that there were at least an extra million unemployed workers who did not appear on the official registers. Most of these were women (Garnsey, 1984: 34). Self-employment has risen by 800,000 since 1971, largely as a consequence of unemployment (see Equal Opportunities Commission, 1988: Table 3.4).

Several reasons for the enormous growth in part-time work have been put forward. First, on the demand side, government policies encourage employers to prefer part-time to full-time workers because employees working fewer than sixteen hours a week are not afforded employment protection rights. Employers uncertain about whether they would be able to offer long-term employment due to product market uncertainty may prefer to hire part-time workers to meet production goals because these can be fired without unfair dismissal suits or extensive remuneration. Secondly, employers can avoid making expensive National Insurance contributions if their employees make less than £34 per week. National Insurance contributions amount to 10 per cent of wage costs (Garnsey, 1984: 25). Thirdly, on the supply side, married women with children who need to work accept part-time work because they have primary responsibility for child care.

Although there were large numbers of men unemployed as a result of the decline of the manufacturing sector, they did not make the transition to the kinds of work for which there was a high demand in the service sector. The unemployed men required well-paid, stable, full-time jobs in areas in which they had been trained or had experience. The jobs on offer in the service sector were low paid, often unstable and part time.

The high male unemployment rates during the early 1980s illustrate that male and female workers are not easily interchangeable. This in turn is important because it illustrates that some of the assumptions upon which protective legislation was enacted, specifically traditional views of women's and men's family obligations, are still structuring the way in which men and women operate in the labour force. This suggests that the assumption on which equal opportunities rests does not accurately reflect empirical reality.

It is in the context of this employment situation that the repeal of the protective legislation should be considered. While, as part of the justification, it was argued that there was a 'high demand for labour', there were large numbers of unemployed men available for work. But it was specifically a high demand for cheap, part-time labour, that is female labour, that caused the Confederation of British Industries to lobby for the repeal of protective legislation. This repeal has to be seen primarily as a victory for employers wanting to promote 'flexible' employment practices rather than a gain for either women or men workers. For nightwork and shift-work have important drawbacks for both men and women workers. First, nightwork for women poses a problem in terms of safety going to and from work. The commission reported that many women went to and from work either by public transport or on foot: they are more exposed to street attacks than men, or at least have the ever-present fear of them. Secondly, it is questionable whether such work contributes to a stable family life. For two-parent families it is doubtful that domestic life is enhanced by solving child-care prob-lems in such a way that one parent works during the day and the other works at night. For one-parent families, nightwork is no solution at all. Thirdly, the government's facilitation of such work practices means that people's opportunities to choose stable, full-time work are restricted. While the commission's survey is inconclu-sive about whether or not shiftwork and overtime is injurious to health and safe working practices, it really is questionable that governments should be encouraging this kind of employment prac-tice. Since the reason that the women in the survey gave for their willingness to accept nightwork and shiftwork was that their hus-bands could provide child care, it must also be asked whether, if affordable good-quality child care was available during the day, these women would not prefer to avail themselves of it. It is surpris-ing that the Commission did not discuss this latter option in some depth.

Conclusions

The repeal of the protective legislation and the introduction of equal opportunities legislation illustrates several major changes in the way in which policies have been made with respect to women. First, and maybe most importantly, women have participated in the introduction of equal opportunities legislation. This has meant that arguments about women's own financial needs have been highlight-ed. And yet, despite greater involvement in decision-making by women, equal opportunities was used by industry to make some gains towards workforce practices that do not particularly help women (in that the development of nightwork and part-time work is not going to substantially improve their economic circumstances) and which certainly hurt men.

Male trade unionists' interests of the 1980s are certainly not served by the increased use of cheap female labour any more than they were in the 1830s or the 1920s. To some extent the male trade union movement has been hampered in its ability to fight for women's employment protection by old traditions of sexism. Male trade union leaders cannot come out and oppose egalitarian provisions, but neither can they effectively argue any more for the old 'male supporter' role without coming into opposition with women. What is needed is the sorting out of common and mutually supportive strategies.

The repeal of protective legislation shows how an emphasis on 'equality' of male and females rather than improvements in material well-being can become a way of ignoring the obstacles which many women, in this case a particular group of women (those with children), face in the labour market. This is not to say that the old protective legislation provisions did not need reform. Their assumptions that *all* women were to be defined primarily as wives and mothers, and their failure to address the financial imperative to work that many women face is out of step with contemporary assumptions and realities for women. Maybe what this repeal illustrates most is that it does not really matter whether legislation is based on strategies of 'equality' or 'difference', since these ideologies obscure the realities that if capitalist concerns dominate the policy process, then it is capitalist needs that will be served. This then forces the conclusion that women must participate actively in the public policy process and must sort out their differences with the male trade union movement if they are going to see their goals advanced, otherwise 'equality' and 'difference' will be used in ways which are against their own interests.

Notes

* I would like to thank Bob Blackburn for his critical comments on this chapter, and Teresa Brennan for her enthusiastic support.

1. Part-time work in Great Britain usually means regular work of less than 30 hours per week.

References

Barrett, M. (1980) *Women's Oppression Today*. London: Verso.
Davidoff, L. and Hall, C. (1987) *Family Fortunes*. London: Hutchinson.

Equal Opportunities Commission (1979) *Health and Safety Legislation: Should We Distinguish Between Men and Women?* Report and Recommendations of the EOC, submitted to the Secretary of State for Employment.

Equal Opportunities Commission (1988) *Women and Men in Statistics.*

Equal Opportunities Review (1988) 'Repeal proposed of discriminatory protective legislation', *Equal Opportunities Review*.

Garnsey, E. (1984) *The Provision and Quality of Part-Time Work, The Case of Great Britain and France*, a preliminary study carried out for the Directorate-General Employment, Social Affairs and Education, Commission of the European Communities. Mimeographed copy obtained from the author.

Garnsey, E. (1988) *Atypical Employment in Great Britain, 1975 to 1985*. Report for the Equal Opportunities Office of the European Commission, Brussels.

House of Commons (1970) *Hansard, Parliamentary Debates*, 795: 914.

Humphries, J. (1981) 'Protective legislation, the capitalist state, and working class men: the case of the 1842 Mines Regulation Act', *Feminist Review*, 7: 1–33.

Hurstfield, J. (1987) *Part-timers under Pressure*, pamphlet 47. London: Low Pay Unit.

John, A. (1981) 'Letter of reply to Humphries', *Feminist Review*, 8: 106–9.

Lewenhak, S. (1977) *Women and Trade Unions*. London: Ernest Benn.

Meehan, E. (1985) *Women's Rights at Work*. London: Macmillan.

Mockett, H. (1988) 'A Danger to the state?: Women and factory legislation 1830–1850', paper presented at the Annual Conference of the British Sociological Association, Edinburgh.

10

Women and Equality in the Irish Civil Service

Evelyn Mahon

Irish policies on equal opportunities have been dominated by a liberal policy model as opposed to a radical policy. The limitations of the liberal model are now being extensively realized. There is still an absence of women in senior posts in the Civil Service and management and organizations remain male dominated. This chapter will examine women and equality policy in the Irish Civil Service and assess its achievements. Before examining the practices, it is useful to look at the kinds of conception of equal opportunities that prevail.

Formal Versus Substantive Equality of Opportunity

Philosophically two interpretations of equal opportunities have been formulated: one formal and one substantive (O'Neill, 1985). Formal equal opportunity as interpreted sees two persons, A and B, as having equal opportunities in some respect if neither faces a legal or quasi-legal obstacle in doing something. Or as Jencks put it, 'the rules determining who succeeds and who fails should be fair' (1972: 3). This principle is part of the liberal classical tradition, an extension of the idea of securing equal liberties for all. It demands that in recruitment and promotional systems fair selection procedures be devised which ignore sex, race or social status and concentrate instead on relevant qualifications. However, many selection systems designed to be non-discriminatory produce results which are still unequal in two respects (O'Neill, 1985). First, they produce societies whose members are extremely unequal in educational and occupational attainment and, secondly, they lead to disproportionate success for some social groups and to disproportionate failure for others. The first result is not a problem for liberals, as they assume that all cannot succeed and so there must be successes and failures. The point is, these are the outcomes of a rational, non-arbitrary system. The second result is a problem in that it suggests, *prima facie*, that new selection procedures might not be after all, truly non-discriminatory; that, for instance, 'promotions are still being made on criteria other than on the job performance' (O'Neill, 1985). This would still reflect their concern with procedures rather than outcomes.

A substantive interpretation of the concept of equal opportunity is more exacting. O'Neill gives the example of a lottery where the same proportion of all kinds of people can win as a case of substantive or actuarial equality of opportunity.

> On this view, opportunities for A and B with respect to x are to be regarded as equal not because neither faces legal or quasi-legal obstacles which the other does not face, but because they belong to social groups whose rates of success at obtaining x are equal.

An equal opportunity society on the substantive view is one in which the success rates of all major social groups are the same. To bring this about, according to this view, preferential or quota admissions and hirings are justifiable, because they confer or ensure equal rewards, not because they apply standards in a non-discriminatory way. In this view, women or minority candidates would be selected on the basis of the proportion of women or minority applicants. Substantive equal opportunity is achieved when the success rates of certain major social groups are equalized. This policy becomes threatening only when a scarce and desirable occupation is at issue. Objections usually come from members of groups who are disproportionately successful under a mode of selection compatible with a formal interpretation and who fear the loss of this privilege. Those who oppose substantive equality argue that action such as preferential hiring might lead to less competent performances and that as such it would be unjust and inefficient. In response to these charges advocates of preferential treatment say that the cost in efficiency will be low since the relevance of job qualifications to job performance is often meagre in existing systems and that, in most cases, people grow into the job. While some concede that an injustice might be done to those who are passed over in the interim period, in the long run overall discrimination will be reduced and the need for preferential treatment eliminated.

There are liberal and radical applications of preferential hiring. The liberal proposes that, if he or she is the *best* candidate or as *equally* qualified for the job as the other candidate, the minority candidate ought to be hired. The radical model holds that if the minority candidate is *at least minimally qualified* for the job, they ought to be hired.

One question which can be initially posed, then, is whether a formal or substantive definition of equal opportunity might be preferable in furthering women's rights, and whether the liberal or radical version of the latter should be implemented.

Jewson and Mason (1986), writing on the development of equal opportunities in the workplace, claim that the liberal formal model assumes that 'all individuals are enabled freely and equally to compete for social rewards'. To facilitate this, any unfair distortions in the operation of the labour market must be removed. Selection must be on the basis of individual, meritocratic characteristics to the neglect of any structural or collective barriers. This requires the removal of legal or social prohibitions which exclude certain groups such as women, in order to enable all individuals to compete as individuals. In the case of women, for instance, the removal of the marriage bar, which prohibited the full-time employment of married women in certain sectors, would be a liberal requirement to ensure fair procedures and enable women to compete with men.

In practice, however, the spirit of the liberal policy is not upheld, and ways are found to apply certain criteria meritocratically, but in a manner which still excludes minority and female candidates. One approach which subverts liberal policy is writing job descriptions in a way which will render some applicants – women and minorities – unsuited. Favoured applicants can, in practice, have a job description designed for themselves; it thus looks as though they are meritocratically appointed to the post. The result is that formal liberal 'fair' policies can perpetuate the status quo. In other cases, selection for jobs which do not require extensive skills or knowledge is performed on the basis of 'acceptabillity' or 'suitabililty'. The result of this is that 'aspects of masculinity and femininity can become established as indicators of suitability' (Webb and Liff, 1988). This has resulted in gendered jobs (Davies, 1988; Webb, 1988).

In other examples, the matching of job demands and individual characteristics is done in a sexist manner in that being a male or having a stereotypical male approach is what is required. Patricia Walters' research, on perceptions of principals in the UK Civil Service of male and female abilities, revealed that, when compared in terms of a list of specific characteristics, men and women were judged to be closely similar in nearly all characteristics. Yet women were found to be different in two respects: they were considered less stable and less likely to be highly dependable, and fewer women as compared with men, were judged capable of functioning in posts beyond the level of assistant secretary. When it came to 'overall style' and approach, women were judged to be lacking when compared with men. This reluctance to be specific facilitates the sexual stereotyping that persists to the disadvantage of women, that women by definition simply cannot possess that classic male quality called 'overall style'.

In practice, a male organizational style dominates organizations to the disadvantage of aspiring women. This lack of belief in women means that 'women have to prove clearly that they are successful, whereas men are assumed to be successful until they conclusively demonstrate that they are failures' (Fogarty *et al.*, 1981: 44). These examples show the possible limitations and abuses of a liberal policy. One could purport to have a 'fair' selection system but its effects would be minimal. In contrast, a substantive policy would try to produce equality in results.

While liberal policy and selection procedures may be invoked in different minority situations (religious, racist, class and so on), the one which preoccupies us is that of gender. Women who wished to advance the rights of women have pursued various policies, loosely described as liberal, radical and socialist.

Liberal Feminism and Criticisms of it

A liberal conception of equal opportunities was initiated by liberal feminists who wished to advance women's rights in the workplace. Liberal equal rights feminism holds that women and men are equal; that is, anything men can do in the public world women can also do. Traditionally, women were confined to the private sphere where their development was restricted. Liberalist John Stuart Mill argued that women's personal development was hindered by their confinement within marriage and the home. To enable women to fully develop their human potential entry into the public world was seen as desirable (Mill, 1861; Friedan, 1963; de Beauvoir, 1963). Discriminatory laws and institutions prevented women from entering this public world, women therefore failed to reach their full potential and so the laws had to be changed. The task was to remove these barriers and then women would gain equality. Access to education, the professions and to paid employment had to be won. Historically, the issue began with the right to vote, then seeking rights to third-level education, and later to equal pay. The aspiration was that over time male/female differences would be removed. Friedan's identification of the 'problem with no name' mobilized women into the public sphere and into career-orientated work.

The political approach taken by equal rights feminists was to stress the similarities between men and women, and not to emphasize their differences, lest the latter would make this difficult for women if they were invoked by those who opposed women's emancipation. In the 1950s and 1960s, 'equality' had a moral value or worth which advanced the rights of women by removing a variety of serious legal obstacles, in a way which an emphasis on 'difference' might have been unable to accomplish. The result was that, while women were incorporated into the labour force, they were accepted according to male organizational norms. Hewlett described this form of feminism as an attempt 'to clone the male competitive model' while denigrating the primacy of motherhood (Hewlett, 1986).

In what has been termed the post-feminist debate, the limitations of the equality approach have been outlined (Rosenfelt and Stacey, 1987). In particular, concerns over the superwoman syndrome and the working mother's frustration and exhaustion as she is compelled to adopt male norms of work practices have been outlined. In some cases, women deferred domesticity and maternity and moved into organizations insisting they be treated as equal to men. The liberal feminist, it is argued, stressed equality and ignored differences between men and women, and in doing so ignored or marginalized women's reproductive role. Further, deeper analysis of the gains of feminism in many countries, if measured in terms of mothers' participation in the labour market, is still quite depressing (Moss, 1988: 4). Pay differences still persist but, in particular, mothers' participation in the paid labour force varies and is characterized by temporary breaks from the labour market, part-time work and persistent gender segregation, both horizontal and vertical. Differences in participation among women and between men and women are related to the type and extent of child-care facilities available. European research shows that the full integration of women into the paid labour force depends on state provision of child care. Denmark has shown that Danish women can show equal labour force participation, given state-supported child care (Moss, 1988). Such policies have not been forthcoming in many countries and the result is uneven participation.

It must be noted here, however, that liberal equality policies are essentially employment based. They do not take into account the reproductive functions of women, the division of labour in the home and the provision or arrangements made for child care. These factors still remain as major impediments to the equal participation of women in the labour market. If women are either reluctant or unable to adopt male norms of work practices, liberal policies have little to offer them. Other initiatives, such as extended maternity leave, job-sharing or career breaks for child-care purposes are policies based on facilitating this involvement of women in their reproductive roles, and could be termed policies based on 'difference', rather than on equality.

This more recent emphasis on difference has helped us to focus on the limitations of a formal equality of opportunity policy. With this debate in mind, I now examine the position of women in the Irish Civil Service and review the impact of an equal opportunities policy in that organization. In particular, I examine the position of mothers in the Civil Service and review whether such a policy facilitates their lives as working mothers.

The National Context

Ireland has the lowest proportion of married women in the paid labour force among European Community member states (20 per cent). In addition, it has by European standards very traditional attitudes towards women in the labour force (Women in Europe, 1987). A patriarchal traditional ideology enshrined the position of women in the home in the Constitution (Mahon, 1987). In practice, a legal ban on the employment of married women in the Civil Service existed until 1973. An example of the sexist attitude which traditionally prevailed can be seen in the Brennan Report, which was a review of conditions in the Civil Service. In this report, the view was expressed that 'when all relevant aspects are taken into account, the woman does not give as good a return of work as the man' (Commission of Inquiry, 1935: para. 180). This legacy of a traditional patriarchal attitude to women is one in which the Civil Service has operated in the past. It is felt by some staff that these traditional views are still strongly held by some departmental secretaries.

The Civil Service

The Civil Service is a hierarchical organization, exhibiting both vertical and horizontal segregation. A comparison over time has shown that this vertical distribution has hardly ever changed (Table 10.1). While, in principle, it is supposed to be a graded structure, in practice it has a two-tier structure. The lower tier recruits school-leavers into the three lowest posts: clerical assistant (CA), clerical officer (CO) and executive officer (EO). In the higher tier, graduates are recruited as administrative officers (AO).

Equal Opportunities Policy

In 1983, an equal opportunities policy was initiated in the Civil Service. This was published in booklet form by the Department of the Public Service, a department subsequently abolished because of cutbacks and its functions absorbed by the Department of Finance. It included a formal statement of a policy of equal opportunities, the introduction of career breaks (for a variety of purposes including

Table 10.1   *Percentage female in general service grades at*
January 1983 and October 1987 (Irish Civil Service)

Grade	1983[1]	1987[2]
Secretary	0	0
Assistant secretary	1	1
Principal officer	3	5
Assistant principal officer	18	23
Administrative officer	31	26
Higher executive officer	35	34
Executive officer	40	44
Staff officer	61	67
Clerical officer	69	68
Clerical assistant	84	83

Sources: [1]J. Tansey (1984) *Women in Ireland*, p. 99. [2]*Equality of Opportunity in*
the Civil Service First annual report (1988: 34)

domestic responsibilities) and job-sharing. A monitoring system
was set up whereby the annual report issued by the Civil Service
Commission would contain a gender breakdown of appointments
and progress on equality would be reviewed. At the end of 1988, a
first progress report on Equal Opportunities in the Civil Service was
published.

From an analysis of the figures presented in this report it is
possible to see to what extent the position of women has changed
since 1983. One way in which to do this is to use a substantive
criterion by making a comparison between the success rates of men
and women at successive stages of the recruitment and promotional
competitions. This will show whether or not the proportion of
women in the higher grades has changed over time.

A comparison of the figures for 1983 and 1987 (Table 10.1) shows
a slight improvement in the representation of women in the higher
grades. Given the existence of the marriage bar until 1973, and the
significance of seniority in Civil Service promotions, it has been
argued that it will take some years before the full effects of the
removal of this bar are to be seen in increased proportions of
women in the higher posts (Lenihan, 1984; Blackwell, 1985). But
the indications from recruitment figures are not promising.

Recruitment at Graduate Level
The proportion of women in the administrative officer grade, a
graduate recruitment grade (the high-flyer grade) has actually de-

creased. A previous analysis of the 1983 figures by Blackwell (1985) claimed that a comparison between eligible candidates and candidates considered for appointment through open competition to administrative officer and third secretary grades could indicate discrimination.

The tables published on success in competitions enables one to see whether there is obvious evidence of discrimination in recruitment or promotion.

An examination of Table 10.2 reveals a success rate of 5 per cent for female applicants for third secretary posts as compared with 31 per cent for men. In the administrative officer (higher-status Department of Finance posts) males had a success rate of 12 per cent compared with only 4 per cent for women: four men and one woman were appointed. Using a substantive criterion, these two grades remain problematic. In view of Walters' (1987) findings about the British Civil Service, it could be that, as these are the 'high-flyer' grades, with subsequent promotion to policy-making roles, Irish women are also disadvantaged by doubts about their overall capacity. The later stages of these competitions are interview based and it may well be that diffuse characteristics, more likely to be 'seen in' male candidates, were sought. In the competition for ordinary administrative officer, the success rate was 7 per cent for women and 3 per cent for men: three women and two men were appointed.

Table 10.2 *Female–male success rates at Civil Service Commission open written/interview competitions in 1987(a)*

Competition	Eligible applicants		Successful written (W) competition		Successful at final interview for place on panel	
	Female (%)	Male (%)	Female (%)	Male (%)	Female (%)	Male (%)
Administrative officer	746(43%)	1008(57%)	43(6%)(W)	62(6%)(W)	3(7%)	2(3%)
Administrative officer D/finance	28(41%)	41(59%)	23(82%)(W)	32(78%)(W)	1(4%)	4(12%)
Third secretary	802(48%)	866(52%)	18(2%)(W)	32(4%)(W)	1(5%)	10(31%)

Source: Equality of Opportunity in the Civil Service
First annual report (1988: 16)

Recruitment to the Lower Tier

One expected result from equal opportunities in recruitment would have been a decline in the proportion of women recruited as clerical assistants, given the existing concentration of women in this grade. In 1983, 183 males (30 per cent) and 417 (70 per cent) women were recruited. Clerical assistant jobs are likely to be seen as women's jobs. By 1987 the proportion had changed little: 243 (31 per cent) men and 525 (69 per cent) women were recruited. Thirty per cent of those recruited were male – lower than their eligibility level. As regards clerical officers, in 1987, despite women's greater success rate in written exams (38 per cent female, 28 per cent male), the success rate of males was 9 per cent as compared with only 2 per cent of women after the interview process. Seventy-six per cent of places on the panels were awarded to men, who constitute only 41 per cent of eligible applicants. Men were more likely to be recruited as clerical officers than women were, while the opposite holds for recruitment to clerical assistant posts.

In the school-leaver competition for executive officer, the success rates were equalized and, in the executive officer adult competition, women gained a slight advantage: 38 per cent as compared with 32 per cent (see Table 10.3). One concludes from these tables that a

Table 10.3   *Female–male success rates at Civil Service Commission open written/interview competitions in 1987(b)*

Competition	Eligible applicants		Successful written (W) competition		Successful at final interview for place on panel	
	Female (%)	Male (%)	Female (%)	Male (%)	Female (%)	Male (%)
Clerical officer	6861(59%)	4768(41%)	2597(38%)(W)	1326(28%)	36(2%)	119(9%)
Clerical assistant	4167(65%)	2221(35%)	1339(32%)(W)	739(33%)	525(39%)	243(33%)
Clerical assistant (typist)	4268(99%)	43(1%)	1130(26%)(W)	11(26%)	148(13%)	2(18%)
Executive officer (school-leaver	3154(61%)	2049(39%)	2741(87%)(W)	1780(87%)(W)	174(6%)	93(5%)
Executive officer (adult)	1541(51%)	1519(49%)	37(2%)(W)	57(4%)(W)	14(38%)	18(32%)

Source: Equality of Opportunity in the Civil Service
    First annual report (1988: 16)

pattern of gendered jobs persists in the recruitment process, perpetuating vertical segregation patterns.

Promotion through Internal Competition within Lower Tier

If one examines the competitions for promotion we can see the progress of women through the different stages: from eligibility to written examination, to interview and to appointment. In one particular internal or confined competition in 1986 from clerical assistant to clerical officer, there was a net candidature of 660 males and 2226 females. Of those 603 and 1890 respectively attended written examinations and 596 men and 1873 women passed. Of those contestants 84 men and 118 women were interviewed. In turn, 79 men and 114 women were considered for appointment; 55 men and 66 women were assigned and eventually 52 men and 62 women took up duty (Local Government Appointments Commission Report, 1986: 24).

This shows, firstly, the low proportion of assignments as compared with the number of applicants who passed examinations and

Table 10.4 *Female–male success rates at Civil Service Commission interdepartmental confined interview (only) competitions in 1987*

Competition	Eligible applicants		Successful at preliminary interview		Successful at final interview for place on panel	
	Female (%)	Male (%)	Female (%)	Male (%)	Female (%)	Male (%)
Principal D/Environment	nil	10(100%)	none held	none held	nil	1(10%)
Principal D/Industry & Commerce	2(8%)	24(92%)	none held	none held	nil	1(4%)
Assistant principal (higher scale)	45(15%)	257(85%)	10(22%)	36(14%)	3(30%)	11(30%)
Assistant principal (standard scale)	73(15%)	405(85%)	14(19%)	56(14%)	6(43%)	18(32%)
Higher executive officer	262(30%)	611(70%)	32(12%)	97(16%)	23(72%)	48(49%)

Source: Equality of Opportunity in the Civil Service
First annual report (1988: 17)

the manner in which the initial gender advantage of women was eroded over the competitive process, which ended up in the appointment of almost an equal number of men as women. Nine per cent of men as compared with 3 per cent of women were assigned. The major fall-out was at the interview stage. This puts into context the very distant prospects of promotion to clerical officer grade for women, in the female-dominated clerical assistant grade.

The 1987 figures also revealed much greater chances of promotion for men in a confined competition for clerical officer posts in the Central Statistics Office: a 71 per cent success rate for males as compared to 36 per cent for women. These figures suggest a 'gendered' job approach, with females more likely to be assigned to clerical assistant posts while males get clerical officer posts (Equality of Opportunity Report, 1988: 19).

The Equality Report suggests that the equality review committee are now concerned about interviewing techniques, procedures and bases of assessment and have recommended special training in this area.

Promotion in Other Grades through Internal Competition
The confined competition for middle grades posts – using a substantive criterion – seemed quite fair to women. However, as can be seen (Table 10.4) there is only a small number of eligible women candidates. This is even more glaring with respect to top posts, where there are no female candidates, and in the lack of success of the few women when they do compete. Appointments to the grades of assistant secretary and higher were all men; it would have been encouraging if even one woman had been appointed (Table 10.5). This is an instance where preferential hiring rather than a substantive criterion would have made a difference.

Awareness of Equality

One might ask to what extent women workers are aware of these persistent inequalities. Two indicators are available, one a case taken by a number of workers backed by their union, and the other the perceptions of women themselves, derived from a recent study.

In the union case, four women who felt they were discriminated against in an internal competition for promotion from clerical assistant (taxes) to the grade of tax officer took the matter to the Labour Court. The published court proceedings are useful in illustrating the evaluation system used at interviews in making such appointments. Candidates were judged on

Table 10.5   *Female–male success rates at competitions for the grade of assistant secretary and higher grades in 1987*

Competition	Shortlisted applicants		Successful at preliminary interview		Successful at final interview	
	Female (%)	Male (%)	Female (%)	Male (%)	Female (%)	Male (%)
Assistant secretary Department of Agriculture	nil	27	nil	5	nil	1
Assistant secretary Department of the Gaeltacht	nil	27	nil	5	nil	1
Assistant secretary Department of Finance	nil	18	nil	5	nil	1
Secretary Department of Finance	nil	18	none held		nil	1
Chief registrar Department of Justice	5	5	none held		nil	1
Secretary Department of the Marine	nil	15	none held		nil	1
Secretary Civil Service Commission	nil	13	none held		nil	1
Revenue solicitor Office of Revenue Commissioners	2	4	none held		nil	1
Registrar Supreme Court	7	8	none held		nil	1
Registrar Wards of Court	6	8	none held		nil	1
Assistant secretary Department of Defence	nil	44	nil	6	nil	1

Source: Equality of Opportunity in the Civil Service
      First annual report (1988: 21)

Length and quality of official experience	100 marks
Intelligence and general knowledge	100 marks
General suitability	100 marks

Additional marks were awarded to candidates who had a record of proficiency in Irish. There were 654 candidates in total for the competition: 26 per cent were male and 74 per cent female. The outcome was that 120 candidates were successful: 49 men and 71 women or approximately 29 per cent of male applicants and 15 per cent of females. In the Cork district, from where the complainants came, the success rate was 73 per cent male and 7 per cent female. Initially, the applicants raised the case of discrimination against the Civil Service Commission. This was rejected so they asked the Irish Tax Officials Union to pursue the matter through the Labour Court, which the union did. The applicants claimed that (1) the success rate of males interviewed by board D was much higher than the success rate of females, (2) that each of the complainants had received a more favourable assessment from their supervisors than at least eight of the eleven successful male candidates, (3) that the educational level and so on of the males would not have given them an advantage over the women and (4) that one female member of the interview board had demonstrated discriminatory attitudes towards female staff in the Cork Tax Office. As the commissioners refused to give evidence which would counteract their allegations, the equality officer in the Labour Court recommended that on grounds 1–3, their case could be upheld and recommended that the women be placed on the panel.

This was a victory for the complainants but it achieved fair treatment for these four applicants only because it did not lead to an entire review of the competition. It does show the limitations of the legislation, which is only useful if *used* by the workers. Regrettably, the Civil Service Commission and indeed the General Sub-committee on Equality of the Commission were of no assistance in supporting the claimants' case, so women had to proceed to the Labour Court. In this case, the substantive procedure was used to support their case together with the fact that they were equal and even superior in qualifications to the male candidates. The interview board claimed in its defence that the interview was a major assessment instrument and that, while they had noted the superior success of the male candidates, this was due to their objective interview performance and not because of favour on the part of the board. However, as they were not prepared to be more explicit in their defence, their view was not upheld by the Labour Court. This was a gain for those advocating fair procedures, but it shows that the diffuse 'general suitability' criterion can be applied in a sexist fashion.

Perceptions of Equal Opportunities
In a recent sample survey of mothers employed in the Civil Service, 52 per cent of the sample felt that women had the same promotional opportunities as men, 45 per cent disagreed, while the remainder were undecided. Among women who had been promoted, 63 per

cent thought that women had the same promotional opportunities as men, as compared with only 42 per cent of those not promoted. The percentage of respondents who agreed that women had equal promotional opportunities was directly related to grade, with only 42 per cent of those in the lowest grades, as compared with 52 per cent in the middle and 82 per cent in the higher grades agreeing that women had equal promotional opportunities (Mahon, 1990).

Assessment

This examination of the recruitment and promotion outcomes, using a substantive criterion, indicates that equal opportunities remain an aspiration. There appears to be some discrimination in the recruitment of women into administrative officer and third secretary positions and in their promotion from the lowest grades.

The overall conclusion of this interim review is that vertical segregation persists in the Civil Service and present liberal policies are not having the desired impact. The result of this is that one has an almost totally female-dominated labour force in the lowest grades, and conversely a totally male-dominated one in the top grades. This gender segregation confirms the subordinance of women, confirms male superiority and facilitates the pervasiveness of a male organizational style. The issues raised are different for women depending on whether they find themselves in the subordinate positions or as a minority among males in the upper grades. The equal opportunity policies do not take such heterogeneity among women into account.

In the following section I will summarize the issues as presented by two groups – women in the two lowest grades and women in the higher grades – and, within that context, assess the merits of an equal opportunities policy.

Women in the Lowest Grades
Women predominate in the two lowest grades of clerical assistant and clerical officers (see Table 10.1). As such, women and subordination are combined and intertwined. In the lowest grades, promotion is generally by open competition which means that established officers compete with school-leavers in an examination system that favours the latter. This affects women disproportionately. All studies reveal high levels of dissatisfaction with promotional opportunities (O'Broin and Farren, 1978; Mahon, 1990).

Because internal or confined competitions are periodic, the chances of promotion from the lowest grades are so distant as to be almost non-existent. Further, in competitions that do arise, women are still likely to be discriminated against. Competitions are unpredictable and, since a public sector embargo, have been very infrequent. Even prior to the embargo, some candidates who were successful and put on a panel were never placed. After two years, the panel expired and the candidates, due to the futility of effort, did not reapply. Those women who might have been ambitious were 'cooled out' at an early stage.

In practice, it means that the majority of women employed in the Civil Service are in dead-end jobs. In addition their payments fall into the category of low pay when compared with the average male industrial wage. Moreover, work in the lower grades can be of a routine and boring nature. In the past this may not have been as great an issue as women left their jobs on marriage and turnover was always very high (Ross, 1986; O'Broin and Farren, 1978). Returns from departments show that it is in these junior grades that married women are mostly located. This is especially the case in regional offices (Mahon, 1990). Women in the two lowest grades with no chance of promotion form the underclass of the Civil Service. While fairer promotional procedures might enable more to be promoted, the reality is one of remaining indefinitely a clerical assistant with no promotional prospects. This is especially so for those in regional offices. In addition, these women had less annual holidays than women in the higher grades. There is no provision for special leave for the care of children who are ill, so if children were sick, women used their holiday leave for that purpose. A common problem experienced by women in the lowest grades was their limited holiday and sick leave and their fears that if their children were sick, they had insufficient leave left to take time off to care for them.

Their low pay has of course an effect on their plans to remain on at work. In practice, the decision to work in the case of mothers is an economically rational one, which in practice means that low pay is a disincentive to work. As I have outlined elsewhere (Mahon, 1988), when they subtract taxation and child-care costs from their low wages, they have little of their wages left for themselves, hence the attractiveness of the career breaks when they have young children. The danger is that the career break becomes a form of retirement from the labour force, and gender differences in participation in the labour force remain unchanged.

Research shows that child care for women in the lowest grades is subsidized by their families' unpaid labour or by low payment to child-minders (Mahon, 1990). Mothers who have more than two children are likely to opt out of paid work. Those who stay on do so because their husbands' salaries are low, uncertain or insecure.

This group of working mothers in continuous employment is a recently formed cohort. In the past, prior to current unemployment levels and with the existence of the marriage bar, a high job turnover rate reduced the number of women who remained employed continuously over a working life in the lowest grades. Without increased pay levels, job enrichment strategies or additional perks, these women exist in a secondary low-paid labour market. The single advantage they have is that their jobs are permanent.

Women in the Higher Grades
As compared with women in the lowest grades, women in higher grades are comparatively advantaged. They could be said to represent the ultimate aim of liberal policy: to see women of ability (with children) get to the top. I will briefly outline their careers.

In all cases of women who had actually made it to the higher grades their early careers had assumed the male norm in that they had deferred both marriage and children, but especially children, until their careers were advanced significantly. This was not as difficult for those women who had been recruited as graduates as many of them had benefited from the guaranteed promotional policy advocated in the 1970s to encourage graduate applications. In practice, after seven years, promotion from administrative officer to assistant principal was guaranteed. These career women had therefore deviated somewhat from the female norm as they pursued a continuous working life. Given the salience of one's twenties and thirties for career steering, this was a wise adaptation (Walters, 1987). Career development dominated their lives. Work had a centrality in their lives that is generally found among professional people: a continuous career pattern, successive promotions and an awareness of career development.

In addition, women at the top had adopted male norms of organizational behaviour: in particular the Civil Service requirement that they must not 'watch the clock' was observed (Walters, 1987). They all worked long hours, were available for late work or for travel within the country or for foreign travel as required.

Without having comparative male data, any explanations of their success are tentative. However, an analysis of their careers indicates that they had postgraduate qualifications or overseas placement, secondment to major international bodies or specialized work assignments which possibly gave them an edge on less successful candidates. They all enjoyed their work and while they felt that some departments were still sexist in orientation, overall attitudes to women were improving. They felt that it 'would be hard to keep a good person down in the Civil Service'. In practice, I feel they may have been superior candidates to their male counterparts.

As a minority group, however, these women did experience some negative effects in the form of what Gerson and Peiss (1985) called micro-level boundaries. Minority women in higher-grade positions felt isolated from the all-male post-work pub networks, where informal knowledge was transmitted and where some aspiring careerists were afforded an opportunity to display their talents. Women opted to go home, instead of the pub on Friday evenings. For some, coffee sessions posed problems as women felt that they could not cope with the intense competitive ethos and scoring practices of male conversation (Fischer, 1985).

Given the fact that women had adopted male norms of behaviour, it is not surprising that specifically female concerns such as maternity leave posed problems for them. In highly competitive mixed departments, women felt that maternity leave was resented. In one instance a mother was forgoing her holidays in order to 'cover' for her colleague who was going on maternity leave. Her colleague had done the same for her the previous year because of growing resentment towards maternity leave. Dedication to the job was their approach.

Children, too, presented problems but, in general, the optimum solution was the delegation of child-care responsibilities to paid help. They were in a position to afford the ideal – home-based care and in some cases additional housekeeping help. One could say that they had found wives by affording their equivalent. Women in the higher grades were able to leave their children and family problems outside the office. They acted and must act as interested servants of the state.

It was this difference which made one realize that just as men and women are not equal, women do not enjoy equal resources or incomes, and in Ireland the only group of women able to afford full-time work are those who can afford to pay for child care.

Satisfaction with child care was a major factor in differentiating full-time working mothers in the Civil Service from job-sharers and mothers on career breaks. Ambivalent career women were tempted to withdraw from the labour market if they had child-care problems, while those women with satisfactory arrangements could concentrate on their careers and adopt work practices similar to those of their male colleagues. In all cases, child care was seen as an individual responsibility, not a collective issue.

The paid employment structure, especially the professional career, is based on the assumption that men will have domestic support services provided by their wives. Women in contrast retain a choice between going out to work or staying at home. The traditional model pulls women towards home and the liberal one treats the issue of child care as an individualistic concern. A woman's choice is in turn affected by her class position and that of her husband's. Women themselves, then, do not compete on equal terms with each other. They still do not compete on equal terms with men as family responsibilities are still not taken seriously or internalized by men. Flexibility, career breaks, job-sharing have all been used by mothers, while fathers' careers remain untouched. For that reason mothers competing in male-dominated organizations will be at a disadvantage unless they can afford arrangements similar to those that men in a traditional family setting have; the support of a full-time wife. Further, maternal responsibilities will always render women unreliable, unless they prove themselves better than men by adopting male norms of behaviour and working even harder than their male colleagues. The delegation of child care is an essential feature of this practice.

Income differentials divide women and determine the way in which they can cope with the double burden. Higher-income group women resort to privately paid child care, while low-paid women are supported by domestic unpaid or low-paid help from their families. Child care remains an individualistic concern, not a collective issue which might require support at an organizational or policy level. Yet, lack of child-care facilities remains a major impediment to the equal participation of women in the labour force. Likewise, the attribution of family responsibilities to women only perpetuates the separate and unequal lives which men and women live in our society, which in turn facilitates occupational segregation. The failure of liberal policy formally to address child-care issues perpetuates the problem.

Policy Implications

Given the limited achievements of a liberal policy and of the practices in place in the Civil Service, what conclusions can be drawn for this review?

Equal opportunity policies should be visible to all staff in a way which demonstrates a political will to improve the situation for women. This, in turn, requires the setting of specific goals and the means by which they will be achieved, giving the policy a dynamic component. Regular critical monitoring of progress towards the achievement of these goals should be initiated.

As regards promotional opportunities, this review shows that promotion to top posts is still denied to women. To make progress in this area, preferential hiring practices must be introduced. The latter can be seen as an expression of political will which endorses the notion that women have the ability to hold senior posts and thereby provide new role models. Further, in reducing vertical segregation, it would erode the dominant male organizational norms and lead to the inclusion of some female experiences, including the acceptability of maternity leave, flexitime and career breaks while acknowledging the rights of workers to have family lives too. Career and life planning for men and women should be encouraged, whereby men and women can opt for job-sharing, career breaks or continuous employment.

A critical progress review would necessitate coming to terms with the structural limitations of equal opportunity policies, such as a realization that all staff will not be promoted due to the scarcity of higher posts and the extensive number of lower posts. This poses the question as to what an equal opportunities policy can offer to staff in the lowest grades. Can their work be structured to increase task diversification and intrinsic job satisfaction? How can the issue of low pay be addressed? Job enrichment policies, the creation of additional perks and increased leave should be introduced with the realization that these posts are now becoming lifelong ones. To improve the situation for workers in these posts is as important as developing processes whereby they can move into higher-level posts.

In the past equal opportunity policies centred on equal pay but a liberal equality approach will not address the problem of low pay for women's work and this must be addressed if women are to remain at work. There is also a need to consider equality in such areas as holidays and sick leave arrangements. Moreover, subsidized child-care facilities or tax allowances towards child care are needed to facilitate women's capacities to be in paid labour. This is partly a matter for the employers who should organize and sponsor child-care facilities. A state policy on child care is also required, which would seek to redistribute child-care costs just as medical and educational costs are distributed. Some women cannot afford child care so some form of subsidized child care is required. A restructuring of work times, that is flexitime and job-sharing, would help retain women in the labour market. Another impediment to women's participation is a reluctance by fathers to share domestic and child-care tasks. This is not a below-market policy issue, but is unlikely to happen until a woman's work is as well paid and her career progression as guaranteed as that of her husband. To assist the latter an equality policy based on substantive criteria is required.

In addition, a consciousness of equal opportunities among women in the organization must be generated, information disseminated and a new power basis among women created. As one respondent put it, 'I think it has been a battle all along . . . now women are coming out of the closet more . . . I don't think women will be treated differently unless women stand up for themselves.'

In conclusion, a liberal approach to equal opportunities is inadequate and fails to reduce gender segregation in the workplace. The full integration of women into the labour market and their representation in the higher levels requires a more radical and dynamic approach.

References

Blackwell, J. (1985) 'Women in the Irish Civil Service: a comment', *Seirbhís Phoibli*, 6(1) Jan: 9–11.

Blennerhassett E. (1983) *Work Motivation and Personnel Practices*. Dublin, Institute of Public Administration.

Commission of Inquiry into the Civil Service (1935) *Final Report* (Brennan Report). Dublin, Government Publications.

Davies, C. (1988) 'Workplace action programmes for equality for women: an orthodoxy examined', paper presented at conference 'Equal Opportunities for Men and Women in Higher Education', University College, Dublin.

De Beauvoir, S. (1963) *The Second Sex*. Harmondsworth: Penguin.

Fischer, M. (1985) 'On social equality and difference, a view from the Netherlands', *Management Education and Development*, 16(2): 201–10.

Fogarty, M. Allen, I. and Walters, P. (1981) *Women in Top Jobs*. London: Heinemann.

Friedan, B. (1963) *The Feminine Mystique*. Harmondsworth: Penguin.

Friedan, B. (1983) *The Second Stage*. London: Abacus.

Gerson, K. (1987) 'How women choose between employment and family: a development perspective', in N. Gerstel and H. Engel Gross (eds), *Families and Work*. Philadelphia: Temple University Press.

Gerson, J. and Peiss, K. (1985) 'Boundaries, negotiation, consciousness; reconceptualizing gender relations', *Social Problems*, 32: 315–31.

Hewlett, S. (1986) *A Lesser Life: The Myth of Women's Liberation in America*. New York: William Morrow.

Jencks, C. (1972) *Inequality: A Reassessment of the Effect of Family and Schooling in America*. New York: Basic Books.

Jewson, N. and Mason, D. (1986) 'Modes of discrimination in the recruitment process: formalisation, fairness and efficiency', *Sociology*, 20(1): 43–63.

Kanter, Rosabeth Moss (1977) *Men and Women of the Corporation*. New York: Basic Books.

Lenihan, B. (1984) 'Leading women astray', *An Seirbhis Phoibli*, 5(1): 15–21.

Local Appointments Commission Report 1986. Dublin: Stationery Office.

Mahon, E. (1987) 'Women's rights and Catholicism in Ireland', *New Left Review* 166 (Nov./Dec.): 53–78.

Mahon, E. (1988) 'Motherhood and the career break', pp. 199–220 in *Proceedings of the Psychology of Women at Work Conference*, London, P(Set) Centre for Psychological Services to Education and Training.

Mahon, E. (1990) *Motherhood, Work and Equal Opportunities: A Case Study of Irish Civil Servants*, prepared for the Joint Oireactas Committee on Women's Rights.

Mill, J.S. (1861) *The Subjection of Women*. Reprint New York: Prometheus Books, 1986.

Moss, P. (1988) *Childcare and Equality of Opportunity*. Brussels: Commission of the European Communities.

O'Broin, N. and Farren, G. (1978) *The Working and Living Conditions of Civil Service Typists*, Paper 93, Economic and Social Research Institute: Dublin.

O'Neill, O. (1985) 'How do we know when opportunities are equal?', in M. Vetterling-Braggin, F. Elliston and J. English (eds), *Feminism and Philosophy*. Totowa, New Jersey: Roman Allanheld.

Rich, A. (1977) *Of Woman Born: Motherhood as Experience and Institution*. London: Virago.

Rosenfelt, D. and Stacey, J. (1987) 'Review essay; second thoughts on the second wave', *Feminist review*, 27 (September): 77–95.

Ross, M. (1986) *Employment in the Public Domain in Recent Decades*, Paper 127 Economic and Social Research Institute, Dublin.

Smith, D. (1987) 'Women's inequality and the family', pp. 23–54 in N. Gerstel and H. Engel Gross (eds), *Families and Work*. Philadelphia: Temple University Press.

Tansey, J. (1984) *Women in Ireland: A Compilation of Relevant Data*. Dublin: Council for the Status of Women.

Walters, P. (1987) 'Servants of the crown', in A. Spencer and D. Podmore (eds), *In a Man's World*. London: Tavistock.

Webb, G. (1988) 'Politics of equal opportunity', pp. 75–100 in *Proceedings of the Psychology of Women at Work Conference*. London.

Webb, J. and Liff, S. (1988) 'Play the white man: the social construction of fairness and competition in equal opportunity policies', *Sociological Review*, 36(3): 533–51.

Women in Europe (1987) *Women of Europe Supplement No 26 Men and Women of Europe in 1987*. Brussels: Commission of the European Communities.

11

Welfare State, Gender Politics and Equality Policies: Women's Citizenship in the Scandinavian Welfare States

Birte Siim

In the highly industrialized countries during the last twenty-five years both women's socioeconomic position and women's relation to politics have radically changed. Women have become mobilized collectively in the women's movement and other social movements, and they have increased their participation in the trade unions and within the political parties. Gender relations in politics have changed. Today, women have to a certain extent become integrated into the political system and they are no longer collectively outside or in opposition to the political sphere. Gender equality has everywhere become a political issue but women's citizenship is still different from men's.

The changes in women's relation to politics have different features in different countries. One of the interesting factors in the political development in the Scandinavian countries (Denmark, Sweden and Norway) has been a parallel increase in women's general political activities in relation to men's and in women's political representation in parliament. In most other countries, women's increased political participation and political mobilization have not resulted in an increase in women's participation in political institutions. In the Scandinavian countries, women today form about one third of all members in parliament. I argue in this chapter that this increase in women's political participation in political institutions is closely connected with women's growing political mobilization. The parallel increase in women's mobilization, participation and representation is one important basis for examining what women's citizenship and the principles of equality mean from a Scandinavian perspective.

In the following I examine the interplay of the expansion of the Danish welfare state in the 1960s and 1970s and changes in women's citizenship and in women's political participation. In the first section I argue that the new understanding of motherhood and care work has given women new social welfare rights and political rights. Citizenship and the principle of social equality, which have been deeply embedded in the Scandinavian politics and culture, have taken on a new meaning in the second stage of the welfare state by incorporating a new understanding of the public–private split. New understandings of citizenship were not articulated with feminism in mind, and feminist scholars debate about whether women in the Scandinavian countries have today become dependent on the state instead of on men. I argue that the new ideas and policies in relation to care work have not only given women more autonomy in relation to their individual husbands but can provide a basis for the empowering of women in society.

In the second section I ask what this political development has meant for women's political participation and mobilization. Although the new policies had a social rather than a feminist perspective, it was feminists who first raised the question of women's citizenship. Since the early 1970s, autonomous women's organizations in Demark have radicalized women in the social movements, trade unions and in political parties on feminist issues. I argue that during the 1980s this broad mobilization of women has helped to bring considerations of women's citizenship into social policies on equality but that there have been limits to the integration of gender policies with social policies.

In the third section I ask what the increase in women's participation, mobilization and representation means in terms of power and influence. What are the limits to the participation of women and to the integration of feminism in political institutions? The understanding of citizenship in Denmark has to some extent come to acknowledge the idea of equality between men and women, but there are important limits to a strategy of equality. The actual practice of citizenship is still gendered, and there are new factors which tend to divide women. One key question is, therefore, what women in the political elite will do with the power they have attained. Another is what can be done when economic developments encourage the reopening of class and cultural divisions. I argue that progress for women implies that women in policy-making positions start to organize themselves around women's issues in the political and corporate structures and to develop new strategies in a dialogue with women in the grass-roots movement. Finally I suggest that the challenges facing women in Denmark and the strategies that they need to develop are common to the movements in other Scandinavian countries.

Scandinavian Citizenship, Equality Principles and Gender Politics

The Scandinavian welfare states have been described as having at their core universal principles of solidarity with groups outside the labour market and with underprivileged groups. In terms of politics this means universal coverage, equal treatment of all citizens and a progressive tax system. It further means that the rights to a greater part of the social services and benefits are not determined by individual payments or by insurance but are part of the individual's social rights as a citizen. On this basis scholars have argued that an understanding of Scandinavian citizenship makes it necessary to look beyond the organization of social security and social services to the social, economic and political history of the different Scandinavian countries (Andersen, 1983; Esping Andersen and Korpi, 1987). While Marxists have stressed that the most important dynamic has been connected with the interplay of the market and the state, and that class organizations have been the most important social actors, feminists have suggested that the interplay of state and family has been another important dynamic in the understanding of the Scandinavian welfare states, and have claimed that other actors than class organizations have been important social actors (Siim, 1987; Hernes, 1988a).

Equality Principles and Social Democratic Citizenship
The political culture of the Scandinavian countries has traditionally placed a high value on the principles of social equality. This attitude, which has sometimes been called 'a passion for equality', is part of the cultural heritage and has not been created by the welfare state. The principle of equality developed during the nineteenth century as a part of the political culture of the specific Scandinavian route to democracy. The social movements, like the folk high-school movement, the peasant and consumer co-operatives, and the high degree of organization for workers were all important preconditions for the abolition of poverty and the creation of a high degree of solidarity and equality in society (Andersen, 1983; Alestalo and Kuhnle, 1987).

Since the 1930s, the social democratic parties have played an important role in the development of the welfare state in the Scandinavian countries and political culture has been strongly influenced by ideals of social equality and solidarity. The political philosophies of socialism have at the same time been closely connected with ideas of fraternity and paternalism. This paternalism has been defined as a specific sense of community and solidarity, which is part of a 'spirit of brotherhood' developed by the Social Democratic Movement (Finneman, 1985; Siim, 1987).

Social democratic parties have attempted to integrate the working class into politics by changing the meaning of citizenship. While the liberal tradition has focused on the rights of the individual *vis-à-vis* the state, the social democratic ideal was to extend citizenship to the workers and to expand citizenship from political to social and economic rights (see Marshall, 1983). Ideas about an active, participatory citizenship were aimed at integrating working-class organizations into the governing of society and did not originally include women. The concept of citizenship was gendered; that is based on the existing sexual division of labour and on a dualist conception of the 'citizen-worker' and the 'citizen-mother' (Hernes, 1988b). As a consequence women's interests have become subsumed under the universal interests of the worker. In contrast to the liberal idea of citizenship motherhood was not, however, isolated from the political sphere, but female citizens were expected to perform their social duties in the family (Hirdman, 1987).

Scandinavian researchers have emphasized that people in the Scandinavian (and Nordic) countries apparently have a different attitude towards the public sector and the government from most countries: the state is seen as a tool to be used, not something to be feared, or respected or worshipped (Andersen, 1983; Hernes 1988b). One common aspect of the development of the Scandinavian welfare states seems to be a greater willingness than in other countries to use public authorities – state as well as regional and local – as a tool towards certain political ends both in economic policies and in relation to social security and services, including child-care services. This attitude towards the state has had important implications for women, and contrasts strongly with the Anglo-Saxon idea that the individual and the private sphere of the family must be protected against state involvement (see Pateman, 1988).

The Welfare State and the Public System of Care

Social democratic politics after the Second World War was built on a class compromise and on corporatist principles of representation. Public politics has during the 1960s and 1970s radically changed the boundaries between the public and the private spheres. Extensive state intervention in the economy and in the family sphere has changed the public–private split and has created a complicated 'public–private mix' (Hernes, 1988b).

This second phase of the welfare state has been characterized by a political process of 'reproduction going public'. This process has gone further in the Scandinavian countries than in most Western countries and has created what sociologists have called 'public families' (see Wolfe, 1988). One important aspect of this development has been women's increasing integration in the labour market and in the public sphere and the increasing importance of the welfare state for women as workers, mothers and citizens (see Hernes, 1987, 1988a; Borchorst and Siim 1987; Siim, 1988).

This state intervention in civil society has resulted in a new organization of the social reproduction of individuals and households. I have argued that this process can be interpreted as a new partnership between the state and the family. *The core is state acceptance of some kind of responsibility for the organization and financing of care for the old, the sick, children and the disabled.* This development has not only changed the boundaries between the private and the public sphere but also the understanding of what is public and private (Siim, 1987).

The changes in social policies and institutionalized social care have touched upon many different areas of what are usually called social or family policies. The cornerstone is local state responsibility for building day-care institutions, nursing and old age homes according to social needs and a system of free health and educational services (Siim, 1988). There is, however, still an informal system of care centred in the family and there is a close interaction between the formal and informal welfare institutions which is important for women.

There is no doubt that the welfare state and the public care system have in many ways been more important to women than to men. In particular, feminist researchers have analysed public provision of care for the old and for children (Borchorst and Siim, 1987; Wærness and Ringen, 1987). From a woman's point of view it can be argued that the changes in child-care policies have perhaps had the greatest significance. Denmark and Sweden today have the highest percentage in the Western world of children between 0 and 6 years old enrolled in public day-care and child-care institutions (Borchorst and Siim, 1987).

The changes were made possible by a political culture dominated by pragmatism and values of social equality, and by state institutions influenced by social democracy. One important point to note about the new public commitment to care is that it was carried out by agreement between different political parties. In contrast to public intervention in the market sphere, there has been to a large extent a political consensus on the new principles of public responsibilities towards children, about free abortion and about the new social organization of care work. Another important point to note is that the new principles and policies about care were not seen as *gender policies* and were not carried through with the intention of improving the situation of women in society. They were understood rather as part of *social policies* intended to create greater *social equality*. Therefore the main protagonist for the new social reform of day-care policies was not the women's movement but social reformers in organized political parties and in the social reform movement.

I find that, even though the policies did not intend to improve women's situation in relation to men, the policies can be seen as *a new form of social citizenship* that has improved women's status as citizens by giving women new social rights as mothers/parents and consumers.

Changes in Women's Citizenship

In the Scandinavian approach to citizenship the concept has a double meaning, because it focuses both upon the bonds between the state and the individual and on the bonds between individual citizens (Hernes, 1988a, 1988b; Petersson, 1989). The right of the citizen is to have 'equal possibilities to participate in the governing of society' (Petersson, 1989: 16). This understanding, which I want to explore, stresses the connection between the political and social aspects of citizenship and relates citizenship to problems of autonomy, participation and power.[1]

Several factors contributed to changes in women's citizenship after the Second World War. Women's entry into the labour market from the 1960s was one important factor that has increasingly made women dependent on their own paid work and has reduced the husband's role as an economic provider for married women. The increase in state support to mothers through soical benefits and services is another factor which has made women less dependent on their husbands. Feminists have argued that women's unequal position in the labour market and their continued responsibilities as mothers have increasingly made women dependent on the welfare state. Helga Hernes has argued that there has been a change from private to public dependency for women, because women have increasingly become dependent on the state as clients in the social system, as workers in the public sector and as consumers of social services like child care (Hernes, 1987).

Feminist researchers have discussed what this new dependency means for women. I have argued that the question of women's dependence on the state cannot in itself be seen as either negative or positive. Women's relation to the state must be analysed in time and space. From this perspective the crucial question is to determine the specific character of women's citizenship and to examine the institutional context, values and concrete policies that are directed towards women as mothers, workers and citizens. It becomes important to analyse the forms of organizations, the concrete cultural values and different co-ordinating principles and rationalities that govern the specific political and administrative institutions (Siim, 1988).

I find the new social and family policies in Denmark have expanded social citizenship by making care work and motherhood part of the public responsibilities of the state and, thereby, have increased women's social welfare as workers and mothers. There has been, however, disagreement about what the political development has meant for women's citizen status in terms of power and influence. The new public policies have been interpreted in two different ways. The negative interpretation argues that public policies are *per se* primarily an expression of state regulation and state control; thus women's increased dependency on the state is a bad thing since it integrates women into a public hierarchy. The positive interpretation argues that the political development is to some extent an expression of the demands of the social movements and has empowered women by creating new social rights and new forms of participation as citizens which can be used to influence institutions (Siim, 1987, 1988).

It is important to stress that the policies of the welfare state did not intend to create equality between men and women in the family or in society. The development has created problems for women in, for example, the labour market, where the sexual division of labour has actually been exacerbated, because women have become employed primarily as service workers in the public sphere, while men have increasingly been employed in the private sector. As a result women experience new forms of dependence and new forms of male domination in both the public and the private sector. This is the basis for the claim that there has been a change in the form of men's oppression of women from private to public patriarchy (Eisenstein, 1984; Borchorst and Siim, 1987).

Today I find that this conclusion is too general and does not do justice to the particular forms of the relationship between women and state agencies. Whether women's dependence on the state is good or bad cannot be determined universally. It can be argued that welfare developments represent a positive step away from women's personal dependence on their husbands. And it can be argued that public provision of care may often increase the independence of the recipients from the personal care of family members (Wærness and Ringen, 1987). What must be avoided is rather the specific forms of dependency, such as *client status* connected with economic dependency, social stigma and ideological control. *Consumer and citizens' rights* have a different rationality. They may give the individual new rights *vis-à-vis* the state and they are often connected with *participatory rights* that make collective political action possible.

There is no doubt that the state has become critical for women. And the welfare state is, in many ways, more important for women than for men. In Denmark women have become dependent on the state largely as *workers and consumers* and to a lesser extent as *clients.* As a result of the expansion of the public service sector women have become employed as white-collar service workers and have come to rely upon public provision of day-care and child-care services. The public commitment to care has made child care a political issue and has created, to some extent, a care culture in the public sector. There is a public commitment to provide for child-care and day-care places according to social needs. But this care culture has never been fully accomplished since social needs have always been defined by the demands of the capitalist economy and have been subsumed under the rationality of the market sector.

I conclude, however, that the integration of care work and motherhood as part of social citizenship has been largely beneficial to women as workers, mothers and citizens (Siim, 1987; Hernes, 1987; Wærness and Ringen, 1987). Women have gained new social rights as mothers and this has given them new potentialities and a new self-confidence to influence politics as *women citizens.* This means that women have gained a new basis from which to attack male domination in both the private and the public spheres.

In Denmark state involvement in social reproduction has weakened the individual power of husbands and made women less dependent on the institution of marriage. Women have become more dependent on their own wages and on state support. There is, however, still a hidden welfare state and a close interaction between formal and informal welfare institutions. The expansion of the welfare state has in some ways weakened the social networks around the family but, at the same time, new social networks and new kinds of extended families have been created to replace the old ones. Also new consumer groups in relation to day care, new citizens' groups and social movements have developed around problems of social reproduction.

Feminist researchers from the Scandinavian countries have emphasized that the public welfare institutions are important for changing and improving the status of women in society (Wærness and Ringen, 1987). And it has been argued that women's political history is closely connected to the second phase of the welfare state.

For women state policies rather than the market are the basis for women's political activities (Hernes, 1987; 1988b). There is doubt that women have *common interests* towards the state as workers, citizens and consumers, but it must be stressed that women also have *different interests* towards the state. Women have different positions in the labour market and in the political power hierarchy. During the economic crisis (with its stronger emphasis on the free play of the market forces and cuts in expenditures in the public sector), class, cultural and power differences between women have become exacerbated. Today it is an important question whether it is possible to create an alliance that can unite different groups of women around common interests in a programme of improving the situation of women in society. That such alliances are possible is evident from Denmark – to which I now turn.

The Political Interests and Mobilization of Women in Denmark

The development of the second phase of the welfare state in Denmark has in important ways improved women's status as citizens. Women are no longer as a group outside politics. Women have become mobilized politically and today they participate actively in all different political channels on almost equal terms with men. It is my claim that there is a connection between women's situation in the family and women's citizenship. Women's political mobilization from the early 1970s has, in contrast to men, been connected with the interplay between the state and the family more than between the state and the market. It is important to analyse in what ways this interplay has influenced women's political activities, participation and representation. Although women's mobilization has spread from women in the new middle classes to working-class women, during the 1980s we find new divisions among women and a new tendency to a polarization in women's political participation.

It is the feminist movement rather than the working-class movement that has raised questions of women's citizenship. The first feminist movement focused on equal rights and the demand for the vote. The second feminist movement focused on citizenship in a broader context by emphasizing the interplay of women's different roles as mothers, workers and citizens and by questioning the definition of politics and the split between the public and the private sphere (Dahlerup, 1986a). In the early 1970s there were ideological and political splits between women in different organizations, between women from the new middle classes organized in the new feminist movement and women organized in the old equal rights organizations, and between women from the new middle classes and working-class women organized in the trade unions and political parties.

Women from the new middle classes joined the new feminist movement during the early 1970s and became part of the political mobilization of the New Left in the new social movements. In contrast, working-class women were organized in the trade union movement and were part of the Social Democratic movement. The themes raised by women in the new feminist movement centred on the emancipation of women from men in the family and society and on the need for an autonomous movement, whereas demands from women in the equal rights organizations and in the trade union movement were centred on equality between men and women in the labour market, in the family and in society in general. An alliance between women of different classes and ideologies was formed at the beginning of the 1970s around the issues of abortion and equal pay. Equal pay was granted in the public sector in 1921 but it was not until 1973 that it came about in the private sector.

The different issues originate from different ideological perspectives: social equality, gender equality and women's autonomy. In view of this it is perhaps surprising that during the 1980s the ideological gap between women of different ideologies and classes has not widened but has diminished. Women in different organizations today support common demands for equality in the labour market through affirmative action, a daily shortening of working time, a 35-hour working week, and equality in the political and administrative decision-making process. They also agree upon protests against cuts in the social state and seem in favour of a shortening of working time for families with small children.

What has been characteristic of the changes in women's political participation and mobilization during the 1970s and 1980s? During the 1970s women increased their political activities in relation to men in all political channels, especially in the new feminist movement and other social movements (Goul Andersen, 1984). The gender difference in participation was largest in relation to activity in the formal political system and smallest in relation to grass-roots activity. Recent studies show further changes in gender relations during the 1980s (Togeby, 1988). Today, there is apparently no longer any significant difference between the participation of men and women. At the grass-roots level women are as active as men in both political parties and trade unions. There is, however, still a significant difference in the participation of men and women at elite level.

One important aspect of women's increased participation has

been a remarkable change in both women's political organization and ideology. The political mobilization of women has grown dramatically, spreading from well-educated women employed in the public service sector to other groups of working women. During the late 1970s and early 1980s women began to organize in equality committees in the different trade unions, and women in the political parties started to demand affirmative action in party committees. This development represents a change in women's political activities and political demands. On an organizational level women have been increasingly active in more traditional forms of political organizations in trade unions and in the formal political system (Togeby, 1988). The new feminist organizations and other social movements are today only one political channel for women's political participation. Paradoxically, during the same time there has been a feminist and political radicalization of women on an ideological level. There is a growing difference in the political attitudes of men and women on specific issues. Women tend to be more positive than men towards the peace movement and the social state and more negative than men towards Nato, defence expenditure and nuclear power. And, since the beginning of the 1980s there has been a tendency for women to vote for the Left compared to men. This tendency is not yet strong, but it has parallels in the other Scandinavian countries (Togeby, 1988).

During the 1970s and 1980s the feminist movement changed and there is no longer organizationally or ideologically one feminist centre. First, feminist ideas have become institutionalized within the public sector, for example by state feminists; secondly, feminist ideas have proliferated to women in other kinds of organizations, such as trade unions and political parties. Thirdly, new feminist institutions have been built with support from public sources. How can we explain the changes in women's political participation? Women's integration in the political parties and their increased political representation can be seen as an expression of women's improved status as citizens and of the growing political mobilization of women in social movements. There is no doubt that the gradual recognition of the principle of equality of men and women as a political issue and as part of labour market, occupational and educational policies is one of the results of women's general political mobilization. Women's political participation has increased but, although women's citizenship has changed, there is still a gendered citizenship where the 'citizen-mother' is subsumed under the 'citizen-worker'.

Equality Principles and Equality Policies

During the 1960s and 1970s the principles of social equality were debated in the Social Democratic Party, in parliament and in society. In 1973 the Social Democratic Party set up a Commission on Equality (meaning social equality) which resulted in a report entitled *The Demand for Equality*. In 1976 the Social Democratic Party set up a Commission on Low Incomes, which submitted its recommendation in 1982. In both commissions the crucial point was the demand for a greater social equality. Equality of men and women was conceived primarily as a problem of social inequality for unskilled, low-income workers. The problems for women workers were accepted as one aspect of the class contradiction, and women's problems were never analysed as independent problems involving their relationship to men. During the 1960s the dominant political strategy was to integrate married women into the labour market and, thereby, increase their economic independence from men.

After pressure from women within the Social Democratic Party the Danish equality policies were institutionalized in 1975 with the establishment of the Danish Equal Status Council (see the English summary in Ligestillingsrådets, 1986). It was confirmed by law in 1978. The council, together with the Equal Treatment Act passed in 1978 and the Equal Remuneration Act of 1976, forms the body of Danish equality law. One characteristic of Danish equality politics is that it has been directed primarily towards the labour market and the educational system and not towards social policies. Another characteristic has been the organizational status of the council, which is part of the corporate system of class representation. Women's representation in the corporate system has historically been very low and today women make up only about 15 per cent of all members in public committees and councils (Ligestillingsrådets 1986). In 1985, the liberal-bourgeois government passed a new Act on Equality in Appointing Members to Public Committees. This may gradually increase the number of women in the corporate decision-making process.

The specific political culture stressing social equality and the corporate system of class representation has influenced both the form and content of women's political mobilization. The feminist movement and the growing mobilization of women have, on the other hand, helped to raise the principle of equality of men and women as a political issue and to raise the issue of gender in politics. As a result, the values of social equality and the ideal of working-class participation during the late 1970s became reconstructed and gradually came to include *equality of men and women and participation of women as citizens*. Educational and labour market policies began, to a certain extent, to be directed towards *gender equality*, and *gender policies* were directed towards increasing women's participation in political institutions and public committees (Ligestillingsrådet, 1987). Social policies, however, did not become integrated into gender policies. And there is still a tension between class and gender politics.

There has been a continuous ideological struggle about the meaning of equality of men and women and about the strategies to accomplish it; for example, between the principle of affirmative action and the principle of comparable worth. The second feminist movement has seldom been directly engaged at the top in changing public policies. The strength of the movement has been its ability to influence people's attitudes and ideologies and to work collectively trying to empower women in their daily lives. Today, the old contradiction between the strategies of women working in the autonomous women's movement or in the new social movements and the strategies of women working within institutions to increase women's power participation in the decision-making process has been diminished. The different strategies may still conflict but they often work together as aspects of the same ongoing struggle to change power relations in politics. Such co-operation is less firmly entrenched in the formal institutions to which I now turn.

Participation, Representation and Women's Power

In all the Scandinavian countries women have greatly increased their political participation and have to some extent become integrated in political and administrative institutions, though only rarely at the top level. Danish women now occupy a quarter to a third of the seats in parliament and local councils. Feminist scholars have started to ask what difference it makes that women have come to occupy positions of power in the political system, and what are the limits to the strategy of equality?

These questions have two aspects that need to be analysed separately both at an empirical and a theoretical level. One is to what extent and on what issues women in the political elite can be expected to articulate and represent the interests, goals and values of all women? The other is what barriers exist against the accomplishment of women's interests and values within the existing power structure?

Experience in Denmark shows that changes are possible, though vulnerable to entrenched political practice and economic crisis. There is no doubt that the increase in women's political representation in the Scandinavian countries is important because it has given

women new institutional resources that they can use to form coalitions to improve their situation. An increase in the number of
women administrators and bureaucrats may also be important for
the formulation and implementation of gender policies. It is,
however, still an open question how women will use the new institutional resources and to what extent women in the political elite have
the political will to work for improvements for the poor and marginalized women in society.

I would argue that the strength of the political mobilization of
women outside the formal political system is one important factor
influencing women in the political elite. The strength of independent organizations of women inside the political and administrative
institutions is another factor influencing the political will of women
politicians. Both factors tend to unite and empower women. Other
institutional factors tend to divide women; for example, the high
degree of centralization and corporatism in political and administrative institutions. The fact that women in the Scandinavian countries
have a relatively high political representation in parliament is an
indication that women are strongly integrated into the party system,
which also tends to divide women.

It is important to understand gender relations as power relations
between men and women and to analyse them as part of political
and economic power structures. Participation and representation do
not by themselves change the sexual power hierarchy in politics.
There is in the Scandinavian countries, next to parliament, a strong
corporatist structure dominated by class interests, class representation and class organizations. This corporatist power structure has
historically been highly centralized and hostile towards representing
women's interests and issues. Today there are signs of change.
Women today make up more than 40 per cent of all members of
trade unions and have become increasingly active, especially at the
local level. This is one reason why the trade union movement has
started to take up issues of gender equality in relation to the labour
market, the educational system and social policy. In order to challenge the strong sexual hierarchy in corporate structures there is a
need for women to organize within the trade union movement and
to form alliances between progressive women and progressive men.

The Limits of State Feminism

Feminist scholars have argued that there is an important difference
between political mobilization from below and women's incorpora-
tion and integration in politics from above. The increase in women's
political representation in Denmark during the last ten to fifteen
years can be interpreted as a combined result of women's increased

political participation and mobilization from below, women's improved status as citizens, and gender equality policies and state feminism. State feminism is a visible result of the integration of women in political and administrative institutions. It has been defined as 'feminism from above' in the form of gender equality and social policies (Hernes, 1988b: 202). The expression then refers both to feminists employed as administrators and bureaucrats in position of power and to women politicians advocating gender equality policies.

Scandinavian scholars have discussed both the potential and the limitations of state feminism (Hernes, 1988b; Eduards, 1986; Siim, 1988). In Denmark, studies have shown that women in parliament have formed coalitions solely on the issue of improving women's political representation in parliament, on local councils, public committees and boards and in the public administration (Dahlerup, 1986b). On most other issues, women in parliament have not formed coalitions and have not agreed on politics. One interpretation could be that women today agree upon strengthening women's political representation and participation but not about how to use the institutional power that women have gained.

Although the general women's political profile on many issues is different from men's, there are important factors, like class, culture and power, that still tend to divide women themselves in policy matters. These differences among women have become exacerbated with the economic crisis, mass unemployment and the political policies of the right-centre and liberal parties in government in Denmark since 1981. Consequently the situation for women in Denmark seems highly contradictory. On the one hand, gender equality has become a public issue and, during the 1970s and 1980s, there has been a remarkable increase in women's political participation and representation and a general political radicalization of women. On the other hand, there are important limits to the dominant understanding of gender equality which does not incorporate the feminist idea of autonomy or the feminist understanding of the interplay of family and public sphere. Women in policy positions have helped to improve women's political representation but they have not agreed upon improving women's economic and social conditions. As a consequence, today there is a growing danger of an economic and political polarization of women, between employed and unemployed women and between women who participate actively in politics and women who remain politically passive.

Feminist Challenges from a Scandinavian Perspective

Feminist scholars have different interpretations of what it means for women to be full and equal citizens and about the strategies that are necessary to obtain that goal (Pateman, 1988; Hernes, 1988b). In this chapter I have argued that it is important for women to increase their rights as citizens and their ability to participate in all spheres of life. From this perspective it is important to ask what are the individual, collective and institutional conditions for full citizenship for women. We need to analyse the institutional and structural barriers against reaching full citizenship for women in the Scandinavian countries.

In these countries women have started the long way through the institutions. The question remains as to whether women have the ability and the power to change institutions or whether the institutional structures will change women. Throughout Scandinavia the challenge for feminists is to develop strategies that combine the aim of the autonomous women's organizations to empower women from below with strategies aimed at changing the unequal power relations in political and corporatist institutions. Today there is a growing need to move beyond equality policies in a narrow sense to policies aimed at the wider aspects of women's citizenship by attacking the unequal distribution between men and women of time, money, work and power in all spheres.

Many scholars have argued that the Scandinavian welfare states stand at the crossroads and that there is a need for fundamental changes in the Scandinavian model. One of the crucial questions for Scandinavian feminists is whether progress for women has come to a standstill with growing economic problems and the weakening of the social democratic parties, as some scholars argue, or whether there is a chance that women may play a significant political role as innovators in the future restructuring of the Scandinavian welfare states. Another related question is what answers Scandinavian feminists have to the ecological, economic and political challenges of the 1990s. There is a need to combine the feminist aim to be able to influence the development of society in all spheres with a global strategy for an alternative paradigm of development that includes a common commitment to a redistribution of resources to the Third World, to peace and to protection of the environment.

Note

1. What I here tentatively call the Scandinavian approach to citizenship is an understanding of citizenship developed by different Scandinavian researchers like Helga Maria Hernes, Olof Petersson and Bent Rold Andersen on the basis of specific

Scandinavian history and culture. They all, in different ways, focus on the interplay of the state and the family and on gender relations as important aspects of Scandinavian citizenship (Hernes, 1988a, 1988b; Petersson, 1989; Andersen, 1983, 1985).

References

Alestalo, Matti and Kuhnle, Stein (1987) The Scandinavian route: economic, political, and social developments in Denmark, Finland, Norway and Sweden, in Robert Eriksen (ed.), *The Scandinavian Model. Welfare State and Welfare Research*. New York: M.E. Sharpe.

Andersen, Bent Rold (1983) *Two Essays on the Nordic Welfare States*. Copenhagen: Amtskommunerne og kommunernes forskningsinstitution.

Andersen, Bent Rold (1985) *Kan vi bevare velfærdsstaten* (Can we preserve the welfare state?) Copenhagen: Amtskommunernes forskningsinstitutionen.

Borchorst, Anette (1986), 'Statsfeminisme eller afledningsmanøvre. Om dansk ligestillingspolitik gennem 25 år" i Årbog for kvindestudier', in *AUC* (Yearbook for Women's Studies). Aalborg University Press.

Borchorst, Anette and Siim, Birte (1987), 'Women and the advanced welfare state – a new kind of patriarchal power?' in Anne Showstack Sassoon (ed.), *Women and the State. The Shifting Boundaries between Public and Private*. London: Hutchinson.

Dahlerup, Drude (ed.) (1986a) *The New Women's Movement. Feminism and Political Power in Europe and the US*. London: Sage.

Dahlerup, Drude (1986b) *From a Small to a Large Minority. A Theory of a 'Critical Mass' Applied to the Case of Women in Scandinavian Politics*. Aarhus: Institute of Political Science, Aarhus University.

Eduards, Maud (1986) 'Kön, Stat and Jämställhetspolitik' (Gender, state and equality politics) in *Kvinnovetenskaplig Tidskrift* 3, Stockholm.

Eisenstein, Zillah (1984) *Feminism and Sexual Equality. The Crisis in Liberal Feminism*. New York: Monthly Review Press.

Eriksen, Robert, Hansen, Erik Jørgen, Ringen, Stein and Unsitalo, Hannu (eds) (1987) *The Scandinavian Model. Welfare State and Welfare Research*. New York: M.E. Sharpe.

Esping Andersen (1985) *Politics Against Markets*. Princeton, NJ: Princeton University Press.

Esping Andersen, Gøsta and Korpi, Walter (1987) 'From poor relief to institutional welfare states: the development of Scandinavian social policy', in Robert Erikson (ed.), *The Scandinavian Model. Welfare State and Welfare Research*. New York: M.E. Sharpe.

Ferguson, Kathy (1984), *The Feminist Case Against Bureaucracy*. Philadelphia, PA: Temple University Press.

Ferguson, Kathy (1986), 'Male-ordered politics. Feminism and political science', in *Political Science and Political Discourse*.

Ferguson, Kathy (1987), 'Work, texts and acts in discourses of organization', in *Women Politics*, 7, pp. 1–21.

Finneman, Niels Ole (1985) *I broderskabets ånd. Den Socialdemokratiske arbejderbevægelses idehistorie 1871–1977* (The Spirit of Brotherhood. The History of Ideas of the Social Democratic Movement 1871–1977). Copenhagen: Gyldendal.

Goul Andersen, Jørgen (1984) *Kvinder og politik* (Women and Politics). Århus: Politica.

Hernes, Helga (1987) *Welfare State and Women Power*. Oslo: Norwegian University Press.

Hernes, Helga (1988a) 'The welfare state citizenship of Scandinavian women', in Jónasdóttir and K. Jones (eds), *The Political Interests of Gender. Developing Theory and Research with a Feminist Face*. London: Sage.

Hernes, Helga (1988b) 'Scandinavian citizenship', *Acta Sociologica*, 31(3).

Hirdman, Yvonne (1987) *The Swedish Welfare State and the Gender System: a Theoretical and Empirical Sketch*. Uppsala: Commission of Power.

Ligestillingsrådets årsberetning (1986) *The Annual Report of the Equal Status Council*, with an English summary.

Marshall, T.H. (1983) 'Citizenship and class', in D. Held (ed.), *States and Societies*. Oxford: Oxford University Press.

Pateman, Carole (1988) *The Sexual Contract*. Stanford, CA: Stanford University Press.

Petersson, Oluf (1989) *Medborgerskab och makt* (Citizenship and Power). Stockholm: Carlssons.

Siim, Birte (1987) 'The Scandinavian welfare states. Towards sexual equality or a new kind of male domination' in Acta Sociologica No 3–4.

Siim, Birte (1988) 'Rethinking the welfare state from a feminist perspective', in Jónasdóttir and K. Jones (eds), *The Political Interests of Gender. Developing Theory and Research with a Feminist Face*. London: Sage.

Siim, Birte (1990) 'Women and the welfare state. A comparative perspective on the organization of care work in Denmark and Britain', in Clare Ungerson (ed.), *Women and Community Care. Gender and Caring in the Modern Welfare State*. Hemel Hempstead: Wheatsheaf.

Togeby, Lise (1988) 'Politisering af kvinder og kvindespørgsmålet' (The politicization of women and the women's question), in J. Elklit and D. Tonsgård (eds), *To folketingsvalg* (Two General Elections), Politica, Aarhus University: Politica.

Wærness, Kari and Ringen, Stein (1987) 'Women and the welfare state: the case of formal and informal old-age care', in Robert Eriksen (ed.), *The Scandinavian Model. Welfare State and Welfare Research*. New York: M.E. Sharpe.

Wolfe, Allan (1988) *Whose Keeper? Social Science and Moral Obligation*. Stanford, CA: Stanford University Press.

Index

Notes on Contributors

Carol Bacchi is a Lecturer in Politics at the University of Adelaide where she teaches feminist theory and policy analysis. Trained as a historian, she is the author of *Liberation Deferred? The Ideas of the English–Canadian Suffragists, 1877–1918* (University of Toronto Press, reprinted in 1989) and a number of articles on Australian intellectual and women's history. Her most recent contribution to feminist theoretical debate is entitled *Same Difference: Feminism and Sexual Difference* (Unwin Hyman, 1990).

Jet Bussemaker studied political science at the University of Amsterdam. Since 1988, she has been working at the same university as a researcher on a project on Gender and Individualism in order to gain her doctorate. She has been a member of the editorial board of Dutch magazines on feminism and women's studies and has published articles on welfare state questions, social movements and Dutch political parties.

Ian Forbes is a Lecturer in Politics at the University of Southampton. He wrote *Marx and the New Individual*, co-edited *The Politics of Human Nature*, and has published articles and chapters on equal opportunities, rights, feminist thought, Nietzsche and international relations. He convenes the Equal Opportunities Study Unit at Southampton, and teaches the MSc in Equal Opportunities Studies.

Jennifer Jarman is a Research Associate and a member of the Sociological Research Group, Faculty of Social and Political Sciences, at Cambridge University. She is in the process of completing a book for Macmillan which compares the various experiments with equal pay legislation in Canada and Britain, and discusses the theoretical premises which underlie this approach to remedying inequalities. She is also working on the ESRC-funded project 'Measuring Changes in Vertical and Horizontal Gender Segregation' which examines occupational segregation indices and twentieth-century occupational trends in gender composition with primary reference to Great Britain.

Evelyn Mahon lectures in Sociology and Women's Studies at the University of Limerick where she is also Director of the Centre for Women's Studies and Course leader of their Postgraduate Diploma in Women's Studies. This article is based on a research project on 'Motherhood, work and equal opportunities: a case study of Irish Civil Servants', funded by the Joint Oireactas Committee on Women's Rights, to be published by the Government Publications Office, Dublin. She has written articles on gender and education, on the Irish women's movement, equal opportunities and women in the labour market. She is at present writing a book on motherhood and work.

Amy Mazur is Assistant Professor of Comparative Politics at Manhattan

College. Her areas of specialization are comparative public policy, Western European politics, French politics and gender politics. She is particularly interested in gender-specific public policy in Western Europe. She has just completed her doctoral dissertation on equal employment policy for women in France and is currently working on projects on gender-specific administration in France, women and political parties in France and women's policy in the European Community.

Elizabeth Meehan has been appointed recently to a chair in Politics at Queen's University, Belfast, having been a Lecturer in Politics at Bath University (1979–90) and a Hallsworth Fellow at Manchester University (1989–90). She is the author of *Women's Rights at Work* (Macmillan, 1985) and one of the co-authors of *Feminism and Political Theory* (Sage, 1986). She has written several articles on European Community equality policies and, with Gill Whitting, edited a special issue of *Policy and Politics* (1989) on this subject. Her current work is on social rights and citizenship in the European Community (in M. Moran and U. Vogel (eds), *The Frontiers of Citizenship*, Macmillan, 1991, and her own *European Citizenship*, Sage, forthcoming). Elizabeth Meehan is a Fellow of the Royal Society of Arts.

Joyce Outshoorn studied political science and contemporary history at the University of Amsterdam. After being Senior Lecturer in Politics at the University of Amsterdam, she became Professor of Women's Studies at Leyden University, the Netherlands. She edited (with Joni Lovenduski) *The New Politics of Abortion* (Sage, 1986). Her current work is on feminist theory, the women's movement and public policy on women.

Tuija Parvikko is a researcher in the Department of Politics at the University of Jyväskylä in Finland. She has just completed her licenciate thesis on the concept of sexual difference in the Italian feminist thinking of the 1980s. Currently she is working on Hannah Arendt's concept of politics in order to gain her doctorate. She has published several articles in Finnish on Italian feminism. A version of the essay published here has been published in Marja Keränen (ed.) *Finnish 'Undemocracy'. Essays on Gender and Politics* (Finnish Political Science Association, 1990).

Selma Sevenhuijsen is a political theorist and professor/chair of Comparative Women's Studies in the Social Faculty at the University of Utrecht. Formerly she was an assistant professor in political science at the University of Amsterdam. She is the director of an interdisciplinary research programme on 'Gender, morality and care'. She has published on such topics as: women and the welfare state; motherhood and reproductive politics; the history and theory of women and family law; feminism and political theory; women, ethics and moral theory. Her publications in English include *Child Custody and the Politics of Gender* (1989, with Carol Smart). She is now working on a book on moral concepts in feminist theory.

Birte Siim is Associate Professor at the Institute of Social Development and Planning at Aalborg University, Denmark. She has researched and written on feminist theory and on women's relation to the welfare state. She is currently working on a research project on gender, power and democracy – women's citizenship in the Scandinavian welfare states.